060 8

D0914398

DATE DUE

Conversations with Louise Erdrich and Michael Dorris

Literary Conversations Series

Peggy Whitman Prenshaw
General Editor

Conversations with Louise Erdrich and Michael Dorris

Edited by
Allan Chavkin and Nancy Feyl Chavkin

University Press of Mississippi
Jackson

Copyright © 1994 by the University Press of Mississippi
Manufactured in the United States of America

97   96   95   94   4   3   2   1

The paper in this book meets the guidelines for permanence and durability
of the Committee on Production Guidelines for Book Longevity of the Council
on Library Resources.

Library of Congress Cataloging-in-Publication Data

Erdrich, Louise.
    Conversations with Louise Erdrich and Michael Dorris / edited by
Allan Chavkin and Nancy Feyl Chavkin.
        p.   cm. — (Literary conversations series)
    Includes index.
    ISBN 0-87805-651-3 (cloth). — ISBN 0-87805-652-1 (paper)
    1. Erdrich, Louise—Interviews.   2. Dorris, Michael—Interviews.
3. Novelists, American—20th century—Interviews.   4. Indians of
North America—Mixed descent—Interviews.   5. Authors, Indian—20th
century—Interviews.   6. Authorship—Collaboration.   7. Indians in
literature.   I. Dorris, Michael.   II. Chavkin, Allan Richard, 1950-   .
III. Chavkin, Nancy Feyl.   IV. Title.   V. Series.
PS3555.R42Z465   1994
813'.5409897—dc20   93-29902
                                                              CIP

British Library Cataloging-in-Publication data available

Books by Louise Erdrich

Imagination. Westerville, Ohio: Charles Merrill Company, 1981.
Jacklight. New York: Holt, Rinehart, and Winston, 1984.
Love Medicine. New York: Holt, Rinehart, and Winston, 1984.
The Beet Queen. New York: Henry Holt and Company, 1986.
Tracks. New York: Henry Holt and Company, 1988.
Baptism of Desire. New York: Harper & Row, 1989.
Love Medicine (Expanded Novel). New York: Holt, Forthcoming 1993.
Best American Short Stories 1993 (Guest Editor). Boston: Houghton Mifflin, 1993.
The Bingo Palace. New York: HarperCollins, Forthcoming 1994.

Books by Michael Dorris

Native Americans: Five Hundred Years After (with photographs by Joseph Farber). New York: Thomas Y. Crowell, 1977.
A Guide to Research on North American Indians (with Arlene Hirschfelder and Mary Lou Byler). Chicago: American Library Association, 1983.
A Yellow Raft in Blue Water. New York: Henry Holt and Company, 1987.
The Broken Cord. New York: Harper & Row, 1989.
Morning Girl. New York: Hyperion Books, 1992.
Rooms in the House of Stone. Minneapolis, MN: Milkweed Editions, 1993.
Working Men. New York: Henry Holt and Company, 1993.
PaperTrail. New York: HarperCollins, 1994.

Books by Louise Erdrich and Michael Dorris

The Crown of Columbus. New York: HarperCollins, 1991.
Route Two. Northridge, CA: Lord John Press, 1991.

Contents

Introduction

Few people would argue with Vince Passaro's conclusion in his interview-profile published in *The New York Times Magazine* that Louise Erdrich and Michael Dorris "are the two most prominent writers of American Indian descent we have, two of the very few to have found a significant audience out in the larger world." In fact, this husband-and-wife team, who collaborate on all their work, can be considered to be among the most important living American writers. They have published nine books and numerous articles, stories, poems, and reviews since 1984 when the publication of *Love Medicine* received international recognition. The immense attention these two writers and collaborators have attracted is suggested by the fact that they have given, in addition to numerous foreign interviews, more than one hundred forty interviews in the United States.

Their unique collaboration has no doubt attracted many interviewers, who want to understand how it works and its relationship to their marriage. In fact, their collaboration and the marriage with which it is inextricably connected are the most frequent topics of the interviews. Passaro stresses the "profound connection between their marriage and their careers" and mentions "the possibility, even, that their most important messages for each other are passed between them in what they write." Although their collaboration is a complex process which they alter as needed for different projects, there are some basic principles upon which it is based. As Michael Dorris explains to Geoffrey Stokes, "We plot the books together, we talk about them before any writing is done, and then we share almost every day, whatever it is we've written—a few pages, a chapter, even a paragraph." But as Dorris explains to Dulcy Brainard, "The person whose name is on the book is the one who's done most of the primary writing." When they each write the drafts, as they did with *The Crown of Columbus,* the work is published with both their names. More often, however, only one person does most of the primary writing. Even in these instances, the books must be considered as products of collaboration, for Erdrich and Dorris together do the research, develop the plot and characters, discuss all other aspects of the work, and ultimately agree on every word before it is submitted for publication. At times, this process of collaboration can result in heated discussions, and in the interviews Erdrich and Dorris mention some of them.

The beginning of their productive collaboration began soon after they married in 1981. At first the newly-married couple, in need of money, published sentimental and romantic stories under the pen name Milou North, which Erdrich explains to Shelby Grantham was derived from "*Mi*chael plus *Lou*ise plus where we live." The usual theme of these stories was "domestic crisis—money, an old flame showing up, that sort of thing." The financially strapped couple were disappointed in how much money the stories sold for, but in retrospect Erdrich thinks that "writing to spec in your formative years as a writer" is not "a bad thing at all." "I do think it's good practice," she tells Charles Trueheart.

The crucial event in their literary partnership occurred when Dorris urged his wife to compete for the Nelson Algren Prize. They had found out about the prestigious contest two weeks before the submission deadline. Erdrich doubted whether she could write a story in so little time, but because of her husband's encouragement decided to try, as she explained to Grantham. With a house full of children and guests, Erdrich "barricaded" herself "at the kitchen table behind closed doors," and in one long day, drafted under difficult working conditions, a substantial part of "The World's Greatest Fishermen." Dorris had sprained his back but collaborated on the story despite being in considerable pain. Finished just before the deadline, the story, one of two thousand entries, was selected for the prize by judges Donald Barthelme, Studs Terkel, and Kay Boyle. There was no question now that their literary partnership should continue.

Not long after this contest, Dorris realized that "The World's Greatest Fishermen" was part of the same world as Erdrich's previously published stories "The Red Convertible" and "Scales," and together the two writers began to work on what eventually would become the novel *Love Medicine,* a series of interrelated short stories. Dorris explains to Dan Cryer how the novel was jointly developed. "We spent a year and a half thinking about these people day and night. We would take walks and imagine scenarios . . . We sat down one day and drew [the characters'] pictures. Just did anything that would help us get a hold of them."

Erdrich wrote the drafts, but Dorris played an important role in the creation of the novel, the interviews make clear. Probably Dorris's most important contribution was helping plot the novel and devising the order of the stories. Although Erdrich resisted changing her original order of the stories for some time, she tells Grantham that in the end Dorris and the editor at Holt convinced her that her order was confusing.

When the novel was published in 1984, it won major prizes, including the National Book Critics Circle Award, and eventually received critical and popular acclaim. In a relatively short time, their literary partnership would publish, in addition to two volumes of poetry by Erdrich, *The Beet Queen* (1986) and *Tracks* (1988) by Erdrich, and *A Yellow Raft in Blue Water* (1987) and *The Broken Cord* (1989) by Dorris. These books not only sold well but won awards and high praise from the critics. On a trip in 1988, while driving across Saskatchewan, they outlined a novel to be published jointly by them, and when *The Crown of Columbus* appeared several years later, it carried both their names.

Despite the success of this literary partnership, some critics and interviewers seem skeptical that two serious writers can possess the same vision and can collaborate so closely to forge one style. Dan Cryer observes that while "Leonard Woolf's aid was indispensable" to his wife's writing and George Henry Lewes's help was indispensable to George Eliot's work, among writers of serious literature, a "collaboration as intense and close as that between Erdrich and Dorris is virtually unprecedented." Cryer remarks that Jack Beatty, former literary editor at *The New Republic,* is astounded by this collaboration because writing fiction "is an exercise in your own creativity" and Beatty wonders "how you can let anybody else in on that." Cryer also quotes others who are skeptical of this collaboration. Erdrich and Dorris have insisted, however, that their collaboration works as they describe it in the interviews, and that it will not only survive but also flourish.

Although some are skeptical, they insist that their collaboration does not require sacrifices in style and vision, as many other collaborations do. As Passaro explains, they "have always insisted on a conception of themselves that is far more romantic and defiant of convention, in which art and marriage are complementary mechanisms. . . . Theirs is an art, as well as a life, directed toward synthesis and unity." The reason some people are so reluctant to accept the authors' description of their collaboration is that such a literary partnership is regarded as an implicit challenge to one of the most widely accepted myths of the writer—that the writer is a solitary genius whose art is purely the product of his or her own creation without any external "contaminating" influences. The interviews in the volume provide evidence that belies that myth; they are full of specific details of how their collaboration functions effectively. That is not to say that their collaboration always proceeds harmoniously. For example, the creation of the masterpiece "Saint Marie" resulted in some tension, the authors informed Grantham. Dorris convinced his wife that the first version of "Saint Marie," a parody of *Heart of Darkness,* was unsuccessful. When she retold the story from the point of view of the sisters, Dorris informed her the "voice" didn't work and the story should be completely rewritten. Furious, Erdrich said she "never wanted to see it again," and stormed off, but by the next day she had completed the version of the story that was published in *Love Medicine.*

Other subjects of some of the interviews are prompted by the Native American heritage of the writers and its influence on their thought and art. Much of Bill Moyers's conversation with Erdrich and Dorris focuses on Native American subjects. They discuss Columbus and the Europeans' first contact with Native Americans, death of Native Americans from diseases brought by Europeans, the failure of the American government to keep the treaties they signed, why Native American influence became more dominant than other influences on their writing, ironic survival humor, their intention not to create "comfortable guilt" but to make Native Americans visible, deliberate outlawing of Native American religions, and the possibility of rejuvenating America by following Native American values of respect for pluralism and cooperation. Erdrich explains to Moyers how the early missionaries' religious zeal could result in coerced conversion and repeats a joke some Indians tell—"When missionaries came here, all they had was the book, and we had the land. Now all we've got is the book and they've got the land." But it would be wrong to assume that Erdrich has an ax to grind. She reveals her objectivity when she remarks to Denis Paiste that while in some instances, the Catholic Church imposed its religion on certain tribes, in other instances, "the clergy worked very closely with a tribe to prevent breakup of tribal lands."[1]

In a number of interviews, Erdrich and Dorris disclose that they like to undermine the stereotypes of Indians. In fact, in an interview with the

Chavkins, Dorris divulges that it is one of the main goals of their fiction. He points out that the stereotyping of Indians from film and television pervades our culture. Erdrich and Dorris see stereotyping of Native Americans as harmful, even supposedly positive stereotypes of Indians as the first ecologists, for any stereotyping simplifies individuals and invariably limits their freedom. Erdrich and Dorris also rebel against those who would stereotype and pigeonhole them; they reject the notion that they are merely "ethnic writers." They emphasize that while they are proud of their heritage, they refuse to be forced into a "literary ghetto." They see themselves as authors who happen to be mixed bloods and sometimes write about Native Americans. They refuse to allow others to limit their subject matter, and they fear that writing by Native Americans will be viewed as insignificant and irrelevant to the main-stream of American literature. In the interview with Laura Coltelli, Erdrich stresses that American Indian literature should be seen as part of American literature, and in the interview with Sharon White and Glenda Burnside, Dorris expresses his fear that Native American writers will not be taught in American and World literature courses but only in Native American literature courses.

Although others frequently consider Erdrich and Dorris spokespeople for Native Americans, they do not see themselves in this role. Actually Native Americans, they repeatedly remind interviewers, are not one people, but many peoples with different cultures, languages, and cus-toms. Historically, the government made the mistake of seeing all Native Americans as "Indians," instead of recognizing that they were Chippewas, Hopis, and members of other tribes. When Michael Huey asks Erdrich and Dorris if it is "legitimate to say that there is a Native American voice, that it had been lost, and is now refound in writers" like themselves, Erdrich suggests that there are many voices from different tribes and that Native Americans never lost their voices but only seemed to when outside interest in them waned. Dorris adds that there are "traditions of expressions, humor, and mythology" for hun-dreds of tribes. He also suggests that the tradition out of which he and Erdrich write is not the same as the one out of which Leslie Silko or others from different tribes write. It is difficult, perhaps impossible, to define what "a Native American perspective" is; it makes more sense to try to define a Chippewa perspective or a Pueblo perspective.

A number of the interviewers ask questions about Dorris's experiences with his adopted son Abel's problems from fetal alcohol syndrome (FAS). In fact, prompted by the publication of Dorris's auto-biographical book *The Broken Cord* (1989), some of the interviews focus primarily or exclusively on this subject. *The Broken Cord* recounts almost two decades of disappointment and anguish as Dorris tried to discover what mysterious affliction was causing Abel's health, behavior, and learning problems. What Dorris finally discovered was that his adopted son's brain was permanently damaged at birth as a result of maternal drinking during pregnancy, and that Abel's numerous problems would never be solved. Reliving almost two decades of his frustration, anger, and guilt by recounting the sad story to interviewers was exceedingly difficult for Dorris, but he felt committed to do so in the hope that he might warn pregnant women not to drink and thereby possibly save their children from FAS, which is totally preventable. Not only Dorris's heartbreak but also his immense love and compassion for Abel are poignantly evoked in some of the interviews.

Collectively these interviews contain much biographical information, and though both Erdrich and Dorris have stated that their fiction is a product of imagination not autobiography, connections between the authors' lives and their fiction can in some instances be illuminating. The interviews also contain some entertaining anecdotes and some details that give one a better understanding of the origins of their work. About ten years before the publication of *The Crown of Columbus,* after reading a translation of Bartolomé de Las Casas's sixteenth-century edition of Columbus's lost diary, Erdrich and Dorris began thinking of writing a novel primarily from Columbus's point of view. As they explain to their interviewers, their original intention was to rewrite the diary, but voices of contemporary characters "took over" the novel. Although *The Crown of Columbus* is not an autobiographical novel, the settings and some of the circumstances do owe a debt to the authors' lives, and these matters are discussed in some of the interviews.

The germ for *A Yellow Raft in Blue Water* was Dorris's recollection of a boyhood encounter with a Jewish concentration camp survivor. Having swum out to a yellow raft, Dorris met a Holocaust survivor who talked to him as if he were an adult, and this transforming experience was still a vivid visual memory twenty-five years later. In the interviews Dorris describes the evolution of *A Yellow Raft in Blue Water* and reveals that this crucial experience from his youth manifests itself in the work in subtle ways.

Other autobiographical experiences had a more direct influence on *A Yellow Raft in Blue Water,* however. As in the extraordinary scene in the novel where Rayona rides a wild horse in a rodeo, Dorris at the last moment substituted for a cousin in a rodeo. He explains to Georgia Croft: "I got thrown off the same horse three times at the Montana State High School Rodeo, and just like Rayona, I thought if you get thrown off, you get back on." Another autobiographical experience that had a direct influence on *A Yellow Raft in Blue Water* occurred when Dorris was working as an anthropologist in a small village in Alaska. While all the villagers were busy with a celebration some distance away, a woman who stayed behind went into labor, and Dorris was the only person available to help her. He volunteered to assist the woman and ended up in the role of obstetrician and delivered the baby. Later his recollection of this experience was useful when he described with a first-person female narrator the process of giving birth.

"The pivotal event in the lives" of the major characters of the novel occurs as a result of a belief that was popular among a certain group of Catholics when Dorris was growing up, he explains to Hertha Wong. In the Pope's possession was a letter given by Mary to a young girl named Lucy, at Fatima. The letter was to be opened on the first day of January of 1960, and then either the Russians would be converted or the world would end apocalyptically. In the novel Christine is raised with this belief and loses her faith when neither of these possibilities occurs after the crucial day. When Christine loses her faith, her mother loses interest in her. "The last major story that Christine tells her own daughter, Rayona, is about this end of the world. So it's a theme that goes into all three" sections of the novel, Dorris explains to Wong.

While Erdrich argues that she should not be regarded as an auto-biographical writer, she does discuss at times aspects of her life that influence her fiction and poetry. For example, in her interview with Joseph Bruchac she reveals that some of the poems in *Jacklight* are based on people whom she knows. In the interviews, she also discusses the importance for her work of listening to her family telling stories. From her mother and grandparents, she heard many stories about life on the reservation during the Depression and other subjects. Her father, too, "is a terrific storyteller and made his relatives and the characters in the towns where he grew up almost mythic."[2] Erdrich suggests that her listening to family stories has been a more significant influence in some ways than literary influences.

Although reviewers and critics have praised the writing of Erdrich and Dorris, these two writers have been the targets of some unusually harsh attacks, and the interviews provide a good opportunity for them to respond. In an article entitled " 'Fetal Rights': A New Assault on Feminism, " Katha Pollitt claimed that in *The Broken Cord* Dorris held the women's movement responsible for fetal alcohol syndrome. She saw Dorris as a part of a "fetal rights" social trend that holds women responsible, "on sketchy or no evidence, for birth defects." In her article, she claimed that Dorris unfairly blamed Abel's alcoholic birth mother for his FAS problems.[3] In a detailed response to Pollitt, Dorris told the Chavkins that Pollitt's "culpably ignorant and elitist" article made him "furious." He suggested that Pollitt misrepresented his position by taking sentences or parts of sentences out of context, and he suggested that her dismissal of maternal responsibility could do real damage because she made one "almost feel that it is politically correct to drink" during pregnancy.

In a scathing review of *The Beet Queen*, Leslie Silko criticized Erdrich for her putative postmodern literary aesthetic that de-emphasized the referential dimension of words and that was outside Native American oral tradition. She claimed that Erdrich's work lacked political commitment and that Erdrich was ambivalent about her Native American origins.[4] While Erdrich informs Gail Caldwell that she is fascinated by some postmodernist writers, she believes that "the emphasis on pure technique and language is a dead end." In her interview with the Chavkins, Erdrich responds to Silko's specific charges and offers a plausible explanation for Silko's diatribe against *The Beet Queen*. She denies that her work lacks political commitment and suggests that any human story has political implications. She and Dorris have stressed that they do not want to become polemical in their fiction and have argued that making their readers identify with Native American characters is political. "If art is one's first concern," she says to Dan Cryer, "whatever politics are behind it will be more effective."

When *The Crown of Columbus* proved to be considerably more commercial than their previous work, some reviewers suggested that

Erdrich and Dorris had sacrificed art for money and that they had no intention of writing an important work of literature. Actually, as Erdrich and Dorris make clear in the interviews, they were as surprised as everyone else about the success of the novel, and regretted that reviewers were suspicious of *The Crown of Columbus* because it was published during the time of the heavily promoted Columbus quincentenary. But Erdrich and Dorris had been planning the book for ten years, and Dorris explains to the Chavkins that they would have written *The Crown of Columbus* "whether there was a five-hundredth anniversary of the first voyage or not." Erdrich and Dorris explain to the Chavkins and other interviewers that they write not for money but out of a compulsion to write serious works, and they reveal that they were surprised when many publishers bid for the idea for *The Crown of Columbus*. Dorris explains to William Craig, Jr., and other interviewers that the novel was a serious one with high goals.[5] In other interviews Erdrich and Dorris discuss the serious themes of the novel, especially the impact of history on the present and the importance of "personal discovery," and the innovative techniques employed to express those themes.

In these interviews Erdrich and Dorris also comment on the writers whom they admire and the influences on their writing. Both state that their collaborator spouse is the single most important influence on their writing and that Native American oral tradition and storytelling are formative influences. Among the numerous writers Erdrich names as favorites are Flannery O'Connor, Gabriel García Márquez, Katherine Anne Porter, Toni Morrison, Willa Cather, Jane Austen, George Eliot, and William Faulkner. She reads *Madame Bovary* over and over. Critics often see Faulkner as an influence, and Erdrich acknowledges that she loves Faulkner's work, especially *Absalom, Absalom!* and *The Hamlet,* and suggests to the Chavkins that white Southerners and Native American writers might have a similar sense of history and of place. While Dorris also admires the work of Toni Morrison, his list of twentieth-century writers who influence his work includes Tennessee Williams, Gloria Naylor, Albert Camus, Sinclair Lewis, Laura Ingalls Wilder, Paul Theroux, John Updike, and Barbara Pym. He does not like avant-garde techniques but prefers an "unobtrusive style in which no word jars you out of your absorption in the story," he explains to the Chavkins.

Throughout the interviews Erdrich and Dorris give many details of their writing habits, and readers can gain much insight into how these two writers work. Dorris states that his best writing time is between 4 A.M. and 8 A.M. He usually is working on more than one project at a time and does not suffer from writer's block. He works intuitively and finds working with an outline "boring." "If it doesn't surprise me line to line, there's something wrong with it as far as I'm concerned," he confesses to the Chavkins. His work is "more character driven than anything else." He revises extensively, and revision is at least as important a part of the writing process as the first draft. He prefers to write in the first person, and in fact, finds writing as third-person omniscient narrator difficult.

Like her husband, Erdrich also works intuitively and even denies having omnipotent control over her characters. She states that she has no rules about writing; sometimes she uses an outline while at other times she writes a book without it. While writing a novel, she skips around, writing her favorite parts first. Like her spouse, she prefers writing with first-person narrators, though she acknowledges the need for using at times third person to compensate for the limited point of view of first person. She likes to write prose each day and feels if she follows a regular schedule connections will form and the work will get done; in contrast, her poetry is the result of strong emotion and often is beyond her control. Like Dorris, she does not have difficulty writing from the point of view of the opposite sex and prefers to work on several projects all at once. She, too, revises extensively. She keeps several notebooks and daily diaries and returns at times to notebooks from many years before for ideas.

While some writers are not astute critics of their own work, and many writers are reticent or evasive when asked to discuss it, Erdrich and Dorris are perceptive critics who answer questions about their work candidly, and their observations about their work enrich one's appreciation of the subtleties of the art of their fiction and poetry. The interviews contain their thoughtful remarks on large theoretical issues and their insights on specific topics. For example, they comment on the role of humor in their fiction, the evolution of their characters through various drafts, the reason for various structural devices, the advantages of telling stories with first-person narrators, the major preoccupations of the works, the sources for *The Crown of Columbus*, the central role of

Lulu Lamartine in *Love Medicine,* Nanapush as a trickster figure, and *Love Medicine* as part of Chippewa storytelling tradition. There is also much factual information about the practical aspects of publishing, such as book sales, editors' influences on their work, and Dorris's role as literary agent. There is much fascinating information that can come only from the authors themselves. For example, as a partial explanation for Lulu Lamartine's character Erdrich provides background information about her that does not actually appear in the work.

In these revealing interviews Erdrich and Dorris eloquently comment on their life and work. Scholars are only beginning to study and to understand the complexities of the art of their fiction, and it is our hope that this collection of conversations will prompt more study and will help scholars in their exploration of the work of these two major American writers.

The interviews selected for inclusion in this book are ordered chronologically according to the dates on which they occurred. As with other books in the Literary Conversations series, they are reprinted without substantive emendation.

Inevitably interviewers focus on some of the same topics and ask some questions previously asked by others; inevitably there is some repetition. Answers to these questions do vary, however, and comparing responses can be enlightening. Furthermore, the writers' repetition can reveal some of their preoccupations and their commitment to certain values and beliefs.

We have selected the twenty-three most informative interviews from the numerous interviews that Erdrich and Dorris gave since the publication of *Love Medicine.* More than half of these interviews were joint interviews, but both writers also gave some interviews individually. We are pleased to be able to include two previously unpublished interviews, a telephone interview with Dorris and an interview by mail with Erdrich, and we thank the authors for their cooperation.

We are grateful to the Office of Sponsored Programs of Southwest Texas State University for a Research Enhancement grant. Our thanks to G. Jack Gravitt, Marion Tangum, Nancy Grayson, and Karen Brown, who helped us to obtain financial assistance for this project. We also are appreciative of Travis Whitehead, Bobby Horecka, and Leticia Perez, for helping in various ways to prepare the manuscript for publication.

We are indebted to the library staff of Southwest Texas State University for providing assistance many times. We also thank our daughter, Laura Michelle Chavkin, for her interest in the project. Finally, we are grateful to Seetha Srinivasan, Associate Director of the University Press of Mississippi, for her encouragement and advice.

This book is dedicated to Gilbert Chavkin, Sylvia Chavkin, Rabbi Saul Kraft, and Marie Feyl and to the memory of Sampson B. Feyl, Sr.

AC

NFC

May 1993

Notes

1. Denis Paiste, "and MORE Books," *Manchester Union Leader,* 27 September 1987, p. 21F.

2. Jan George, "Interview with Louise Erdrich," *North Dakota Quarterly* 53 (Spring 1985): 242-43.

3. Katha Pollitt, "'Fetal Rights': A New Assault on Feminism," *The Nation,* 26 March 1990, pp. 409-418.

4. Leslie Silko, "Here's an Odd Artifact for the Fairy-Tale Shelf." *Impact/Albuquerque Journal,* 8 October 1986, pp. 10-11. For a discussion of Silko's attack on Erdrich, see Susan Pérez Castillo, "Postmodernism, Native American Literature and the Real: The Silko-Erdrich Controversy," *The Massachusetts Review* 32 (Summer 1991): 285-94.

5. William Craig, Jr., "An Exploration of Discovery," (White River Junction, Vermont) *Valley News,* 19 April 1991, p. 6.

Chronology

Louise Erdrich

1954   Karen Louise Erdrich born in Little Falls, Minnesota, on 7 June; the first of seven children of Ralph Louis and Rita Joanne (Gourneau) Erdrich.

1972   Enrolls at Dartmouth College, member of the first coeducational class

1975   Awarded Academy of American Poets Prize

1976   Receives a B.A. degree from Dartmouth College

1977–78 Visiting Poet and Teacher, North Dakota Arts Council

1978–79 Receives a fellowship and teaches expository and creative writing at Johns Hopkins University

1979   Awarded an M.A. degree in the Writing Program from Johns Hopkins

1979–80 After graduating from Johns Hopkins, becomes communications director and editor of *The Circle,* a Native American newspaper sponsored by the Boston Indian Council; later she is a textbook writer for the Charles Merrill Company and a Macdowell Colony fellow.

1981   Becomes a Yaddo Colony fellow and later a visiting fellow at Dartmouth College; *Imagination* is published; marries Michael Anthony Dorris on 10 October.

1982   Receives Nelson Algren Fiction Award for "The World's

Greatest Fishermen"; receives National Endowment for the Arts Fellowship.

1983   Receives Pushcart prize for "Indian Boarding School" (poem) and National Magazine Award for Fiction for "Scales." "Scales" is included in *The Best American Short Stories, 1983,* and "The Immaculate Conception of Carson Du Pre" is chosen for PEN Syndication Fiction Project.

1984   *Jacklight,* a book of poems, and *Love Medicine,* a novel, are published. Receives National Book Critics Circle Award for Best Work of Fiction, Sue Kaufman Prize for Best First Fiction from The American Academy and Institute of Arts and Letters, and the Virginia McCormick Scully Award for Best Book of 1984 Dealing with Western Indians. "The Resurrection of Linus" is chosen for PEN syndication Fiction Project.

1985   Awarded Guggenheim fellowship; receives *Los Angeles Times* Award for Fiction, American Book Award from the Before Columbus Foundation, and Great Lakes Colleges Association Award for Best First Work of fiction for *Love Medicine.* "Saint Marie" is included in *Prize Stories: The O. Henry Awards.*

1986   *The Beet Queen* is published and nominated for Best Work of Fiction of 1986, National Book Critics Circle.

1987   O. Henry Prize (First Place) and National Magazine Award for "Fleur." The story is published in *Prize Stories: The O. Henry Awards.*

1988   *Tracks* is published and is on the New York Times Bestseller List. "Snares" is included in *The Best American Short Stories 1988.*

1989   *Baptism of Desire* (poems) is published.

1991   With Michael Dorris, publishes *The Crown of Columbus*
            and *Route Two*

1992   Receives Western Literary Association Award

1993   Guest editor of *The Best American Short Stories 1993;* the
            expanded version of *Love Medicine* is scheduled for
            publication.

1994   *The Bingo Palace* scheduled for publication

Michael Dorris

1945   Michael Anthony Dorris born in Louisville, Kentucky on 30
            January; the only child of Jim Dorris, who is killed at the
            end of World War II, and Mary Besy (Burkhardt) Dorris.

1963   Enrolls at Georgetown University on scholarship

1967   Graduates *cum laude*, Phi Beta Kappa from Georgetown
            University with a B.A. in English and classics; receives a
            Woodrow Wilson fellowship and a Danforth graduate
            fellowship; appointed editor of *Viewpoint*.

1967–68   Graduate student in department of history of the theatre,
            Yale University

1968–71   Graduate student in department of anthropology at Yale
            University; receives a M.Phil. from Yale University.

1971–72   Assistant professor of anthropology at Franconia College,
            Franconia, New Hampshire; awarded a National Institute of
            Mental Health research grant.

1972   Joins Dartmouth College faculty in Hanover, New
            Hampshire; appointed chairman of Native American Studies
            Department.

1973–74   Becomes chair of Native American Council; begins serving
           as member of editorial board of *American Indian Culture
           and Research Journal*.

1977   Thomas Y. Crowell publishes *Native Americans: Five
           Hundred Years After*.

1978   Awarded Guggenheim fellowship

1980   Receives a Woodrow Wilson faculty development fel-
           lowship and is a visiting senior lecturer in anthropology and
           Maori studies at Auckland University, New Zealand.

1981   Marries Louise Erdrich on 10 October

1983   Publishes *A Guide to Research on North American Indians*,
           which is selected as an "Outstanding Academic Book" by
           Choice

1985   Appointed Rockefeller Foundation Research Fellow and
           receives Indian Achievement Award

1987   Publishes *A Yellow Raft in Blue Water*

1988   PEN Syndicated Fiction Award for "Name Games"

1989   Awarded a National Endowment for the Arts creative
           writing fellowship. Harper publishes *The Broken Cord*,
           which wins the National Book Critics Circle Award for Best
           Nonfiction Book. To devote more time to writing, resigns
           from full-time faculty position and is appointed adjunct
           professor, Dartmouth College.

1990   *The Broken Cord* named Outstanding Academic Book by
           Choice; receives Christopher Award and Heartland Prize for
           the book.

1991   With Louise Erdrich, publishes *The Crown of Columbus* and

Route Two; board of directors, Save the Children Foundation; receives Sarah Josepha Hale Literary Award.

1992   Publishes *Morning Girl* and receives Scott O'Dell Award for best historical fiction for young readers; receives Center for anthropology and Journalism Award for Excellence and Overseas Press Club citation for Zimbabwe essays. A film based on *The Broken Cord* receives the Scott Newman Award, Gabriel Award for National Entertainment Program, ARC Media Award, Christopher Award, Writers' Guild of America Award, and American Psychology Association annual "Media Award."

1993   *Rooms in the House of Stone* (essays) and *Working Men* (stories) scheduled for publication

1994   *PaperTrail* (collected essays) scheduled for publication

Conversations with Louise Erdrich
and Michael Dorris

Life, Art Are One for Prize Novelist

Malcolm Jones/1985

From *St. Petersburg Times,* 10 February 1985, 1D, 7D. Reprinted with permission of the *St. Petersburg Times.*

New York—Louise Erdrich's novel, *Love Medicine,* which just won the National Book Critics' Circle prize for fiction, is so full of voices, young and old, aggrieved and at peace, that a reader might expect Erdrich to be nothing less than a wizened sage with a motley life and a long shelf of books to her credit.

Yet the author's picture on the dust jacket shows a handsome young woman whose expression is so warm and beatific that she might have known no hard experience at all, and the jacket copy tells us that this is her first novel.

The jacket copy also says that Erdrich is a member of the Turtle Mountain Band of Chippewa; that she is a wife and mother; that she won the 1982 Nelson Algren Award for fiction; has written a book of poetry, *Jacklight*; and has published short stories in national magazines and seen her work selected for *The Best American Short Stories of 1983.*

Impressive stuff, but not extraordinary, and it certainly doesn't explain how this 30-year-old woman came to write such an accomplished novel on the first try. *Love Medicine* is both emotionally and literarily sophisticated, a novel that begins near the present, drops back to the '30s, and then spins out several tales of several lives of Indians living on a reservation in North Dakota.

The tales swap narrators, scenes are seen from more than one perspective, generations pass, and new characters come forward to interact with their elders and to carry the saga forward. It is not a conventional novel, but it is altogether plausible and even logical after awhile.

Yes, logical, for while a lot has been said about Erdrich's precise language, that ought to be a given with a good writer (it's remarkable only when a good writer isn't much good with words, e.g., William Golding, Theodore Dreiser, Philip K. Dick). What is remarkable about her writing is its scrupulous logic.

She takes a set of characters, puts them together and wonders, What

now? And, Then what? And, given that, What then? She doesn't shy
from ugly conclusions, and the stories in *Love Medicine* are the more
credible for that.

All right, so relentlessness is part of her talent, and neither a small
nor negligible part, since most writers aren't brave enough to stare too
long at life. But relentlessness taken alone is a close cousin to callous-
ness, and Erdrich isn't a callous writer.

I would say she was sensitive, but that might make her sound weepy,
so I'll settle for saying that she seems to have a good grasp on who she
is and where she's from.

When we met a couple of weeks ago to talk about the book, I asked
about the way her novel trades narrators from chapter to chapter and
sometimes even skips about in time.

In a melodious voice with an almost narcotic lilt, she replied that, as
a fan of William Faulkner, William Gass, Toni Morrison and some of
the Latin American writers, she isn't afraid of experimentation; and so,
while she knew the plot and could have written it as a traditional novel,
she decided against that because the form the book was taking—with
stories almost but not quite independent of one another—was a legitimate novelistic form, "something I have always loved reading."

Then she said, "It also reflects a traditional Chippewa motif in
storytelling, which is a cycle of stories having to do with a central
mythological figure, a culture here. One tells a story about an incident
that leads to another incident that leads to another in the life of this
particular figure. Night after night, or day after day, it's a storytelling
cycle. It's the sort of thing where people know what they're going to
say. They're old stories, but the stories have incorporated different
elements of non-Chippewa or European culture as they've gone on, so
that sometimes you see a great traditional story with some sort of fairy
tale element added to it."

We met on a cold January morning at her aunt's apartment in Manhattan one day before Erdrich was due to collect her award from the
NBCC. I was barely out of my overcoat before I began seeing more
evidence of how life and art are not long separated for this writer.

Her husband was there, as were two of their four children, as was the
author's editor, whose job it was to spirit the children off to nearby
Central Park for the morning. Erdrich herself was in the kitchen brewing

coffee, while her Aunt Jenny bustled about, seeing to everyone's comfort.

For me, the smell of coffee brewing in a household always welds the image into whatever part of my mind takes stock of domestic matters, so, walking in, I couldn't help thinking of one of *Love Medicine's* opening scenes in which a young Indian woman goes home to the reservation and is immediately swallowed up in a makeshift family reunion.

That scene is painful, the scene I saw was not; but they shared a welter of domestic activity, and Erdrich assured me that things are usually even more chaotic around Aunt Jenny's during family visits.

It isn't too surprising that family life should occupy such a big spot in her fiction, since both Erdrich and her husband, Michael Dorris, who is also half Indian, come from large families. Likewise, given the accommodations that big families make to get along, maybe it isn't too shocking that Erdrich and Dorris collaborate to a much larger extent than do most writers.

"The only part (of *Love Medicine*) that I was not involved with was the writing of the drafts," said Dorris, who runs the Native American studies program at Dartmouth College and is an author himself.

"We talked about the plots, the characterization, the conceptualization, the order, all that stuff, and then, as a draft or part of a draft is finished, Louise gives it to me, and I read it, and make suggestions and comments or reinforcements, as the case may be."

Once the coffee was perked and tea brewed and the children were out the door, Erdrich and Dorris settled down in the living room to talk. Each took turns talking, and each would take a turn answering the telephone that never stopped ringing in the back room.

Dorris is tall and rangy and loquacious, and Erdrich is his compliment: tall but in no way angular, articulate but somehow meditative in her answers.

"Basically, I think she and I have the same 'ear,' in the sense that as an artist has an 'eye,' a writer has an 'ear'," Dorris said. "Sometimes, since Louise is a poet, there will be certain combinations of words that will be just irresistible, and it is my unfortunate task to say, That's a beautiful combination, but that person would never say that. Then we argue about whether they would or not and in the process figure out a little more about who that person is.

"With *Love Medicine*, we read it out loud to each other when it was finished twice, slowly and did some integration between the various stories to tie them together and figure out the chronology and the relationships and all that stuff in a way that would be comprehensible to someone who didn't know these people as well as we did.

"Then, after that, I was the agent and sold the book. And before it was far out of manuscript, we were at work on the next book, and had already worked on a previous one. There are basically four books related, two of which are much more than half completed, and one of which is about a quarter or a third completed."

Okay again, many of us have large families, many of us know how to collaborate with others, and still we do not write good novels. So what, other than the fact that her father paid her a nickel every time she brought him a story when she was a kid, set Erdrich on the way to getting all of this on paper?

After watching her that morning, and listening to her talk, I decided that a lot of her talent has to do with affection for people who are up against trouble, even when they misbehave. It's not sloppy affection, though. Her characters were more warts than haloes.

Part of her fondness for the people comes from a nostalgia for the place where she grew up, Wahpeton, N.D. and the North Dakota reservation where her mother grew up. Erdrich and her family now live on 17 acres in rural New Hampshire, and while they are fond of the land and the house (laughing, they say that visitors always tell them the place has "a lot of possibilities"), it's a far cry, geographically and emotionally, from the Great Plains.

"We miss the West quite a bit sometimes," she said, "because that's where the writing is set, and maybe the book is informed by that kind of nostalgia or longing in a way for openness. That's the thing I really do miss, that and my family.

"Michael and I both have a strong sense of family and community. I grew up with storytellers in the family. Both sides, my father and my mother, had a *lot* to tell about the Depression," she says with a humorless chuckle, "and so there's a lot of Depression in this book. When we look at the book and the time span, it's our parents' lifetime and our lifetime and it's probably because we both listened a great many hours."

At this point Dorris was quick to point out that the novel "really isn't autobiographical. It's a curious blend of details that we picked up, either from Louise's life or mine, sometimes we can't remember which. And a lot of invention."

"More than anything else, it's invention." Erdrich says. "There are things that family members recognize or small incidents that are embroidered upon. It's something that's fabricated, but out of real observations and real aspects of people we might have known or imagined. But people that are totally fictional, that we've never met in our lives, became the most compelling of all to us. Like Lulu."

Lulu Lamartine, part earth mother, part strumpet, is a human pivot round which much of the novel's action turns. As her complicated love life affects more than one household, so do the children from these households slowly uncover relationships of both blood and spirit that have their foundations in Lulu's actions.

"No one like her has ever existed in my life," Erdrich said, "and yet to me she's completely real. Certainly we both imagined her in great detail as being real.

"Another thing is that we don't really have a social community. We're out in the country, we're isolated. So, the characters become a sort of fictive community, and when we talk about them and think about them, it's really, it's really . . . well, it's great fun."

Although both Erdrich and Dorris, especially Dorris, are active in Indian organizations and causes, and although *Love Medicine* is grounded in the realities of Indian life, it is not a "cause" novel nor is it particularly political.

One of the characters is involved with the American Indian Movement AIM, and one represents his people in Washington on occasion, but the rest are, if not apathetic, generally not too absorbed in headline making.

According to Dorris, "*Love Medicine* focuses on the community and not on the conflict between Indians and non-Indians. It's sort of out there on the periphery. We decided to focus everything on the community in order to remind people that in the daily lives of contemporary Indian people, the important thing is relationships, and family and history, as it is in everybody's life, and not these sort of larger political questions, although they do impinge."

Impinge is a polite word for the occasional mule kicks awaiting unsuspecting throughout *Love Medicine,* as when one of the characters leaves the reservation and tries his luck in the white world. One of his jobs gets him into the movies, but the employment holds no satisfaction once Nector Kashpaw realizes that "Death was the extent of Indian acting in the movie theater."

But, as Dorris pointed out, "With people growing up on reservations, the first time they're in a minority or think of themselves as in a minority is when they leave. While you're there, it isn't a big issue."

Both of them see reservations as places to be fought for and preserved.

"One thing that I hope is clear in the book is that people aren't incarcerated there," Erdrich said. "Sometimes people will read this book as depressing, as though people are trapped on this place, but it's land, and it ought to be increased. Michael described a reservation as a homeland, and I think that's true. It's a place where culture has been kept alive.

"Now, although the places have seemed in former times very rocky and barren and sort of end of the earth and that's why they got 'em, it now is true that these lands are quite uranium rich, oil rich, water rich, and Native American people of all different tribes are having enormous problems on a whole new front."

"Not only that," Dorris says, "they are the people who have suffered most under this last administration. Half the money allocated for Indian education is gone. A third of the money for Indian health has been eliminated, including all the money that was paying for Indian students in medical school. And it's an invisible cut, because we're talking about 200 different tribes, none of whom have enough political clout, except possibly the Navajos, to make a stink.

"And it's money that many people believe shouldn't even be coming, because they think of it as the dole rather than as an installment payment on North America, which is what it in fact is.

"The whole basis for Indian land and sovereignty is 'You give up Wisconsin and keep this one little bit, and we will pay you so much money a year in perpetuity.' But then people forget why that came about, and think, 'Gee, they're getting something for nothing.'"

Erdrich and Dorris are newcomers to fame, and they say that so far *Love Medicine's* success has wrought no great changes in their lives, aside from buying an answering machine to keep the outside world a little more at bay. The biggest, and most positive, change they anticipate is the freedom to keep working, to have the chance to publish more books.

In the meantime, they are enjoying the book signing at the local bookstore back home, and the sight of the *New York Times* advertisement for the book taped to the cash register of the local country store. Otherwise, there is life as usual, which at present includes the pleasant anticipation of the birth in two months of their fifth child.

And, oh yes, Erdrich wished aloud that some profit from the book might give them leave to think of hiring a carpenter who can afford to advertise in the Yellow Pages.

Intimate Collaboration or "A Novel Partnership."

Shelby Grantham/1985

From *Dartmouth Alumni Magazine,* March 1985, 43–47. Pre-printed by permission.

"I like old, old yellowed paper," explains Louise Erdrich '76. "I know that's silly. But I love finding boxes of old paper at office supply sales. I will write on anything—lined, unlined, scrap—but I savor the pages that I write on old, brittle paper."

The author of the recent bestseller *Love Medicine* crosses her ankles and slumps back into an overstuffed couch. Beside her lies an unhappy tiger cat with a swollen paw. He has an appointment with the vet in a couple of hours, but in the meantime, Erdrich will answer another batch of impertinent questions. Publicity is important.

"I always write with a pen. Actually, I write with anything I can find. But I prefer a black felt tip. I write by hand and type it up afterward on an electric typewriter. I have a lovely new one now, that I'm almost scared to use. I was fond of the old one, even if it did stick on pica 80."

She is softly handsome, a full-lipped, broad-nosed, and strong-jawed woman who seems younger than her 30 years. Her handshake is tentative and a girlish awkwardness lingers about her. But it takes only a short while to discover that she cannot be pushed around in conversation; and no one could write the way she does without an unflinching mind and a very brave heart.

As early as 1975, when Erdrich was a junior at Dartmouth, English professor A. B. Paulson cited her for literary excellence. "Ms. Erdrich is a writer and poet of extraordinary talent," he wrote, and that same year another English professor commended her gifts as a lyric poet. She was also praised that year for "impressive work" in his course by Dartmouth Professor of Anthropology Michael Dorris—more of whom later.

After winning The American Academy of Poets Prize, taking a master's degree in creative writing from Johns Hopkins University, reeling in two PEN newspaper awards, and receiving a National Endowment for the Arts fellowship, she returned to Dartmouth in 1980 for a year as writer-in-residence. In 1982, writer-judges Donald Barthelme, Kay Boyle, and Studs Terkel chose her short story "The World's

Greatest Fishermen" from among 2,000 entries and awarded her *Chicago Magazine*'s $5,000 Nelson Algren Prize. The next year she was represented in *The Best American Short Stories of 1983*. Then separate chapters of a novel began to appear in such top-flight journals as *The Atlantic Monthly, Ms.,* and *The Kenyon Review.*

In 1984, Judy Karasik, an editor at Holt, Rinehart & Winston, was told in a dream that *Jacklight,* Erdrich's volume of blank verse poetry, ought to be published—and so it was. Later that year, Holt also brought out Erdrich's novel, *Love Medicine,* which was in short order proclaimed an alternate selection of the Book-of-the-Month Club, a "New Voices" selection of the Quality Paperback Book Club, and winner of both The American Academy and Institute for Arts and Letters' 1984 Kaufman Prize for the best first piece of fiction and The National Book Critics Circle Award for the best book of fiction published in 1984. As her agent Michael Dorris says, "It's hot stuff."

Love Medicine is actually the result of a collaboration, according to Erdrich, who explains that when she writes she works closely with her editor, Michael Dorris. The basis of the collaboration, says Dorris, is talk—"weeks of conversation" about a character's looks, his clothes, her jewelry. "The details of clothes and action are invented and thought about between the two of us," says Erdrich. "Often Michael notices things about people I don't."

Erdrich will do a draft, or part of one, according to Dorris, and then give it to him to read: "If she is really happy with it, she reads it aloud. Most often she just gives it to me, and I make suggestions. It's a draft at this point, an idea struggling to get out. She knows her stuff well. I am a gentle reader, a sounding board."

This intimate collaboration works, Erdrich and Dorris say, because of the similarity of their backgrounds, which they describe as "lower middle class" and "mixed blood." Erdrich was born and raised in Wahpeton, North Dakota, one of eight children born to a Chippewa mother and a German-American father, both of whom taught in the boarding schools run by the Bureau of Indian Affairs. Dorris, 39 grew up in many places—Kentucky, Montana, Washington State and is the only child of a Modoc father and a mother from Kentucky. Neither Erdrich nor Dorris was raised on a reservation, but both often visited relatives there, and for each of them, the reservation became a sort of second home.

One result of sharing such experiences, says Dorris, is familiarity with the same idiom. That allows Dorris to be what he calls "a language testing ground" for Erdrich's work, checking what she describes as "the things people wouldn't do or say, the psychological veracity of a scene."

Overwriting is a problem for her, Erdrich feels—"too many words, labored attempts at comparison, too many metaphors"—and Dorris is a help there, too. He explains it this way: "Louise has the largest vocabulary of anybody I know. Esoteric words often mean exactly what she wants, but sometimes they are not words that characters would say. They jump out at you. I tell her, 'It's a beautiful word, a great choice—*but* it's inconsistent with the mood.' "

Erdrich and Dorris first met in 1972, on the day each arrived in Hanover for the first time, he as an instructor in anthropology, she as an undergraduate. "Once, she took a seminar I gave," recalls Dorris. "We were friends, and after she graduated, we kept in touch with Christmas cards." Then, in 1979, Erdrich returned to Hanover to give a reading at Dartmouth. By that time, Dorris had adopted three children and become a tenured professor teaching anthropology and chairing Dartmouth's Native American Studies Program. He attended her reading: "It was exclusively poetry, which was what she was writing then. I was tremendously impressed, especially with her reading ability. Louise is as good a reader as she is a writer." Shortly thereafter, Dorris took the children to New Zealand, where he spent a sabbatical year studying early Maori-English relations. He and Erdrich corresponded.

According to a 1984 interview by Georgia Croft, Erdrich decided at 21 that she wanted to be a writer—but, she says, she didn't really go into it full-time until she was 26. "I began with a switch from poetry to fiction in 1980. I was happy about that because—as was often pointed out by readers of my poetry—my poems are narrative, more like stories than poems." Before that, she says, she had not had the patience to write a novel.

"At Johns Hopkins, midstream, I made a rambling stab at a novel. 'The burden is on me now,' I remember feeling. It was Time to Write a Novel. It was a search for a voice, a very serious, very ponderous novel. It just went on and on. I tried everything I could think of out and put everything I could think of in."

Dorris, meanwhile, had decided to try his hand at creative writing, too—although as a single parent with a heavy teaching load, he found precious little time for it. "I published some poetry in *The North Dakota Quarterly* and *Suntracks,*" he says. "Two of my poems were anthologized in *Best American Verse,* and I published some little stories—commercial stories." He sent the stories to Erdrich for comment, and she sent him her story "Red Convertible."

Dorris returned from New Zealand, and Erdrich reappeared in Hanover as writer-in-residence under the auspices of the Native American Program. She was still at work on the manuscript of her "very serious novel," which by then had acquired a title—*Tracks.* She showed it to Dorris, he recalls, and they started working on it together.

"It was exciting, beautiful writing," recalls Dorris. "Working on *Tracks* was fun, and I felt I was making a contribution. We started on it in January, fell in love, and were married in October."

Soon after they married, Erdrich and Dorris took their first shot at co-authorship. "We did some domestic, romantic stuff, drawn from our experience, for our own enjoyment," recalls Erdrich. "We published it under one name, a pen name, "Milou North"—*Mi*chael plus *Lou*ise plus where we live. No one seemed to think it was a strange name, which is weird. One of those stories has been in *Redbook,* but the rest have appeared in Europe. The general theme was domestic crisis—money, an old flame showing up, that sort of thing. We thought it would make a lot of money. It didn't."

Then Dorris's aunt read about a new literary prize—the Algren Award—and sent the couple a notice about it, which arrived in Cornish 12 days before the submission deadline. Erdrich and Dorris pondered this temptation to "fame and fortune" and then decided to try for it.

"Why not, we thought," recalls Erdrich. "Or rather *Michael* thought, *I* thought, I don't feel like it. I had a story I wanted to work on, but it was winter, we had houseguests, and the children were home because it was a school holiday. I didn't believe I could write straight through in two days. But Michael said, 'Try it, just try it. What harm is there?'"

Since her study is also the guest room, Erdrich had to set up elsewhere: "I hate having to block off a quiet part of the house, but I barricaded myself at the kitchen table behind closed doors. It seemed very depressing. But as soon as I got the first section down, I knew I couldn't stop writing. It was upsetting, and I had to go on."

The first part of what became "The World's Greatest Fishermen" was drafted completely by the end of the day. "I had thought of an episode—a family reunion—with events, but no conversation or details yet," recalls Erdrich. "In the meantime, however, Michael had sprained his back, and the guests were trying to tend to themselves and to the children. Michael couldn't move—he took Tylenol and tried to relax on the sitting room floor all that day and through the night. I would bring in parts of the story and he would hold them over his face to read them."

When the story was finished, just under the wire, Erdrich and Dorris typed it up together—that, says Erdrich, was hard for her: "I have a lot of trepidation about letting anyone else type up my work. It's a superstition. But it was necessary. By then, Michael had gotten up off the floor."

It won. The Erdrich-Dorris literary partnership was a success. After the Algren, one or the other of them realized that two stories Erdrich had published earlier—"The Red Convertible" and "Scales"—belonged to the same world as "The World's Greatest Fishermen," and Erdrich embarked on a second novel built around them. Thus was *Love Medicine* born and Erdrich launched on a tide of critical acclaim such as every writer yearns for and at the same time mistrusts. Philip Roth has declared her "greatly gifted" and found in her work "originality, authority, tenderness, and a pitiless and wild wit," and Toni Morrison has written that "the beauty of *Love Medicine* saves us from being devastated by its power."

The book consists of 21 stories—"the related stories of the intertwined lives of two families living on a North Dakota reservation from 1934 to 1984," as the book jacket explains. A few of the stories are omnisciently narrated, but most are brilliantly immediate monologues by the characters themselves. The fact that the characters are on a reservation is important, says Erdrich—but not as important as the linked themes of survival and the healing power of life: "The people are first, their ethnic background is second." It is a point all too many reviewers have missed, and, as she told *The Wall Street Journal*, Erdrich sometimes worries that *Love Medicine* "will be perceived as another 'plight of the Indian' novel." In fact, Erdrich's characters are no more "ethnic" than William Faulkner's or Eudora Welty's—no less, admittedly, but certainly no more—and their "plights" are universal.

The first chapter of *Love Medicine* is a revised version of "The World's Greatest Fishermen." It opens in 1981 with the poignant story of the last days of June Kashpaw, who dies walking home in a blizzard on Easter day. Her death occasions a family reunion at the home of her adoptive parents, Grandma and Grandpa Kashpaw, and this first chapter ends with the despoilation of a large number of freshly-baked pies. It is followed by a flashback of 47 years to 1934, when the separate lives of Marie Lazarre (Grandma) and Nector Kashpaw (Grandpa) intersect, and Nector, in "an instant that changes the course of his life," is diverted from the pursuit of a ripening Lulu Nanapush into marriage with Marie. From there the book moves forward, collecting lives right and left like a burdock burr.

Despite losing out to Marie in the matter of Nector, the wise and lusty Lulu is perhaps the most engaging character in the book. She is Dorris's favorite and has become for Erdrich "one of the most real characters I know." Lulu has "bold, gleaming blackberry eyes" and "smooth tight skin, wrinkled only where she laughed, always fragrantly powdered," and she "let the men in just for being part of the world," because she was "in love with the whole world and all that lived in its rainy arms."

"And so," she says, "when they tell you that I was heartless, a shameless man-chaser, don't ever forget this: I loved what I saw. And yes, it is true that I've done all the things they say. That's not what gets them. What aggravates them is I've never shed one solitary tear. I'm not sorry."

Lulu has a child, Gerry, by Old Man Pillager and then marries Henry Lamartine, who endures patiently her prolific production of sons not his own. Lulu's son Gerry and the young June Morrissey (later June Kashpaw, whose death opens the novel) produce their own illegitimate son, though June does not acknowledge him and he is raised by Grandma and Grandpa Kashpaw in ignorance of his origins. This son, Lipsha Morrissey, is the finest voice in the novel.

"Lipsha sat down," recounts his cousin Albertine, "with a beer in his hand like everyone, and looked at the floor. He was more of a listener than a talker, a shy one with a wide, sweet, intelligent face. He had long eyelashes. . . . Although he never did well in school, Lipsha knew surprising things. He read books about computers and volcanoes and the life cycles of salamanders. Sometimes he used words I had to ask him the meaning of, and other times he didn't make even the simplest sense. I loved him for being both ways."

Lipsha's discovery of his origins and his acceptance of them provide the ballast for this episodic novel. All the grieving and drinking and lusting and dying, the loving and torturing and birthing and joking, the working and musing and wising-up packed into this magnificent chronicle culminate in Lipsha's realization that "there was good" in his life, appearances to the contrary notwithstanding. The book is finally a celebration of such acceptances, and of patience, toleration, endurance, and passion. Reading *Love Medicine* is as reassuring as looking on the Sistine sybils—those ageless, full-fleshed, monumental custodians of creation, those smiling and unflappable *mothers*.

Lipsha, having discovered who his mother was and found his father, brings the book to its triumphant conclusion. "The sun flared up," he says, having just driven his father, escaped convict and Indian hero Gerry Nanapush, across the river into Canada. "I'd heard that this river was the last of an ancient ocean, miles deep, that once had covered the Dakotas and solved all our problems. It was easy to still imagine us beneath them vast unreasoning waves, but the truth is we live on dry land. I got inside. The morning was clear. A good road led on. So there was nothing to do but cross the water, and bring her home."

Erdrich recalls the ordering of its parts as one of Dorris's most significant contributions to *Love Medicine:* "'Scales' and 'The Red Convertible' were written at the same time (I collected sentences over a period of time for them—on pieces of paper, napkins at restaurants). But I let them sit a long time. I kept at the long, tortuous novel and tried to write another short story. They didn't become a novel until Michael entered the picture. I did not see that the bunch of episodes was really a long, long story. They all meshed and became a novel through a lot of late-night conversations between Michael and me until the plot was discovered."

Erdrich originally had the book in an "entirely different" form. "I didn't have it chronological," she says. "I had no real theory behind the form. I started it way in the past with 'St. Marie,' then went to the present, and then back and forth without any real structure, just a kind of personal liking." Both Dorris and the editor at Holt found Erdrich's order confusing. She resisted changing it for some time, she says, but in the end they convinced her, and now she is pleased that the book has only the one jump backwards in time.

Dorris may be, as he says, "a gentle reader"—but he is a thoroughly hard-nosed editor. "Originally," he recalls, "the 'St. Marie' chapter was

a parody of *Heart of Darkness*. I said it should be more serious. Louise
was not pleased. She rewrote it from the point of view of the sisters.
Very pleased with that, she was. I could tell she was pleased—she was
asking me to read it *now*. I didn't like it. That was bad news. But I told
her so, said the voice was wrong. I told her to make it first person. That
is a thing I encourage her to trust. She's so good at it, she makes it so
vivid, so real. She chucked it in the other room, said she never wanted
to see it again, stomped out of the house, and took a long walk in the
woods. I sort of lay low and let her deal with it. The next day, there was
a new draft on my desk. We had no other words about it—it just
appeared there. And it was absolutely right."

"Michael has a writer's mind," says Erdrich. "I doubt if he would
ever give up teaching, but he dreams books. Words overwhelm him
every so often, and he has to write them down. But he has almost no
time—no time. The last time he wrote, he did it in the car with one
hand on the wheel. That's part of what this is all about."

Sometimes, says Dorris, he contributes "whole episodes." "Sister
Leopolda in the 'St. Marie' story was a character I knew well in the
fourth grade—the closet, the shoe, the window-stick. And suddenly that
appeared, subsumed, as a story. Louise said, 'The complete image
popped out of my head.' But I recognized it."

One of the most ticklish decisions Erdrich and Dorris had to make
was whether to publish jointly. They decided not to. Dorris may have
his fingers in a good many pies, but Erdrich is the writer. "I read with
pencil in hand," says Dorris, "and I mean *pencil*. The final decision is
Louise's."

Dorris is easy—perhaps, he feels, easier than Erdrich is—about his
remaining in the wings. "I'm not like a frustrated writer who wishes it
were me. I'm glad it's Louise. What I do now may be the best thing I
can do literarily. It's such a kick to be more than just a cheerleader. I
have no problem with the fact that my name is not on the books." He
shrugs. "Louise is always careful to give me credit."

When *Love Medicine* was sent out to an agent, it didn't move, and
finally Dorris decided to become Erdrich's agent himself. As he told
Wall Street Journal reporter Helen Dudar, "I figured that chutzpah and
my monomaniacal devotion would work. And it did. We made a number of magazine sales before Holt took over. I would send out sections
of the book with long letters about Louise and how they should get in on

the ground floor. I even had 'Michael Dorris Agency' stationery printed up. I did everything but open my shirt down to here and wear chains around my neck and call everybody baby."

Dorris admits that he learned the agent's trade by trial and error. He feels that he didn't know enough in the beginning to demand the best royalty arrangements and that he reserved for himself and Erdrich too few options. "The cover choice, for instance, we got only because of the intercession of our editor at Holt. Holt had originally selected a cover of a coffeepot in a window. It was too domestic and tame. We wanted—and finally got—a photograph of the Aurora Borealis." And their decision to subcontract the movie rights is giving them second thoughts, since they disagree with the sub-agent's recommendation of a television mini-series.

Being an agent is fun, says Dorris—"the gamesmanship of it—the negotiation, the deals, having my own stationery printed." And in that role, he points out, eschewing the byline has its advantages. "Playing agent would be difficult if my name were on the book. This way, I can call up and go into raptures and *sound* selfless."

"The whole experience may have averted my mid-life crisis," says Dorris, grinning happily. Erdrich, too, has found the success of *Love Medicine* to be a watershed: "Now I have to go back to *Tracks* and do without the tension that was present when I had to sit down at writers' colonies with the weight of the world on the shoulders of My Novel. It was a logical progression. I am now not as serious about writing, am much more anxious to have a good time doing it."

Dorris is also eager for her to have a good time doing it. "She's impervious to critical acclaim," he says with wry affection. "If she goes three days without working, she feels, 'I've lost my talent!' I used to take all that much more seriously than I do now. I feel like giving her a pie in the face sometimes now."

Still, it is true that Erdrich has not yet achieved her greatest ambition. "I want you to be able to buy my book at the Minot, North Dakota, airport," she says. But that surely, is only a matter of time. Probably not much time, either.

Louise Erdrich and Michael Dorris

Laura Coltelli/1985

From *Winged Words: American Indian Writers Speak,* by Laura Coltelli (Lincoln: University of Nebraska Press, 1990), 41–52. Reprinted by permission of the University of Nebraska Press. Copyright © 1990 by the University of Nebraska Press.

Louise Erdrich was born in 1954 in Little Falls, North Dakota, and she attended schools at Wahpeton. Her father is of German descent and her mother is a Turtle Mountain Chippewa. After graduating from Dartmouth in 1976 with a major in English and creative writing, Erdrich returned to North Dakota, where she conducted poetry workshops throughout the state under the auspices of the Poetry in the Schools Program of the North Dakota Arts Council. She later entered the creative-writing program at Johns Hopkins University, directed by Richard Howard. After receiving a master's degree in creative writing, she moved to Boston, where she became editor of the Boston Indian Council newspaper, *The Circle.*

Michael Dorris arrived at Dartmouth College in 1972 to join and later to direct the Native American Studies Program. Erdrich and Dorris met at Dartmouth and were married in 1981.

First a poet and then a novelist (her collected poems, *Jacklight,* were published in 1984), Erdrich's short stories have appeared in many important magazines. Working with Michael Dorris, she turned the stories published between 1982 and 1984 into a novel, *Love Medicine* (1984), which received enthusiastic praise. Among its many awards, the novel was named the best work of fiction of 1984 by the National Book Critics Circle.

Michael Dorris was born in 1945 and grew up in Washington, Idaho, Kentucky, and Montana. A member of the Modoc tribe on his father's side, he received a bachelor's degree in English and classics from Georgetown University in 1967 and a master's in philosophy from Yale University in 1971. He has recently left Dartmouth College, where he was professor of anthropology and Native American studies, to devote himself to writing.

19

His many scholarly publications include *A Guide to Research on North American Indians* (1983), with Arlene Hirschfelder and Mary Lou Byler, and *Native Americans: Five Hundred Years After* (1977).

The unique collaboration between Louise Erdrich and Michael Dorris is explained by Michael himself: "We go over every word and achieve consensus on every word; basically we agree on every word when it's finally finished." They are currently writing together a four-volume family saga, three volumes of which have been published under Erdrich's name: *Love Medicine* (1984), *The Beet Queen* (1986), and *Tracks* (1988). In addition, they have collaborated on *A Yellow Raft in Blue Water* (1987), a novel, and *The Broken Cord*, a book on fetal alcohol syndrome in Indian reservations. Both of these are under Dorris's name.

Erdrich and Dorris live in Cornish, New Hampshire, with their family. They are the parents of six children: three children adopted by Dorris as a single parent whom Erdrich has since adopted and three children born since their marriage.

On September 17, 1985, I met with the Dorris family at Northfield, Minnesota, where Michael was spending a sabbatical. Incessant, simultaneous activities were going on in their house: Dorris, who acts as the couple's literary agent, was constantly interrupted by the telephone; Louise was busy with the youngest child, Pallas; Madeline, eleven, kept trying to find peace from her three-year-old sister, Persia; the computer printer was noisily doing its job somewhere. The creative process seemed to be perfectly shared.

LC: What's the source of your storytelling technique?

Dorris: Louise had two stories that were independent stories, "Scales" and "The Red Convertible." They were published independently and then there was a contest for the Nelson Algren Award for which they solicited stories of some five thousand or so words. We got the announcement that it was due by the fifteenth of January, and this was the first of January, and we just got back from vacation, and so we started talking about it and out of that grew "The World's Greatest Fishermen," the opening story of the novel *Love Medicine*, and we sent it off and thought of all the things that were wrong with it and what we would revise when it came back, and lo and behold, it won that contest.

There were thousands of entries. We said, if it's that good maybe we ought to think about expanding this and telling that same story because there are many stories in that story, from other points of view. And that expanded to developing the characters of Nector and Marie and Lulu and on and on. At first it was, I think, a series of stories, many of which were published independently, and then in the last several drafts we went back and tied them together. We realized some of the people who had different names were in fact the same character and that they would unite, very much the same way that this book has now turned into four books, because the next book, which is titled *The Beet Queen*, takes place in a small town just off the reservation where *Love Medicine* takes place. And some of the characters, Eli, for instance, are in that, and one of the main characters in *The Beet Queen* is Dot Adare, who married Gerry Nanapush in that book, and we didn't realize who it was until it was almost done. And then *Tracks,* which is the third book, takes the older character in both *Love Medicine* and *The Beet Queen* back a generation into a traditional time; and the fourth book, to be titled *American Horse,* will take the younger characters forward for a few years. It's a saga that takes place over about eighty years, a hundred years, and is an analogy in a way, of all the processes that people in this part of the country have gone through.

The Turtle Mountain Chippewa people are an interesting group because they came originally from northern Minnesota but are heavily mixed with French and Cree, and so the language that they speak up there is called Michif, which is a combination of all those. And for instance, Lipsha, the character in *Love Medicine,* is Michif bastardization of *le petit chou,* the French expression of endearment, "my little cabbage," and that's where the name comes from. The traditional music in Turtle Mountain is fiddle music and there are a lot of French names up there.

LC: So is it a kind of traditional tribal storytelling technique?

Dorris: It's cyclical in that respect and that's why it's disturbing that the last line of the Italian translation does not bring her back into it,[1] because basically this is the story of the reverberation of June's life even though she is the one character who does not have her own voice. Bringing her home is finally in fact resolving her life and death in balance.

[1]*Medicina d'amore* (Milan: Mondadori, 1985).

LC: Can you speak about the point of view in *Love Medicine?*

Dorris: It's what Louise does best, basically. Every one of these stories went through seven, eight drafts, some in third person, some in the voice of a different character, and basically the voices that emerge are the ones that work best. One of my roles in this was to tell Louise that she really did it well. We all think we should be able to do that thing which was hardest for us rather than things which are easiest for us. First-person narrative is easiest for Louise; she does it best. It's not easy, but she does it best. It is a story cycle in the traditional sense. One of the interesting reviews of the book was talking about the fact that nobody in the book is right, that in fact it is community voice, that the point of view is the community voice and the means of exchanging information is gossip, and so consequently there is no narrator; there is no single protagonist, but rather it is the entire community dealing with the upheavals that emerge from the book and now will emerge from four books. [Louise returns from feeding the baby.] Now you can speak for yourself.

LC: In *Love Medicine,* one character, Lipsha, was happy because he hadn't yet acquired a memory, and Granpa was happy because he was losing his. Memory then is a burden instead of being a source to shape a new identity and as a link between past and present.

Erdrich: That's an interesting tie. I guess for Nector the events of his life and his guilt made his memory a burden for him. It's certainly not a burden for everyone in the book. But for him I think the guilt of his association with his mistress, with Lulu, his rejection of her and burning her house down, whether he causes it directly or not, made memory something he is not happy to live with.

LC: The multiethnic family is at the center of *Love Medicine.* How do you see the future generations of American Indians from this perspective?

Dorris: The only multiethnic person, really, is King's wife, Lynette. Marie is a mixed-blood herself.

Erdrich: Well, everybody has a lot of French, but in particular the French and the Indian had been so blended by that time, it's a new culture. I don't know what to think about it; I haven't really thought a lot about what the future would be. I suppose more of the same. [To Michael.] What do you think? Have you thought about that?

Dorris: Well, I think one question people ask us and have been asking since 1620 is "Are Indians vanishing?" "Are Indians going away?" I think the answer to that question would be no. Maybe native tribal culture has changed like all cultures, and *Love Medicine* is a story about a contemporary group of people that are in some ways indistinguishable from other rural North Dakota people who are not rich, but in other ways they are very much unique, very much who they were; they have the same kind of symbols that inspired Chippewas in the past, the water and the water god, and they have the kind of family connection which has always been the core of the tribe, I think. It is more subtle than when people dressed differently and when people spoke different languages and everything but not less real.

LC: Your poems in *Jacklight* show a remarkable narrative power and a tense poetic language. What's the impact of the storyteller upon the poet?

Erdrich: Probably it's more the other way around. I began as a poet, writing poetry, I began to tell stories in the poems and then realized that there was not enough room in a poem unless you are a John Milton and write enormous volumes of poetry. There was not enough room to really tell the story. I just began to realize that I wanted to be a fiction writer; that's a bigger medium, you know. I have a lot more room and it's closer to the oral tradition of sitting around and telling stories. But I think in the book you try to make the language do some of the same things, metaphorically and sensuously, physically, that poetry can do. So the poems had a real effect on the storytelling. But when I wrote the poetry I never had tried writing fiction before, so it was prior to all of the other stories.

LC: But do you consider yourself a poet or a storyteller?

Erdrich: Oh, a storyteller, a writer.

LC: Humor is one of the most important features of contemporary Native American literature. Is there a difference in the use of humor in the old Indian stories and in the contemporary ones?

Erdrich: The humor is a little blacker and bleaker now.

Dorris: Louise, have you talked about the ways in which we sort of consciously saw this book differently from much other contemporary fiction by American Indians? Most of the others, I am sure Laura is aware of, deal with contact in one way or another—what is the impact of leaving the reservation, coming back to the reservation—but the outside world very much imposes on the characters. In some of the drafts of *Love Medicine* that was the case, the characters went to Washington, or one thing or another, and basically we made a conscious decision, in the way Louise wrote the book to have it all centered in a community in which the outside world is not very present or very relevant in some respects. This is a world that is encompassed by that community, and it isn't so much the outside world of discrimination or wealth or anything like that, but rather this is how a community deals with itself and with the members of itself.

Erdrich: To go back just for one second, I really think the question about humor is very important. It's one of the most important parts of American Indian life and literature, and one thing that always hits us is just that Indian people really have a great sense of humor and when it's survival humor, you learn to laugh at things. It's really there, and I think Simon Ortiz is one person who has a lot of funny things happen, but a lot of terrible things as well in his work. It's just a personal way of responding to the world and to things that happen to you; it's a different way of looking at the world, very different from the stereotype, the stoic, unflinching Indian standing, looking at the sunset. It's really there, the humor, and I really hope that beside the serious parts in this particular book, people would see the humor.

LC: Do you see, then, American Indian literature as a multiethnic literature?

Erdrich: One of the big mistakes that a lot of people make in coming to American Indian literature is thinking, oh, if it's Indian it's Indian. It's just like being in Europe and saying French literature is European literature. Well, of course, French, Italian, German, any culture, has its own literature, its own background, its own language, that springs from that culture. The thing that we have in common is that English is a language which has been imposed on Indian people through a whole series of concerted efforts. Almost all American Indian writers speak English as their main language, as their first language, but they all come out of a different heritage, background, a different worldview, a different mythology.

LC: Do American Indian writers have a large audience among Indian people? Do Indian people see the writer's work as a means to preserve their culture?

Erdrich: My first audience that I would write for, that we write for, as a couple, is American Indians, hoping that they will read, laugh, cry,

really take in the work. One of the problems is the distribution of
literature. For instance, how many Indians can afford to buy *Love
Medicine* right now? It's pretty expensive and it's the way publishing
unfortunately goes on. One of our hopes was to have it available in a
nice, cheap edition everywhere, so that people could get it easily.

LC: Does literature develop a sense of Pan-Indianness?

Erdrich: Oh, yes, I think it does. There is a whole rich mine of Pan-
Indian culture people circulate, and I am sure literature is certainly one
of those things. Michael has had lots of mail from readers of *Love
Medicine,* Indians from different tribes who have read it and said,"This
is what happened here and it's so much like what happened to me, or to
someone I know." It's a kind of universalizing experience. The book
does touch some universals, which is what we're talking about, Pan-
Indianism. We wanted the reservation in *Love Medicine* to kind of ring
true to people from lots of different tribes.

LC: American Indian literature in mainstream American literature.
What's its place and its contribution?

Erdrich: I don't distinguish the two. I don't think American Indian
literature should be distinguished from mainstream literature. Setting it
apart and saying that people with special interest might read this literature sets Indians apart too.

LC: I am not distinguishing, I am not setting American Indian
literature apart from mainstream literature. Still, in American literature
you have black, Jewish, Chicano literature, and so on.

Erdrich: I was thinking ours contributes to literature as a whole in a
way that any book would. You have a view into someone's life that you
could not have had without this particular book and its vision. It's
contibuting in that way. I think that Jean Rhys said something about her
contribution being a small tributary to the great lake of literature. I think
that's the same way any writer feels. To contribute to the great run of
literature is very worthy.

LC: Can you speak about the contribution in terms of themes and
style?

Erdrich: Writing is different from tribe to tribe, the images are
different from tribe to tribe.

LC: What do you think of non-Indian critics and readers of your
work and of American Indian literature in general?

Erdrich: I never expected to get a letter back about this book, and there have been letters you would not believe; people just baring their souls. I think they really felt some kind of kinship with people in the book. People who are not Indians are writing these letters, too; it doesn't matter to me, I am glad for readers, as any writer is, I think, so I feel grateful. I want to be able to present Indian people as sympathetic characters, nonstereotypes, characters that any non-Indian would identify with. If they read the book with a certain kind of sympathy, I'm glad. What can I do but to be grateful for non-Indian critics who bring the work into a greater circulation and interest other people in it.

LC: What about the European approach toward American Indian literature?

Erdrich: I suppose I don't really know. I know that Karl May had a great effect on the German imagination. Anyway I think more interest is there, because so much of what is being written now is breaking the stereotypes and giving a different view of American Indians than Karl May could have. Because of his writing there's this fertile kind of ground, a thirst for American Indian literature, but goodness, there is more than Karl May. There are people writing who really write out of the tradition, who really are fascinating writers. There is that romanticizing aspect too, at least I am familiar with some Germans' attitude toward American Indian literature, but I think the distance between American Indians and Europeans is another factor, because people who live near Indians have the worst kind of prejudice—people who are competing for the same land. Probably there is less prejudice in Europe toward American Indians. I think that's how Indians feel in general; there is just less prejudice.

LC: Has there been any one major influence on your writing?

Erdrich: Michael, of course. He has been a major influence. He really is. I am indebted to him for organizing and making the book into a novel. I tended to be a person who thought in terms of stories and poems and short things. The book became a novel because of Michael. He came one day and said pretty much, "Oh, this is a novel," and you know, we began to write it in that way. So it's Michael. I would probably be a poet or a short-story writer, not a novelist. And other writers have influenced me. Certainly Toni Morrison, Barbara Pym, the English novelists.

LC: You mentioned Faulkner before.

Erdrich: (William) Faulkner, (Italo) Calvino. For me Calvino is one

of the most wonderful writers, and the magic in his work is something
that has been an influence, as well as the South American, Latin
American, writers.

LC: Are you going to write a screenplay from *Love Medicine?*

Dorris: It may be; it's not clear. I am doing a book, two books, this
year myself, with my name on them, but we are doing them together, in
the same way. One is a nonfiction book on fetal alcohol syndrome on
reservations, and another is a novel which is about people on a reservation farther west than this. *The Broken Cord* is about what happens
when on some reservations a very large percentage of children are born
with birth defects that come from their mothers' drinking during pregnancy. They are very subtle birth defects, sometimes that you can't see,
but they paralyze the ability to think abstractedly and they complicate
long-term choices. And how these communities cope with that. I was at
a reservation last week doing some interviews for that.

LC: How large is the percentage and where is this syndrome most
widespread?

Dorris: Fetal alcohol syndrome is a condition that exists, mostly
undiagnosed, in all parts of the world where women consume alcohol
during their pregnancies. Countries in which it is reported to be most
serious include the Soviet Union, France, Sweden, the United States,
and Japan. In some communities in this country, including some American Indian reservations, it is estimated that if current trends continue
something in excess of 50 percent of all babies born in the year 2000
A.D. will be impaired to some degree by FAS or FAE (fetal alcohol effect). The only truly safe policy is no drinking at all during pregnancy
or breast-feeding, since alcohol affects different women in various
ways.

LC: Could you describe your writing process?

Erdrich: Now we don't know what to do because we don't have a
big table in the living room. Back in New Hampshire, we put the table
out, and we could work with the whole manuscript at the end, when it
was about finished. But Michael will have a draft and show me and we
will talk it over, or I'll have a draft, talk about the whole plan of it,
characters out of it, just talk over every aspect of it.

Dorris: We get to know the characters very well and talk about them
and every situation. If we are in a restaurant we imagine what so-and-so
would order from the menu, and what so-and-so would choose from this

catalog, so that we get to know them in a full way, and when they appear on the page, they have that fullness behind them even though it doesn't all get written about.

LC: But who actually writes down the page?

Dorris: Louise. In *Love Medicine.*

Erdrich: Michael writes down on his page, or I write down on my page. I go and work in my room, and in *A Yellow Raft in Blue Water,* Michael goes and works on his computer. He can write right on the screen, right on the keyboard.

Dorris: And we edit it together. We go over every word and achieve consensus on every word; basically we agree on every word when it's finally finished.

LC: Did it work that way for *Love Medicine* too?

Dorris: Yes.

Erdrich: Yes, we go through—

Dorris: Every sentence!

Erdrich: Any!

Dorris: Many times, many times. Two times at the very end when it's all finished, then we sit down with the entire manuscript and talk about the manuscript and read it aloud at each other. We just did this with *The Beet Queen,* and it took about four weeks to go through what we thought was the finished manuscript, and in the course of that we cut thirty pages because it was like pinching it and squeezing it and thirty pages fell out.

LC: Could you speak a little bit more about your works in progress?

Erdrich: Michael's work is what we're working on now. He's writing a novel (*A Yellow Raft in Blue Water*) that has to do with a young teen-age girl who has a series of comic and tragic and explosive experiments. She gets into situations. One of my favorites is when she takes over for one of her cousins who is incapacitated, who can't ride his horse in a rodeo, and she rides the horse.

Dorris: She is a combination ethnically; her father is black and her mother is Indian, and so there is another multiethnic combination.

Erdrich: It hasn't been written very much at all, it's really fascinating.

Dorris: Not so uncommon. It's very common in certain parts of the country. *Tracks,* the third book in the *Love Medicine* quartet takes place from 1915 to 1927 and acts as a kind of "pre-quel" to *Love Medicine* and

The Beet Queen. It is narrated by an elderly man, Nanapush, and a young girl, Pauline. Parts of it have or will appear in *Esquire* (August 1986, "Fleur," which went on to win the National Magazine Award for fiction and the O. Henry first prize), *Harpers* (May 1987, "Scales"), and the *Atlantic* (March 1988, "Matchimanito"). *Tracks* will be published by Henry Holt in September 1988, and in paperback by Harper and Row a year later. The fourth and last book of the quartet, "American Horse," is under way and should be published in a couple of years. It will begin in 1972 and go to the present. My next novel, "The Cloud Chamber," is also under way, as well as a new collection of poems by Louise and a coauthored novel by both of us. *Tracks* was the first one to have the finished draft, but it will be the third one to be published, and it's going to be thoroughly revised and changed in the light of the characters that we know from the other books.

LC: By Louise Erdrich or by Michael Dorris?

Dorris: By Louise.

LC: I understand that your names are interchangeable.

Dorris: In some ways, yes. We actually write some stories for popular consumption under the pen name of Milou North, and they have been published a lot in England and also in this country. So actually we write some less serious things together.

LC: Considering that you write as a couple, is there any significant change in *Yellow Raft* with respect to *Love Medicine* and *The Beet Queen*?

Dorris: The answer is yes. It's about different characters, and therefore the voices are different, as is the setting. While we labor closely with each other in all phases of making a book, Louise and I each have our own relationships with the particular work.

LC: Can you see any evolution in your work?

Erdrich: It's the hardest thing for a writer to get a grasp on. I mean, you almost have to be removed to see.

Dorris: I think more confidence, maybe, and a greater risk-taking.

Erdrich: It's true. The forms of the work are loosening up.

Dorris: We have written so many pages between the two of us, only a very small tip of the iceberg actually sees print.

An Interview with Louise Erdrich and Michael Dorris

Hertha D. Wong/1986

From *North Dakota Quarterly* 55.1 (Winter 1987), 196–218. Reprinted by permission.

Louise Erdrich, of German-American and Turtle Mountain Chippewa descent, was born in Minnesota and raised in Wahpeton, North Dakota. In 1972 she went to Dartmouth where she majored in English and Creative Writing. During her years at Dartmouth she met Michael Dorris who was a faculty member there. Upon graduating from Dartmouth in 1976, she traveled throughout North Dakota conducting poetry workshops. Later, she received her Master's degree from the Writing Program at Johns Hopkins University and worked as editor of an Indian newspaper in Boston.

Since then Louise's poetry and short stories have been published in numerous journals. Within one short year, Louise received acclaim both as a poet and as a fiction writer. In January 1984 *Jacklight,* her collection of poetry, was published. The San Francisco *Chronicle* named it one of the ten best books of poetry of the year. Ten months later, in October 1984, *Love Medicine* was published. Already it has been translated into several languages and published in over fourteen countries. *Love Medicine* has received the 1984 National Book Critics Circle best fiction award, the Sue Kaufman Prize for the Best First Novel, the Virginia McCormick Scully Prize for the Best Book of 1984 dealing with Indians or Chicanos, and many others. Louise's second novel, *The Beet Queen*, was published in September of 1986. She is now working on *Tracks,* the third of her quartet of novels.

Michael Dorris, part Modoc Indian, has an undergraduate degree in English and Classics from Georgetown University and a Ph.D. in Anthropology from Yale. He founded the Native American Studies Program at Dartmouth where he is a full professor teaching Native American Studies and anthropology. His field work has taken him to New Zealand, Alaska, Montana, New Hampshire, and most recently to

South Dakota. Currently, he is on sabbatic leave from Dartmouth to study fetal alcohol syndrome at Pine Ridge reservation. Michael has presented scores of papers and talks and received at least a dozen awards. Recently he received the 1985 Indian Achievement Award, a Rockefeller Foundation Research Grant, and the Outstanding Academic Book of 1984-85 Award. He has published two scholarly books on Native Americans and numerous articles. But Michael is not only an academician. He is a talented creative writer as well, having published both his poetry and fiction. His first novel, *A Yellow Raft in Blue Water* will be published in March 1987.

Since Louise and Michael do everything together, from taking care of their five children to writing internationally acclaimed novels, it seems only appropriate to interview them together. It's an April afternoon in Northfield, Minnesota, where Louise and Michael are spending the 1985/86 academic year. Louise had just returned from a full day of parent-teacher conferences. Michael has just descended from upstairs where he has been working at his word processor, editing *A Yellow Raft in Blue Water*. Abel, Sava, and Madeline, the three oldest children, do their homework at the dining-room table, while we settle into overstuffed couches in the living room with cups of cranberry tea.

Hertha Wong: Do you consider yourselves Native American writers? What do you think of such labels?

Louise Erdrich: I think of any label as being both true and a product of a kind of chauvinistic society because obviously white male writers are not labeled "white male writers." However, I suppose that they're useful in some ways. I could as well be "woman writer" or whatever label one wants to use. But I really don't like labels. While it is certainly true that a good part of my background, and Michael's background, and a lot of the themes are Native American, I prefer to simply be a writer. Although I like to be known as having been from the Turtle Mountain Chippewa and from North Dakota. It's nice to have that known and to be proud of it for people back home.

Wong: What about something like *The Beet Queen* which is not, from what I've heard, going to be focused entirely upon the lives of Native Americans?

Erdrich: Not all of the characters are, just as not all the people in my background are. It's true to the way I've grown up and the way I've lived. And the four books are about a region, a small area.

Michael Dorris: I think it's entirely possible hypothetically that either or both of us could write a book that did *not* have an Indian character in it. It just has not happened in a book. Short stories certainly. There have been short stories in the Milou category [published under the pen name Milou North] that have not had any Indian characters.

Wong: Michael, do you have any response to how you wish to be labeled?

Dorris: I would agree with Louise. It adds a level of complication to say that you are a Native American writer because it sets up expectations in readers which you may or may not fulfill for them. Then they like or don't like what you've written based on whether you've fulfilled their expectations. One would hope that one gets a reputation for writing with some sensitivity about the subjects one deals with. And if it were just a question of whether this person is a Native American and also a writer, fine. But "Native American writer" strikes me as a little cumbersome.

Wong: Michael, in your article in *College English* on "Teaching Native American Literature in an Ethnohistorical Context," you write that there is "no such thing as Native American literature." Will you elaborate?

Dorris: Native American literature is about as descriptive a term as non-Native American literature. If by definition non-Native American literature is about and by people who are not Native Americans, fine; except that doesn't tell you a great deal. I think what Louise and I do is either within the tradition of a particular tribe or reservation or it is within the context of American literature. Some of the comments on *The Beet Queen* so far are how *American* it is. I don't think that either of us, by any extension of the imagination, could presume or even dare to speak for or write about themes that were important for Navajos or for Iroquois or for people from other regions or other tribal backgrounds. I made the point in the article that I think it is entirely conceivable to write within an existing tradition. Somebody like Simon Ortiz is a perfect example, and to a certain extent, so is Leslie Silko. Pueblo literature begins, like Western literature, in an oral tradition and works its way up into a literary tradition. In the present day it maintains an oral and written tradition simultaneously. But by the same token, they're not writing about Chippewas and they're not writing about Montana. To that extent, I think it is a clustering that non-Indians tend to make and that, in many cases, Indians would sometimes find useful, but not take very seriously.

Erdrich: I totally agree with that.

Wong: There has been extensive discussion about a Native American Renaissance. Is there such a literary revival? Hasn't there been activity all along?

Dorris: According to Lavonne Ruoff and other scholars who have meticulously chronicled the continuity of Native American literature (even when it did not have a popular audience), there has always been a great deal of activity. You find it more prevalent in contemporary times. There has been a recent abundance of well-received Native American writers, people like Jim Welch, Leslie Silko, Janet Campbell Hale, Linda Hogan, Simon Ortiz, and Gerry Vizenor—all of whom have gained regional or national attention. You might say there is a change in accessibility. Within a tribal tradition there has always been strong storytelling and literary art. But to come outside of one's own culture and make it accessible, that's probably something new.

Erdrich: The recent abundance of Native American writers follows the course of Native American fortunes in general. Things got better for Native Americans in education, in health, in many areas. I'm one who has benefited from Bureau of Indian Affairs money and education. The program at Dartmouth really stresses the importance of keeping your heritage. All of these things really work together. If things continue as they are now under the Reagan administration, we can expect to see a corresponding absence of younger Native American writers—as well as Native American doctors, lawyers, everything—who don't have the educational advantages. These things are linked to a national governmental attitude toward keeping those promises of providing education and tribal assistance.

Wong: Are there any other factors involved in this revival?

Dorris: I think there is such a thing as the creation of an audience. If you go back to some books (some by Indians and some not) such as *Bury My Heart at Wounded Knee* and Vine Deloria's books (especially, *Custer Died for Your Sins*) and then Scott Momaday winning the Pulitzer Prize in 1969, suddenly there was consciousness that there were

Indians around and they had interesting things to say. I think that created a climate in which writers could both write and be read. People were encouraged to write because there was an interest.

Wong: In his article, "Towards a National Indian Literature: Cultural Authenticity in Nationalism" [*MELUS*, Summer 1981], Simon Ortiz writes that "indigenous peoples of the Americas have taken the languages of the colonialists and used them for their own purposes," and thus they "have creatively responded to forced colonization. And this response has been one of resistance." The fact that oral traditions continue today is "evidence that the resistance is on-going" and this is the basis of contemporary literature by Native Americans. Would you respond to Ortiz's conclusion that it is "this literature, based upon continuing resistance which has given a particularly nationalistic character to the Native American voice"?

Dorris: Well, I would disagree with the notion of *the* Native American voice, certainly. I think that national traditions are, in fact, national. A national tradition would be Pueblo and Lakota or Winnebago rather than an Indian national tradition. Also, I would respectfully disagree that the oral traditions are primarily in English. Trying to come to terms with culture contact is often done in English because it speaks to an audience on both sides, but the resistance is often done in one's language.

Erdrich: I think very much the same as what Michael was saying. The people who are really continuing oral traditions are probably continuing to further them in their own language. The resistance is keeping your language.

Wong: The resistance, then, is internal to the group. It's not an overt political resistance, but a cultural maintenance.

Erdrich: Oh, but it is political. It is very political to keep your own language. There has been an incredible effort to make Native American people speak English. And in many many cases it certainly worked. It's interesting to look at how many people writing from Native American experience are speakers of their native language. I know I'm not. Michael speaks Tanaina and has experience of living in a non-English speaking culture. But I have no idea how many writers do or do not speak a native language, how many have access to the real oral tradition, that is not translated, that is ongoing.

Wong: In a recent book review, Karl Kroeber says that what is unique about American fiction is its "texture of multiple ethnicities." In reference to *Love Medicine,* he writes: "much of the 'Indianness' in Erdrich's novel is linked to her sensitivity to the peculiarly polyethnic character of Americanness" [*SAIL,* Winter 1985]. How do you respond to this?

Erdrich: Well, that's tough. I guess I respond, "Okay. All right. Fine."

Dorris: Well, I don't know what "much of the Indianness" refers to. *Love Medicine, The Beet Queen,* and *A Yellow Raft* all deal with people in a multi-ethnic environment, but I don't think that in itself is Indianness. Bea Medicine once said the Indian people have to be far more adept at manipulating a multi-cultural world than non-Indian people do because they have to live in both parts of it—the mainstream and the non-mainstream—whereas mainstream people never have to learn those skills of working in both worlds. It may be that Karl means "Indianness" in that respect—to be able to empathize and see in a perspective of varying ethnicities. In that case, I think it's true.

Wong: Collaboration is an idea that makes many writers who emphasize individual creativity uneasy. You two work together. Would you describe your collaborative process?

Erdrich: It's not very mysterious.

Dorris: We'll start talking about something a long time in advance of it—the germ of a plot, or a story that has occurred to us, or an observation that we've seen. *A Yellow Raft in Blue Water* started out with the title. The title came before the book. After we talk, one of us, whoever thought of it probably, will write a draft. It might be a paragraph; it might be ten pages; it might be something in between. We then share that draft with the other person. Shortly thereafter they will sit down with a pencil and make comments about what works and what doesn't work, what needs expanding and what might be overwritten. Then they give that draft with their suggestions back to the person who wrote it who has the option of taking or leaving them, but almost always taking them. Then that person does a new draft, gives it back to the other, and goes through the process again. This exchange takes place five or six times. The final say clearly rests with the person who wrote the piece initially, but we virtually reach consensus on all words before they go out, on a word by word basis. There is not a thing that has gone out from either one of us that has not been through at least six rewrites, *major* rewrites. In fact, we thought *The Beet Queen* was completely done in November. We sent it out; it was duplicated at the publishers. It was even sent out to some other writers for comment. But it just nagged at us and nagged at us. Right after Christmas, we started rewriting it from page 206 on. In a month we rewrote pages 206 to 393 and made a whole new ending. The last fifteen pages are completely new.

Wong: Rayona, the protagonist of *A Yellow Raft in Blue Water,* was conceived of initially as a male. How did you decide that "he" should be a "she"?

Erdrich: We decided we would talk about *Yellow Raft* on the way out here in the car. We had hours to talk.

Dorris: When we left New Hampshire the book was about a young boy who was coping with his mother's death, and by the time we reached Minnesota it was about a young girl whose mother lives. Since then it has expanded into three parts. One of which is the mother's voice, and the next is *her* mother's voice. All of that really evolved out of changing the main character from a male to a female. Louise, I think, proposed that originally. It was hard to think of. It's like sending somebody to Sweden for a sex change operation, but it just worked better.

Erdrich: Dot in *The Beet Queen* was Wallacette throughout most of the book. Then we were sitting at dinner one day, and Michael looked up in amazement and said, "Do you know who she is?" So we went to check *Love Medicine* to see what the years were to see if they would work out. And indeed it turned out to be Dot Adare. But the book was almost written. That's one of the wonderful things. I don't think I would have seen it, but it was obvious once Michael pointed it out. And that happens often.

Wong: Some people like to think of your collaboration as one of the examples of why this is a Native American novel. Would you give that any credence or is it just because you two work well together and you like each other?

Dorris: And we trust each other's judgment.

Erdrich: Good, I'm glad you said that.

Dorris: Oh, see, she's lobbying for me to put back a line. [Laughter from both. To Louise:] I put it back, while you were gone, but I left the second line as was. [To Hertha:] We have done things like trade. Louise will say, "I will get rid of this line, if you will get rid of that line."

Erdrich: Yes.

Dorris: We both have a real proprietary sense of all the books. We *both* have that sense regardless of whose name is on them. We take a lot of pride and feel very personal about them and the characters. Louise's last word before she left the house today was: "I'm going to fight you for that line." [Laughter.] She doesn't have to anymore because I know that she'll win.

Erdrich: I'm so thrilled to hear that [laughing]. This whole after- noon, driving back and forth, I was thinking I'll go and I'll get the galleys, after Michael thinks they're gone. I'll take them to the post office [laughs]. I'll open them up; I'll change it. I won't let that line go. We're not saying there is no individual creativity. Obviously you have to bring all of your experience, something very personal, to write. But it is really mixed in with collaboration.

Dorris: You know that if the other person feels strongly about it, that they're right. One of the things I learned from Louise is that if some- thing doesn't work no amount of arguing with another person, to say, "Well, this is what I meant," matters. If it doesn't work, it doesn't work. No matter how devoted one was to the initial line, it's better when it works for the other person. I mean we may just be the common denominator American reader.

Erdrich: I think we are, yes.

Wong: Early in your literary relationship you collaborated on several short stories which were published in *Redbook* and *Woman* under the name Milou North. Other than the obvious union of names, [*Mi*chael and *Lou*ise], why did you publish under a pseudonym?

Erdrich: It's mysterious. You really think that's probably a female, but you don't know. It's one person. I think that when readers read a story they want to read one by one person. But we liked having the romance of it. [Laughter.]

Wong: What about North? Did that have a special meaning?

Dorris: Well, we were in New Hampshire. It sort of sounded literary. [Laughter.]

Wong: You have mentioned that William Faulkner, Toni Morrison, and Barbara Pym have all influenced your writing. Would you say a little about what, in particular, they contributed to your work?

Dorris: Louise, I'll leave you William Faulkner because I think he's more you than me. Barbara Pym could take absolutely ordinary words and combine them into simple sentences in such a way that they sometimes just made you gasp. She demonstrates that tremendous insight can come from utter simplicity.

Toni Morrison is absolutely magic in *Song of Solomon*. I never will forget the fact that Pilate did not have a navel. Here's something that, again, is very simple, but a total surprise. It cuts off the whole chain of being back to origination. The sense of the mysterious within a story that is tightly and interestingly plotted is part of her influence.

Erdrich: As for William Faulkner, I guess I can't really pin down what his influence is. I think one absorbs him through the skin. He is just such a wonderful storyteller. He is so much of an *American* writer. I have read him over and over. I really like the other writers you mentioned as well. Everybody that you read is a literary influence. I had a literary education so the entire literary canon is a background. I'm very fond of John Donne.

Wong: Besides a literary tradition, what about an oral tradition? Have family stories influenced your work?

Erdrich: Sitting around listening to our family tell stories has been a more important influence on our work than literary influences in some ways. These you absorb as a child when your senses are the most open, when your mind is forming. That really happened, I know, in our family, and [to Michael] certainly with yours. In Michael's family not a thing happens, but that it is *really* a tale.

Dorris: And an interesting tale. My aunt writes us a lot. She told of the exterminator coming to her apartment. It's like an epic saga. She worked it into the space shuttle, and made it a really gripping story. I've never heard her tell an uninteresting story.

Wong: What kinds of stories? From both sides of your family? Louise, you mentioned your father was a good storyteller.

Erdrich: Yes, he's very good and has a great sense of humor. His stories are always funny. He's also literary. He and my mother and Michael's family all told stories about their experiences during the Depression. That has made a very strong impact on our work. Both of our work has people living through the Depression. That's probably because to us it was a *real* time, very real. My grandparents also told stories.

Dorris: Mine too. I mean people vie for air time.

Erdrich: My brothers and sisters, in fact, are always telling stories.

Wong: What about the kids?

Erdrich: Yeah, they do too. I guess it is just a family thing. It's probably the case in lots of families. Some of my father's stories are just indelible.

Wong: Kathleen Mullen Sands claims that the root of your "story-telling techinique is the secular anecdotal process of community gossip" [*SAIL*, Winter 1985]. Would you comment?

Erdrich: I think that's great.

Dorris: I thought that was one of the most perceptive comments of any reviewer. In fact, it's one of those comments that you don't think of beforehand, but once I read that I've never thought of *Love Medicine* without thinking of that comment.

Wong: The reader gets the sense of *hearing* bits and pieces of gossip. We don't have an omnisicent narrator to tell us how it *really* is. There is no one with authority that imposes some kind of order and stasis on a character or a character's life.

Erdrich: No, I really agree with that. We both grew up in small communities where you were who you were in relation to the community. You knew that whatever you did there were really ripples from it. I don't think you can grow up like that and ignore it once you start writing.

Wong: What about films? Have any films influenced your ideas on narrative and imagery?

Erdrich: Not for me. I didn't grow up watching film or T.V. I really didn't watch any, even when I was in college. So I don't think it's much of an influence.

Dorris: It is more with me. I was totally weaned on television. There's a lot of television reference, which is a marker of time and class and all sorts of things, in my book. My characters aren't snobs about T.V. and neither am I [laughs]. I really enjoy it.

Wong: Louise, in an interview with Jan George [*North Dakota Quarterly,* Spring 1985] you said "if there's a story there, that's enough." How do you know if "there's a story there"?

Erdrich: Well, don't you think it's when you can't control your characters any more? That feeling of *"Oh, no."* You just can't believe that "Oh, this is what they're doing." It's when you get really taken away by it yourself.

Wong: So they start to have a life of their own somehow?

Dorris: Yes. The funniest thing about writing is how anxious you are to sit down and write to see what happens when you don't really know. Or when you have a sense of the ultimate end, but you don't know how they get there, and it almost unfolds on a line by line basis in front of you. I never knew that before I started writing fiction. It's like the story is inside of you or inside of the characters. The writing is the vehicle for telling it, and you hear it yourself as you're telling it. It is so different, we have found, writing at the beginning of the book then at the end because in the beginning anything is possible. It's hard going because you're kind of carving out a path, but at the end you have the whole weight of the book behind you. You know the characters and you know what they're capable of and the parameters in which they can move, and it works itself out much faster.

Wong: So the fewer possibilities are really . . .

Dorris: Liberating.

[Louise goes to pick up the kids.]

Wong: Michael, tell me about your shift from academician to poet to fiction writer.

Dorris: Writing poetry is the one thing I have done consistently over the years. I've published in *Sun Tracks, Akwesasne,* and *Wassaja.* I've even been anthologized a couple of times. When I was teaching full-time and raising three kids of my own, I didn't have a lot of time for fiction nor did I know that I could carry it off. As you know, when you're working for tenure you have to do your scholarly stuff first. I really like the novel form, and Louise does too. She started out as a visual artist, then she moved into poetry, then into short stories, then into novels, and now she's into epics [laughs].

The editor of the *Paris Review* called yesterday afternoon. She had just read the draft of *Yellow Raft* and liked it a lot. Actually she hadn't read the last section, and she asked if one particular character was going to come back. I said no, and she was *so* distressed that she really made me think we should write a sequel [laughs]. There are people who don't get to articulate their stories in this book. It's three women talking, and they all start basically in their fifteenth year. The first person is a fifteen-year-old girl, and she ends up being fifteen. The real action of the novel takes place between May and August of 1986. Yet each of them go back to their pasts. She starts fairly early, but her mother starts when she is fifteen and tells her story in the second section, working her way up to the present time. Then the grandmother starts when *she* is fifteen and takes it up to the point when the mother is fifteen. So there's a kind of interweaving.

Wong: Is there any magic about fifteen?

Dorris: No. Oddly enough, the pivotal event in the lives of the characters is the belief that was very big among a certain group of Catholics when I was a kid. The Pope had a letter—a letter given by Mary to a little girl named Lucy at Fatima—that was going to be opened on January 1, 1960. This was something I heard about from the time I was in the second grade until 1960. This letter was going to be opened, and either Russia was going to be converted or the world would come to an end. So Christine, the mother in *Yellow Raft,* was raised with this belief. When she gets to fifteen, she stays up all night waiting for the world to come to an end. It doesn't, and she loses her faith. Her mother is very much involved in the idea that Christine have a faith. When Christine loses it, she loses her mother's interest. The last major story that Christine tells her own daughter, Rayona, is about this end of the world. So it's a theme that goes into all three.

Wong: And the daughter, Rayona, is half black, half Chippewa?

Dorris: No, no. We don't specify. The action takes place on a reservation in eastern Montana. There are about five reservations in eastern Montana. We have discovered that it's easier if nobody thinks it's about them. It's not. None of these books is about real people. People from other parts of the country have confronted us: "This is my uncle's story" or "my aunt's, my mother's, or my story. How did you hear it?" [Laughs.] So I made it vague as to exactly where it takes place. I went to high school on a reservation in eastern Montana so I know the country, but . . . .

Wong: Are these composite characters then? Just bits and pieces of people you've observed, or knew or are these just out of your head?

Dorris: There are elements in some characters . . . . I mean I had a nun who was known for her window pole and who did, in fact, throw it at a little boy in the back room and send him into the closet. So Sister Leopolda in *Love Medicine* incorporated those facts. But there really isn't anybody upon which a character like Lipsha or Lulu or Gordie or Marie or any of the characters in *Yellow Raft* is based.

In some respects it's kind of funny. *Love Medicine* was the main selection of the Finnish Book-of-the-Month Club. They drew their version of what each of the characters looked like. On the front page of the Book-of-the-Month Club News from Finland there is the photograph of Louise from *Love Medicine* with her T-shirt on, except they've amended the T-shirt to look like a blanket thrown around her shoulders. And there are big mesas in the background [laughter]. Then on the inside, you have pictures of Lulu and Nector and Marie, and they *all* look like Italian prostitutes. The picture of Albertine is a line drawing of Louise's photograph on the cover.

Wong: I was waiting for that.

Dorris: There's the assumption that because this character has some education she must be Louise. And it's certainly not. But nobody's going to think that Rayona or Christine is me. That's another benefit to the gender change.

Wong: How do you feel writing in a woman's voice? In other words, creating a female character?

Dorris: I think it's the riskiest thing we're doing. If it doesn't work, it dramatically doesn't work. It sets you up for being roasted, as it should. But I was raised by women, by strong women—a mother, three aunts, two grandmothers. I heard their version of the world much more clearly and consistently than I heard anybody else's version. So if I have a point of view to draw on other than myself, it's a woman's point of view. Time will tell.

We do a very risky thing in this book. I describe giving birth from a first-person perspective. Those who have read it so far like it, but somebody said, "I don't know whether they'll ever sell it at a feminist bookstore in San Francisco." [Laughter.] I hope they do because I participated closely in the birth of two of my daughters as a *helper*, and then I delivered a baby when I was doing field work. And I've talked to a lot of women about their experience of delivery.

Wong: How do you balance your creative and scholarly work? Do you prefer one over the other?

Dorris: It remains to be seen. This year was a real departure because it allowed me to spend a great deal of time thinking of myself as a creative writer and seeing whether anybody else did. It was a big question. I *love* writing fiction. I've now got to turn around and write a non-fiction book that I've contracted for. It's a really important subject and . . .

Wong: Is this on fetal alcohol syndrome?

Dorris: Yes. The title is *The Broken Cord*. It's important to a lot of

Indian people. It's important to do a good job on it, and that is really challenging. But there's a part of me that thinks: how am I going to go on without making up some stories in the process? It's a slower process, when you're cooking as it were, to have to check sources and be in command of all the literature. When you do fiction, you're in command of the character. Your only real requirement is to make him or her consistent to themselves. You gain affection for them in a way that I have never found affection for scholarship. I come from a family in which nobody went beyond grade school on either side. Their aspirations really were for me to graduate from high school. I don't have a scholarly tradition to draw on. It has always surprised me to find myself professing. But storytelling is a much more common thing in my family. They may even take me seriously if I'm a storyteller. [Laughter.]

Wong: What do they think about you being a professor and running all over the world?

Dorris: They're not impressed. I think they may be impressed when they tell their friends. But my aunt told me one time about her boss's son who worked for the Chamber of Commerce. He had gotten a divorce. He had a fourteen-year-old daughter, and he hired a full-time housekeeper to come in and care for the fourteen-year-old daughter. At that point, I had just been promoted to Associate Professor, I had three children on my *own*, and I was doing a lot in terms of career. I said, "Why are you so impressed with *him*? I don't have a full-time housekeeper, and my kids are young." And she said, "Oh, he's got a *real* job." [Laughter.]

Wong: In your and Louise's *New York Times Book Review* article, "The Writer's Sense of Place," you reflect upon the importance for you of the North Dakota landscape. Does your home in New Hampshire move you in the same way? What about Alaska and Montana?

Dorris: I have a very strong feeling for Montana. I have a very strong feeling for Alaska, but I'm pretty adaptive. I guess you find out about your sense of place when you see what you write about. I didn't expect that the first long thing I wrote would be set in Montana, but it just naturally happened. I don't think either of us, as long as we've lived in New Hampshire, would automatically say we're *from* New Hampshire. It's the kind of place that you have to be from for many generations to feel that you're native. We like it. It's beautiful. It's convenient. But we both have a real response to the plains—not even the plains around here (this is more the prairie), but once you hit that stretch of land between Fergus Falls and the North Dakota border. It is absolutely flat and the sky is the dominant thing. It gives us a real thrill in its simplicity. It's like a white room as opposed to wallpaper in some respects.

Wong: There's a kind of exhilaration that comes from feeling the land is in your blood. It's not just lovely and somehow distant?

Dorris: I think distance helps you write about it, though. It makes you think about it in a way that you don't think about it if you see it everyday. It lets you mull it over and distill it so that you can actually translate it to paper. I think that's what Louise found about being in New Hampshire and writing there. She, in fact, did say that if she ever wrote about New Hampshire, it would have to be far away from it. [Louise and the kids return.]

Wong: We've been talking about "The Writer's Sense of Place." I'm wondering about the whole notion of living in New Hampshire and writing about North Dakota.

Erdrich: I wonder about that too. I feel a lot of affection for New Hampshire. It's just lovely as a place, but I don't have the history there, the connections with a particular culture, the family connections, the feelings for the history that one gets over time living in a certain place. I'm so attached to our home, in particular, that I really love being there, but I certainly miss North Dakota and this area a lot. Those are the two places I've really *been*. I haven't really lived anywhere else, and so most of my work is set out here. And my . . .

Dorris: . . . flowers are planted back there. [Laughter.]

Erdrich: My flowers are planted out *there*. Sometimes I think that the sheer nostalgia sends me back emotionally in a stronger way. I certainly have a great wish to spend more time out here or in the plains, at some point. But I get very upset about the idea of raising children around all of those Minuteman missiles. North Dakota is a nuclear arsenal for the entire country. And people don't really make much of it.

Wong: Would you elaborate on the water/river imagery in *Love Medicine*?

Erdrich: That's absolutely there, and it's elaborated on in other books. In *Love Medicine* the main image is the recurring image of the water—transformation (walking over snow or water) and a sort of transcendence.

Dorris: The river is a boundary.

Erdrich: The river is always this boundary. There's a water monster who's mentioned in *Love Medicine*. It's not a real plot device in *Love Medicine*. It becomes more so in *Tracks*.

Wong: I have heard that the imagery of your quartet of novels—*Love Medicine, The Beet Queen, Tracks,* and *American Horse*—is patterned after the four elements. What is the grand plan of your quartet?

Erdrich: We really think of each book as being tied to one of the four elements. There's a lot of other imagery as well.

Dorris: Oh, sure. It's not neat. But *Beet Queen,* as you will see, is clearly air.

Wong: What about *Tracks*?

Erdrich: That's earth.

Dorris: And then *American Horse,* if it turns out to be titled that, probably will be fire.

Wong: This design sounds like a literary medicine wheel.

Erdrich: I think that's a lovely image. But I don't know if we really . . .

Dorris: That's what the elements of the universe were supposed to be made up of. At least in Greek mythology, it's those four things. The number four is, of course, a cardinal number, and the magic number in a number of Native American traditions.

Erdrich: It's the number of completion in Ojibway mythology. There are different myths, but one of them is the bear coming through different worlds, breaking through from one world into the next, from the next world into the next world. The number of incompletion is three and the number of completion is four, so four is a *good* number. It has good things associated with it—the four directions. It works in a lot of different ways.

Wong: Louise, you started as a visual artist, then became a poet, short story writer, and now a novelist. It seems that there's still a lot of visual emphasis in your writing. Is the visual artist a conscious influence?

Erdrich: I don't think so. Well, but in a way it is conscious. You try to create an image that hits the reader, something in your mind that is very powerful, so I guess it is conscious. But what happens and how it works is really unconscious.

Dorris: It's one of those questions we always ask each other. What

do they look like? One of the first things we did fooling around with
Love Medicine one night was draw the characters.

Wong: Louise, you've described your perspective as one you remember as a child—lingering unnoticed on the outskirts of a group of
grown-ups, hanging on the fringe of conversation. In "Fleur" your
narrator is literally on the outside. In *Love Medicine,* Albertine remembers that Aunt June never kept her on the "edge of conversation"; the
Kashpaw's house is on "the very edge of reservation"; many of the
characters are on the edges of society. How does this point of view
inform your writing?

Erdrich: In a way it's the condition of a writer. You're not always
the most *popular* person, the center of attention, everybody looking to
you for the answers. I always felt like I was more the one who listened
in on everything else.

Wong: It seems to me a more positive version of Henry James's
observer. Because even if this observer is outside, he/she is concerned
and involved with what's going on in the inside whereas Henry James
always seems so detached to me.

Erdrich: Yeah. I think it's just that you're observing people you
love, and you want to be part of their lives. But part of it, too, is that I
wasn't married for a long time. As a single woman I always felt like I
was on the fringe of a lot of things that were happening between people
who had much more settled lives. I would be involved, but a little self-
conscious. So that was prolonged for me—that period of adolescence.

Wong: Do you experience anything like that at all, Michael? That
whole idea of observing from the outside?

Dorris: Yes. A lot. In a way it's kind of a mixed-blood condition as
well. When I lived with my father's side of the family, I was too light.
And when I lived with my mother's side of the family, there was a kind
of distancing because of my other experience. I may be internal and
psychological more than it's real. I think it's something that a lot of
mixed-bloods relate to—going to a new situation always feeling periph-
eral, although other people might not feel that way. When I got the
Indian Achievement Award this year, I talked about that condition in
my acceptance speech. Afterwards, a number of people, who growing
up I would have given my eye teeth to look like, came and said to me,
"Don't be silly. You're really part of it. You wouldn't be getting this
award if you weren't." It made me think that maybe it was my problem

rather than something real. But it's also an anthropological thing—to stand on the outside and try to be objective, and to see a situation clearly even though you're involved in it.

Wong: Some critics think of *Love Medicine* as a collection of short stories rather than a novel (much like the argument about Faulkner's *Go Down, Moses*). How would you defend the claim that *Love Medicine* is a novel? Or do you feel it's necessary?

Erdrich: I don't even worry about it actually. It's a novel in that it all moves toward some sort of resolution.

Dorris: It has a large vision that no one of the stories approaches.

Erdrich: Yes. But I think that's not for people who read just for enjoyment. It's for people who want to quibble about the form. I just don't think of it as an earthshaking question so I don't worry about it [laughs].

Dorris: I think the answer to the question, though, is that *we* think of it as a novel. If it had been a collection of short stories, it would have been very different. Some of them existed as short stories before, and then were adapted and incorporated. There were a couple of short stories and then the rest were written—three—really as part of the novel although with different perspectives. Then we went through the entire manuscript. We wove in all the changes and resolutions and threads to tie them all together. By the time readers get half way through the book, it should be clear to them that this is not an unrelated, or even a related, set of short stories, but parts of a large scheme.

Wong: *Love Medicine* has received all kinds of acclaim. Like many others, Ursula Le Guin is unrestrained in her praise of *Love Medicine* which she calls "a work of really startling beauty and power" and of you, Louise, whom she refers to as "a true artist and probably a major one" [*SAIL*, Winter 1985]. How has success affected both of you?

Dorris: We have met some really nice people as a result of it—both people who are well-known, like Philip Roth, and people who are our readers who have written to us. That's certainly an important thing. It gives you confidence.

Erdrich: But you know, life is so schizophrenic because, on the one hand, you read all these magnificent things and it seems like. . . . Well, I'm just sitting here thinking, "I better go and take the fish sticks out of the oven." [Laughter.] Really it's hard to think of the two as happening to the same person or people.

Dorris: Gail Godwin gave us this marvelous quote for *The Beet Queen* which, in part, says that the writing in *The Beet Queen* "cleanses perception and makes reality magic." We had been up *all* night with one of the babies the night before. I was upstairs and took this call. I came down and Louise was sitting on a little red bench in the kitchen—kind of shell shocked, her hair limp and mine was standing straight up. [Laughter.]

Erdrich: Just a mess [laughs].

Dorris: We looked at each other and I said, "Do we look like the kind of people who would 'cleanse' anybody?"

Erdrich: "Perception"? [Laughter.] We have such a chaotic family life, as anyone who has a number of children does. This reality just supersedes anything else. Sometimes, on our rare trips out, like when we go to New York, it seems incredible that now there is access to people to whom previously we were down on our knees, "*Please* read us." Certainly I can't argue with that. Getting acceptance of that kind means that people will read your work, and that's a very important thing. And it's very hard to do. It's tough, and I *appreciate* it. But also, literary fame is comparatively tiny. You can go anywhere and nobody's interested in *books*. So within a certain world, it's wonderful to have people read your work now. In other areas, it's not so important. You've got to have a certain sense of perspective on it.

Wong: Having five kids keeps you down to earth regardless.

Dorris: Or somewhere. [Laughter.]

Erdrich: I don't know. We were up last night too. I'm sort of reeling. . . . Sometimes we walk through our day and I'm thinking, "Oh please, I'll tell you anything." I just remember that this is the way they used to break prisoners during the war—deprive them of their REM hours of sleep. And that's what happens when you have babies who are going through some sort of gastric disturbance. They wake up at those particular moments and you just feel like, "You've broken me."

Wong: I guess that covers how having 5 children has affected your writing. [Laughter.]

Erdrich: Well, that's all that bad stuff, but it's really wonderful. One is in love with each child in a different way. It *is* wonderful.

Wong: A student of mine from Pine Ridge Reservation burst into my office the other day. "I just read *Love Medicine*," she said, "and I *know* those people!" What about Native American responses to *Love Medicine*?

Dorris: Yesterday afternoon I talked to a woman at Pine Ridge who is working very closely with me on *The Broken Cord*. I had given her that chapter of *A Yellow Raft* that Louise read at St. Olaf College because it really was inspired by driving through the snow in that particular stretch of territory. She had just driven up to Rapid City to pick up her husband, a tribal judge. They had had a freak snow storm. She said she thought of the chapter every mile of the way and that she and her husband liked it. I say that not to promote that particularly, but because that's the kind of response *Love Medicine* got from Indian people too. One of the things that has just *really* reinforced us and made us feel comfortable and good about writing is the reactions of Indians to it—which have been widespread and very encouraging and positive.

Wong: You have mentioned that non-Indians often either miss, or choose to ignore, the humor in *Love Medicine*.

Erdrich: I think that's often been the case. In talking to tribal people who've read the book, the first thing they say is, "Oh yes, that funny book." It's not like they self-consciously pick out the humor, but on the whole it's funnier than a lot of critics who read it who were kind of saying this is devastating.

Wong: Describing the characters as "doomed and durable" reminds me of the "doomed Indian" stereotype of the 19th century.

Dorris: Yes. There were sad things that happened and there were unhappy people, but we never thought of it as a book about poverty or depression. The other interesting thing that one Indian woman said is: "At last people write the way Indians really talk." Some critics have said, "Oh, it's a literary voice." One would hope it's in part a literary voice, but it's also a reflection of a real idiom that we admire.

Erdrich: It is. There are a lot of words used in the book that are probably quite sophisticated that just get incorporated into people's everyday language. I think that's very true.

Wong: Like Nector's analysis of *Moby-Dick* and Lipsha's commentary on the Bible. These are wonderful revisions of the English language and mainstream interpretations.

Dorris: There's a part in *The Beet Queen,* the naughty box part, that I think is one of the funniest things. The first time I read Louise's draft of that I laughed for twenty minutes.

Erdrich: That was actually quite autobiographical. I was put in the naughty box as a first grader and never forgot it.

Wong: I bet a lot of people ask you about how much of *Love Medi-*

cine is autobiographical. Michael said that the Finns thought you were
for sure Albertine.

Erdrich: I know. Well, actually . . . I think that's quite a compliment. Most people now say, "You are Marie." [Laughter.]

Wong: Louise, recently you spent a week on Manitoulin Island,
Ontario, with Delia Beboning, probably the best traditional porcupine
quill artist in North America, who taught you the intricacies of birch
bark quill work. Is this a creative pastime you would like to emphasize?
Is it an artistic form that might influence your writing?

Erdrich: I like doing things with my hands. [Turns to Michael and
laughs.] One of the first presents I ever gave Michael was a piece of
quill work, my first piece of quill work. I've always wanted to learn
more. I wanted to go there partly because a lot of Ojibway people live
on the island. I just *love* it. It's an important place to me, but I don't
know about it as being something . . .

Dorris: It is kind of a metaphor for writing. You take quills and
you lay them down one by one. Using the natural colors, you create a
pattern that emerges in the course of laying them down. That is what
you do with dialogue or with anything.

Erdrich: That's very true. It's a beautiful image really. I'd never
thought of it.

Wong: You said, Michael, that you were working on the final revisions of *The Yellow Raft*? What else are you working on now?

Dorris: Yes. I'm working on that. And I'm also working on *The
Broken Cord* which will be published by Harper and Row.

Wong: Is that going to be a summary of your fieldwork on fetal
alcohol syndrome at Pine Ridge?

Dorris: It's basically a book about modern Indians, using as the
centerpiece this particular issue.

Wong: So it's basically a scholarly work?

Dorris: It's a popular work on a serious theme. We made the decision to publish it with a trade publisher, rather than a university press
because there's a lot written about it for specialists and very little for a
popular audience. It will be aimed at a popular audience.

Wong: Louise, what are you working on right now?

Erdrich: I'm starting on *Tracks* which is the next book that goes
before *The Beet Queen*—just writing the first drafts of it.

Dorris: But really the answer to your question is more complicated.
I mean Louise is working on . . .

Erdrich: I was just thinking . . .

Dorris: . . . revisions for *Yellow Raft*.

Erdrich: . . . that I am working on Michael's. I'm really getting so up to working on *The Broken Cord*. I think it's a terribly important book. Right now I'm really in love with *A Yellow Raft in Blue Water* because as something is being finished, you feel this mixture of can't let it go and glory because it's beautiful. Right now my primary concern is go keep Michael . . .

Dorris: . . . from taking out that line.

Erdrich: . . . from taking out that line. [Laughter.] Exactly. That's what I'm working on. I'm very worried that he doesn't know how much this means.

Dorris: You might as well tell her the famous line. This is the opening line of the last section.

Erdrich: This is a woman who's at once so fierce and so generous. She's just this engima. Her first line is: "I never grew up, but I got old." To me that says everything about knowledge gained over hard experience, realizing that you have really not matured, but you've wrinkled. It's just everything to me. I just love that *line* [laughs].

Wong: It's beautiful.

Erdrich: And it's really her.

Wong: What's the next line?

Dorris: Well, the next line was, "I'm a woman who's lived for 60 years and carried a grudge for 45." But that's going to get changed a little bit . . .

Erdrich: You want to change it?

Dorris: . . . because she's . . . Well, I think it's more resentment.

Erdrich: Well, I would go with more resentment, but I just think those numbers are really important to have in there.

Dorris: Yeah, but I don't know whether she's a person who thinks in numbers.

Erdrich: Not her . . .

Dorris: Don't press it. [Laughter.] You won one big one for today.

Wong: You have to wait until tomorrow and wage a new battle. [Laughter.]

Erdrich: Oh, I know.

Wong: How did you come up with Marie peeling three bags of potatoes in response to Nector leaving her?

Erdrich: I don't know. Except that my mother peels potatoes [laughs] and I peel potatoes. I don't know. That's just what she would have done. Right, Michael?

Dorris: Yeah. There are some lines and some things in *Love Medicine* that if you ask we would be able to tell you long anecdotes about, but not that one. That one I think was in your first draft.

Erdrich: Yeah, I think we just think she would do that. But you know what was interesting? I never told you this [to Michael], about when I was visiting the quill worker on Manitoulin. Here she has created gorgeous things. It takes her a year to make a box. She sews each quill down so it's upward. That's the tucked quill box I was telling you about. And she says, "Yes, well I really like doing this, but then, my favorite thing, much better than doing quill work or knitting" (you know, she had all these other things she liked to do when she took a break from quilling), she said, "I really like to peel potatoes." [Laughter.] She said, "I just get myself a sack of potatoes. I can peel and peel and peel." That's what she does. There's no one else in the world who does her particular art and she likes to peel potatoes better. She just reminded me of Marie.

Wong: One final question. You are spending a busy 1985-86 academic year in Northfield, while Michael is on sabbatic leave from Dartmouth. Both of you have been writing, giving readings and talks, and traveling. Would you share some reflections on this year in Minnesota?

Dorris: We were talking about this the other night. We both feel perpetually behind on everything—that we're not doing as much as we should, especially the writing, and sometimes the parenting, and sometimes any number of things. I think the only way that we can, or at least I can, get away from that feeling is to look over the long picture. If you look over the period of the whole year, we finished editing *The Beet Queen* to our liking, finally. We'll finish editing *A Yellow Raft in Blue Water* before we leave. Sixty to seventy pages of *Tracks* will be underway and . . . we're alive. [Laughter.]

Erdrich: And the kids are.

Dorris: And the kids are alive. Yeah.

Erdrich: When I first married Michael I couldn't believe he was such a busy person. Always, always I thought to myself: we're in the last month of Michael's being busy and then our life will change and we'll settle down. I was busy too, but I never thought about it, I guess. Now I've just come to accept this. We're always behind in everything, but we've been very happy here.

As for Minnesota itself, it's a beautiful place. We go walking sometimes at night when everybody's settled down. We just really *love* it as a
place. To me that's been very important. One of our favorite places is
this stretch of flatness as you drive between Fergus Falls and Wahpeton.
So we've been able to experience that flatness several times [laughter].
And that's very good for the soul.

Behind Every Great Woman . . . ?
Louise Erdrich's True-Life Adventures
Geoffrey Stokes/1986

From *Voice Literary Supplement,* 48 (1 September 1986), 7–9.
Reprinted by permission.

A sign on the 18th century New Hampshire house—a barn-red frame
structure that's sprouted some typical New England els over the past
couple hundred years—reads "Pumpkin Pond Farm." The pond,
pumpkinless at the moment, sits across the dirt road; up a hill behind the
house, a tractor purposefully hays the meadow, the noise from its
engine floating distantly through the soft morning sunshine. There's a
pleasant scatter of bright plastic from a few children's toys in the yard
outside the "official" front door (friends and family routinely come in
through an el near the driveway). After this folksy introduction, the
sterile interior of the house comes as a surprise. Not simply that it's
been modernized—walls have been removed and windows opened up so
that light spills across the high-tech kitchen; a metal staircase mounts in
a tight corkscrew to an office loft above what was probably a wood-
shed—but that it is almost medicinally uncluttered. From my time in the
madly coincidental, slam-bang world of Louise Erdrich's fiction, I'd
expected at least a touch of chaos.

Here, for instance, in her award-winning 1984 first novel, *Love
Medicine*, is Albertine Johnson, come back to the reservation from
nursing school:

> I stumbled straight into the lighted kitchen and saw at once that King
> was trying to drown Lynette. He was pushing her face in the sink of cold
> dishwater. Holding her by the nape and the ears. Her arms were whirl-
> ing, knocking the spoons and knives and bowls out of the drainer. She
> struggled powerfully, but he had her. I grabbed a block of birch out of
> the woodbox and hit King on the back of the neck. The wood bounced
> out of my fists. He pushed her lower, and her throat caught and gurgled.
> I grabbed his shoulders. I expected that Lipsha was behind me. King
> hardly noticed my weight. He pushed her lower. So I had no choice then.
> I jumped on his back and bit his ear. My teeth met and blood filled my

mouth. He reeled backward, bucking me off, and I flew across the room, hit the refrigerator solidly, and got back on my feet.

His hands were cocked in boxer's fists. He was deciding who to hit first, I thought, me or Lipsha. I glanced around. I was alone. I stared back at King, scared for the first time. Then the fear left and I was mad, just mad at Lipsha, at King, at Lynette, at June. . . . I looked past King and saw what they had done.

All the pies were smashed. Torn open. Black juice bleeding through the crusts. Bits of jagged shells were stuck to the wall and some were turned completely upside down. Chunks of rhubarb were scraped across the floor. Meringue dripped from the towels.

"The pies!" I shrieked. "You goddam sonofabitch, you broke the pies!"

Now this is writing as violent as the scene it depicts, and while I didn't anticipate gore-spattered walls in Erdrich's own kitchen, its Calvinist serenity—no messages piling up near the wall phone, not even a shopping list to mar the gray, lablike plane of its extrawide counters—felt somehow wrong. Even if she wrote like Jane Austen, there would still be five kids living in this house.

When I hinted disappointment, Erdrich—a slim 32-year-old whose pale skin and light-brown hair owe more to her German-American father than her Chippewa mother—laughed indulgently. She and her anthropologist husband, Michael Dorris, head of Dartmouth's Native American Studies program, had just returned from a year in Montana and the Dakotas, where he'd been working on a study of fetal alcoholism, and they hadn't settled in yet. (The reason I'd been offered tea instead of coffee was that they couldn't find the coffee filters.) Besides, with the oldest child out haying, the next two away at camp, and the babies off with their regular sitter, the house was untypically quiet. "It's not usually like this at all," she grinned. "I promise."

With what turned out to be the easiest riddle of the Erdrich-Dorris household explained, we sat and talked about "coming home." Home—and homelessness—matter enormously to the characters in her novels, and though she'd been an undergraduate at Dartmouth, entering with the first class of women in 1972, nothing could be further from the Dakotas of *Love Medicine* and *The Beet Queen* than New England academia. With her imaginative life rooted half a continent away, where was *her* home?

At first, Erdrich was hesitant, "I don't know what to say, really. We've been taking this route back and forth between Hanover and North

Dakota, and now Montana, and I've got strong attachments out there
. . . my folks, brothers and sisters, the *landscape*, but it's really this
place, this place and Michael." And then, after a brief pause, she spoke
more firmly, "*Michael* is home."

In a way more true for Erdrich and Dorris than for most couples, they
are home for each other. *The Beet Queen*'s jacket copy notes that "she
lives in New Hampshire with her husband/collaborator," and as our
triangular conversation continued, I noticed each of them unselfcon-
sciously using the plural "we" to talk about her books. Gradually, the
nature of a collaboration extending almost to a single, shared imagination emerged so clearly that it seemed hard to determine why the books
bear only one by-line. Dorris, whose own first novel, *The Yellow Raft*,
is due in a few months, said authorship goes "to the person who writes
the drafts. That's the difference, really. We plot the books together, we
talk about them before any writing is done, and then we share, almost
every day, whatever it is we've written—a few pages, a chapter, even a
paragraph. I'll give it to Louise or she'll give it to me, and then the
other person goes over it with a red pencil: 'This works. This doesn't
work. How about *this* here? How about *that* there? Strengthen this
character . . .

"We give it back and then the other person rewrites the draft. We've
gotten to the point now where we just don't even *argue* anymore. We
just take the suggestion of the other person. And then it goes back and
forth, and then before the book goes out, we sit around for a couple of
weeks and read it out loud to each other. So before it leaves the house,
we agree on *every word*.

"And that's not just the books. It's articles. We had a thing in the
Times travel section a couple of weeks ago—"

"Well, that had both our names on it," she interrupted, "because we
each wrote drafts of part of it. I wrote one draft, then he went through
and added to what I wrote. But the novels, it's either I wrote it or
Michael wrote. *But*," she amplified, "when you're writing it, you're
always remembering the characters, the plotting, the talking . . . the
very shape of the books."

"Right," he said. "When you look back at the books, what you remember are the conversations we had about this or that particular part.
When you think, 'how did this particular development come about?'
you remember that we were out there," he gestures toward the garden

beyond the window, "talking about it. And of course it comes to your mind *while* you're writing, too."

"Now, I've started to record," she says. "I have a journal where I keep entering things as each work goes along, and I've got all these arrows going 'Conversation on the road to such and such,' and then revisions of the plot."

This is, in a way, the sort of iterative process that used to be the norm back in those primitive publishing-industry days when editors actually edited rather than merely "acquired." What's odd about Erdrich and Dorris is the ease of agreement they described, and a couple of disquieting possibilities need to be considered. First, one wonders, without quite asking, whether Dorris, nine years older, is a sort of Svengali; if they are Erdrich's drafts, after all, it is always she who has to yield. When I'd called her publisher to set up the interview, I was told, "You'll have to talk to Michael Dorris. He's her manager." The role, even the word, is unusual in the context of literary writing. But as I discovered when I replayed the tape, whenever he left the room—as did a couple of times for phone calls—she shifted, with apparently equal unselfconsciousness, from "we" to "I." Could there be some *Star Is Born* trip playing out, as the young overnight sensation at once protects and inflates her older spouse?

No, I think, to both. The literary world is nasty enough that if there were any plausible hope of successfully dismissing Erdrich by portraying her as Dorris's cat's-paw, the whispering would already have begun—and Erdrich's fictional women knock the second for a loop. Not simply in ones or twos, but universally, they radiate too much power for their creator to be involved in Judy Garlandish self-immolation. Finally, though I confess to being relieved when I discovered that Dorris was working on his own fiction, when they describe their collaboration and its history, it seems as natural, if as fragile, as apple pie.

It began when she was an undergraduate, he was already at Dartmouth, brought in at the tail end of the civil rights movement to reaffirm the school's somewhat half-hearted historical commitment to the education of Native Americans. Though her major was English and creative writing, the two not unnaturally became friends. Both were half-Indian, both had been "missionized" Catholic, and both were unquestionably achievers. When she returned to North Dakota as a teacher in 1976, they began sending each other manuscripts in the mail. The flow abated a

couple of years later, when she entered the graduate writing program at
Johns Hopkins, then began building as she moved slowly north—to
Boston, where she edited the Boston Indian Council newspaper; to New
Hampshire's MacDowell Colony for a 1980 fellowship—finally resum-
ing its face-to-face character early in 1981, when she came to the Native
American Studies Program as writer-in-residence. By then, she'd
written a textbook, her poems had been published in a dozen little
magazines, and some had been anthologized. By then, too, she was no
longer a student, but Dorris's colleague. The collaboration flowered
when she moved into the farmhouse with Dorris and the three children
he'd adopted as a single parent.

"It was clearly fate," she laughed. "We'd gotten to trust each other,
and when we got married, after what seemed like a lengthy courtship,
but was really quite short—we look back, and it was only six months,
but it seemed like, 'My goodness, we're being so restrained'—and once
we started living in the house, it just seemed like the right way to
work."

He added that they'd actually written together before they married—a
series of domestic short stories, one published in *Redbook,* the rest in
England—under the name of "Milou North," a blend of their first
names and their geographical setting. "For a while, that was the area
where we did the combination, but then it really spilled over into the
more serious fiction. Though it was a gradual process, we used to argue
a lot more. You know, a person said, 'this doesn't work,' and the other
person would storm away and throw the manuscript down and be
furious for a while. But then we always, literally *always,* took the other
person's suggestion ultimately."

Not even, I asked, a tiny demur? And suddenly they were both talking at once, going on about the word *Doppler* in *Love Medicine.* He'd
thought it should go; she'd wanted it to stay. "There was nothing wrong
with *Doppler*," he said. "I just didn't think the character would use that
word."

"Which I agree with," she replied quite firmly, "but I *liked the
word.*"

The precise, efficient choice of words is most obvious in Erdrich's
poetry, but both the love of language and the respect for characters'
speech are fully evident in the interrelated novels. Though almost
everyone in them is blood-tied (a *Times* reviewer despairingly noted that

it "would take genealogists or canon lawyers to track the consanguin-
ity"), and though the Indian characters repeatedly draw metaphors from
Dakota's landscape and natural life, the voices—*Love Medicine* has
seven narrators; *Beet Queen* has six, plus 16 third-person fugues—
remain unfailingly distinct. Thus in *Love Medicine*, Albertine sees
Grandma Kashpaw and thinks, "When I was very young, she always
seemed the same size to me as the rock cairns commemorating Indian
defeats around here. But every time I saw her now I realized that she
wasn't so large, it was just that her figure was weathered and massive as
a statue roughed out of rock." Yet toward the end of the book, when a
widowed Grandma Kashpaw is in the nursing home, the rock imagery is
tellingly altered. As she administers postoperative eyedrops to fellow
patient Lulu Lamartine, her longtime (and occasionally successful) rival
for her husband's love, Lulu's eyes blink open. "The light was cloudy
but I could already see. She swayed down like a dim mountain, huge
and blurred, the way a mother must look to her just born child."

That first novel, rather like Grandma Kashpaw herself, is composed
of enormous compassion and damn few compromises. The narrative
voices leap back and forth, often flatly contradicting each other, across
50 years and three generations. Erdrich constantly thrusts responsibility
on the reader, saying, as poets effectively do, "Here it is. Here it *all* is.
I've done my best, now it's *your* turn."

In *The Beet Queen,* she takes it a little easier on us. Though her
canvas is almost as large as *Love Medicine*'s—the narrators carry the
story across 40 years rather than 50—the book doesn't hopscotch
through time."I'm not sure," she said of the earlier book, "that the
structure really *had* to be that complicated." In addition to its more
linear narrative structure, *The Beet Queen* is punctuated by third-person
interludes that let Erdrich explain a little more, filling in the shadings
when a character sees only in lovers' stark black-and-white, or height-
ening the contrasts when one self-protectively washes the world in gray.

The cool reserve of these passages comes almost as a relief after each
narrator's passionate intensity, and in that sense, they fulfill a psychological need for the reader in much the same way that the collaborative
process functions for Erdrich. "Doing all those different voices, I
become those characters," she said. "It's sort of a low-level schizophrenia, and being able to go back to Michael—and to our family—lets
me escape."

Escape is necessary—for reader and writer—because Erdrich, unlike most of her novelistic generation, has no truck with wan, attenuated minimalism. Her characters scream with pain, roar with laughter, and her plots overflow with Dickensian complication. This is resolutely unfashionable fiction, made even more so by its moral under-pinning. Good and evil are real, they count, and even though *The Beet Queen* lacks the substructure of Indian religion that informed *Love Medicine*, its judgments are as impassioned and unsparing. In a way, Erdrich's ability to control her whirling sprawl in a world of mainstream white culture makes *The Beet Queen* even more impressive than her first novel.

It begins not with death, as *Love Medicine* did, but with abandonment, when Adelaide Adare, a desperately impoverished mother on the brink of being evicted one more time from lodgings, climbs into a buck-a-ride carnival airplane. Behind her on the ground are 14-year-old Karl, 11-year-old Mary, and a nameless, still-nursing, newborn son. Mary tells the story:

> Karl stared in stricken fascination at the sky, and said nothing as the Great Omar began his stunts and droning passes. I could not watch. I studied the face of my little brother and held myself tense, waiting for the plane to smash.
>
> The crowd thinned. People drifted away. The sounds of the engine were harder to hear. By the time I dared look into the sky, The Great Omar was flying steadily away from the fairgrounds with my mother. Soon the plane was only a white dot, then it blended into the pale sky and vanished.
>
> I took Karl's arm, but he pulled away from me and vaulted to the edge of the grandstand. "Take me," he screamed, leaning over the rail. He stared at the sky, poised as if he'd throw himself into it.
>
> Satisfaction. It surprised me, but that was the first thing I felt after Adelaide flew off. For once she had played no favorites between Karl and me, but left us both.

As in the first book, Erdrich's women are stronger medicine than her men, and *The Beet Queen* is largely the story of three women: Mary, raised behind her aunt and uncle's butcher shop in Argus, North Dakota; her slightly older and much prettier cousin, Sita Kozka, who's both jealous and envious of Mary; and their schoolgirl best friend, Celestine James. Though Celestine, half-Chippewa, is a Kashpaw by blood, she lives in town, off the reservation, and much of *The Beet Queen*'s

dialogue is conducted in the flat, emotion-denying language of Great
Plains whites. What magic these people do practice—Mary's yarrow
sticks, for example, cast and read only "according to some mail-order
instruction"—is ineffectual, and the consequent loss of hope makes *The
Beet Queen* the darker of the two novels.

Almost as compensation, though, it is genuinely if grimly funny.
More than 20 years after Mary's arrival in Argus, her niece Dot (the
somewhat casual offspring of Karl and Celestine) tells her that the
kindergarten teacher put her in "the naughty box." Dot describes it with
great detail—a red box under the clock in the back of the room, "it's
big. It's made of wood. It has *splinters*." Not thinking for a moment in
the face of such circumstantiality that the naughty box is a chalked
square on the blackboard where the teacher writes the names of children
who've misbehaved, Mary sails forth to avenge her niece:

Beneath the clock, in the precise spot Dot had described, there was a
glazed box painted a sinister and shining red. It was long as a coffin and
twice as broad . . .

I pointed at the box, then lifted one end and dumped the toys out.
Blocks, fire engines, plastic doll furniture and bright rubber rings spilled
across the floor. I let it fall with an empty crash.

"Mrs. Shumway. Come here," I said.

She walked over to me, not obediently, but with a nervy terrier's
menace.

"What is the meaning of this!" she cried. "Who are you?" Her blue hat
seemed to lift off her hair in surprise . . .

I put my hands on my hips, butcher's hips, used to shifting heavy
loads and moving hams down the smoke rails.

"Your little game is up, Mrs. Shumway," I said.

She coughed in surprise. "What are you talking about?" she squeaked.
She stepped backward, laughed uncertainly. I suppose thinking of it
now, she merely thought I was a harmless lunatic, but at the time I took
her nervous laugh as an admission of guilt. I reached out and grabbed the
shoulders of her camel coat. I dragged her toward the red box.

At first, she was so shocked that her knees buckled and her heels
dragged, but when we reached the box, and when I tried to force her in
by pushing her and bending her arms and legs up like a doll's, she
suddenly regained her poise and stood fast. She was surprisingly agile,
and very strong, so that I had a harder time than you would expect
shoving her inside the box and crushing all of her limbs in besides. Also,
she was proud. For she made no outcry until she was trapped and all was
lost. And then, once I'd sat down on top of the red box, breathing

heavily, recovering my composure, Mrs. Shumway began to hammer and howl.

The deadpan brilliance of the set piece is typical. The "woodpecker-ish" Shumway, moving from cry to squeak to howl, is good, but Mary's impervious certitude is better. Though she tells the story well after learning of her mistake, it nonetheless stretches to include the reader when she mentions she had a harder time *than you would expect . . .* crushing all of her limbs in besides." This splendid wrongheadedness is totally natural, totally Mary—and one feels almost as sorry for Dot, bearing the burden of this overwhelming and manipulable love, as for the imprisoned Shumway. Though this is a book in which the characters take almost nothing but false steps (Dot herself is merely one among many), Erdrich's language is cat-footed sure.

It moves certainly even when she avoids fire and considers repression. Here Mary's brother Karl, whose fathering Dot was an aberration, thinks about his relationship with a lover, the hapless Wallace Pfef, an Argus Chamber of Commerce bulwark so closeted he can barely think of what he and Karl do after they've done it: "As his only experience, I was some sort of God he worshipped by acting like he was my personal maid. He ironed everything I wore, washed my shirts fresh, brought coffee, squeezed oranges because I said I liked real juice, and cooked up big dinners every night. An ash wouldn't drop from my cigarette but that he'd catch it in his bare palm and brush it into a wastebasket. Sleeping with him was no different from that. He'd do anything to please me, but didn't have the nerve to please himself."

Unlike Erdrich's Indian characters, who are victims of external forces, Pfef guards his own prison, but his condition—and his pain—echo theirs. As we talked, Erdrich was at first hesitant about making the connection. "Wallace, in his *particular* life is a person who's kept this secret," she began, "kept it almost from himself." But after a pause, she added, "I think the one thing about reservation life is that the people who are talking in these books almost take oppression for granted, to such an extent that it's a part of their lives they never talk about."

Erdrich—it is perhaps the best way of summing up her strengths—tells secrets her characters don't know they have. For the most part, she stands back and lets the force of her language do it; the shifts from voice to voice, the calming interludes of third-person reflection, are necessary escapes from the depths she plumbs.

And, too, from the heights. For if her language limns physical and psychic pain with a hypochondriac's obsessive detail, it takes on joy like a roller coaster. In *Love Medicine*, for instance, Dot is older and increasingly pregnant with the child of Gerry Nanapush, an Indian escape artist "mainly in the penitentiary for breaking out of it," his original three-year assault sentence having long elapsed. In Albertine Johnson's phrase, Dot "weighed over two hundred pounds, most of it peanut-butter cups and egg-salad sandwiches," and Nanapush was even bigger. On those frequent occasions when he busted out of jail to visit her during her pregnancy, "she was hard-pressed to hide him. . . . Hiding a six-foot-plus, two-hundred-and-fifty-pound Indian in the middle of a town that doesn't like Indians in the first place isn't easy," so though he had escaped to be with Dot during childbirth, he wasn't hanging around her house.

Somehow, though, once Dot was hospitalized, she got word to him to fetch Albertine:

"I was surprised when Gerry rumbled to the weigh-shack door on a huge and ancient, rust-pocked, untrustworthy-looking machine that was like no motorcycle I'd ever seen before.

"She asst for you," he hissed. "Quick, get on!"

I hoisted myself up behind him, although there wasn't room on the seat. I clawed his smooth back for a handhold and finally perched, or so it seemed, on the rim of his heavy belt. Flylike, glued to him by suction, we rode as one person. Whipping a great wind around us. Cars scattered, the lights blinked and flickered on the main street. Pedestrians swiveled to catch a glipse of us—a mountain tearing by balanced on a toy, and clinging to the sheer northwest face, a scrawny half-breed howling something that Dopplered across the bridge and faded out, finally, in the parking lot of Saint Adelbert's Hospital.

I don't think *Dopplered* is such a bad word here. Do you?

Writers and Partners

Gail Caldwell/1986

From *The Boston Globe*, 26 September 1986, 15. Reprinted by
courtesy of *The Boston Globe*,

CORNISH, N.H.—The scene has all the earmarks of an American pastoral.
The two-century-old farmhouse where Louise Erdrich and Michael
Dorris live with their five children is a rambling, brick-red structure set
in the midst of 17 acres, their back boundary demarcated by a field of
wildflowers. On a flawless autumn day, the only sound is that of an
occasional car driving down nearby Route 120, on the road to Cornish.
This is pond-and-barn country, where the pace of living is measured by
the height of the corn in fall gardens.

Last Friday, the idyll was upended over the course of an afternoon by
a UPS delivery, a photographer's visit, a spate of long-distance calls
from New York and the arrival of 16 long-stem roses. The flowers came
from Bantam Books, which the day before had acquired the paperback
rights to Erdrich's second novel, *The Beet Queen,* after a day-long
auction in New York. While Erdrich and Dorris won't discuss the figure
involved, they admit to being "very pleased" with the arrangement.

Published earlier this month to excellent reviews, *The Beet Queen* is a
featured alternate of the Book-of-the-Month Club; foreign rights have
already been sold to England, Denmark, Norway, Finland, Sweden,
Germany and France. This Sunday, just three weeks after publication,
the novel will appear on the *New York Times* Best Seller List. The
evocative story of two families in North Dakota that spans some 40
years, *The Beet Queen* is the second book in a projected tetralogy; like
Erdrich's first novel, *Love Medicine*, it draws its strengths from a
Native American sensibility and an understated, luminous narrative.

Erdrich and Dorris appear unruffled by all the fanfare, finding time
to serve a seemingly effortless lunch and oversee the schedules and
whereabouts of five children, who range in age from 18 months to 18
years. Certainly this renovated 18th-century farmhouse in southwestern
New Hampshire is a far cry from Erdrich's native Wahpeton, N.D.,
where her parents taught in the Indian Boarding School. It may be that

Erdrich and Dorris are used to incongruity: When *Love Medicine* was published in the fall of 1984, it initially met with a quiet reception, but news of its remarkable prose vision soon spread among reviewers and literary patrons. (Philip Roth called Erdrich "the most interesting new American novelist to have appeared in years.") That winter, despite scant attention in the press, the novel came out of nowhere to win the National Book Critics Circle Award.

But perhaps the most peculiar aspect of this Cinderella publishing story is the partnership-of-letters behind it. Erdrich names Dorris as her "collaborator/husband" in *The Beet Queen*, which is dedicated "To Michael. Complice in every word, essential as air." He also acts as general agent and editor of the work, which, as he says, never leaves the house "without six or seven drafts" having passed between them.

Of Chippewa and German descent, Erdrich first met Dorris in 1972, when she entered the Native American Studies program at Dartmouth College, where he was an instructor. (He now heads the program.) His first impression of Louise was of her wearing red cowboy boots.

Erdrich returned to North Dakota in 1976 to work as a poet in the schools, then went on to take a masters degree in creative writing from Johns Hopkins University. She met Dorris again when she came to Dartmouth to give a poetry reading ("Actually, our glances locked across a glass of tonic water," she laughs). An anthropologist with graduate degrees from Yale, Dorris was working on his own fiction. The two started exchanging manuscripts through the mail; in 1981, when she returned to Dartmouth as a writer-in-residence, they were married.

At 32, Louise Erdrich is a confident and eloquent woman who gestures easily as she speaks, her dark eyes almost as expressive as her hands. Dorris, 41, who is part Modoc Indian, is the more outwardly vivacious of the couple. There's a rough-and-tumble grace between them that suggests a well-worn familiarity; they often interrupt each other to laugh or disagree.

"It's sort of a conversational process; we just talk about it all time," says Erdrich about their collaboration. "We take lots of walks around here. It's nice walking. And we talk about ideas for characters, and one of us gets excited about a conversation and starts writing something."

Dorris breaks in. "Then the person who isn't doing the writing takes the piece of paper and brutalizes it," they both burst out laughing, "and tries to balance off the criticisms with little stars in the margin. It's much stronger editing than we would tolerate from anybody else. We've gotten to the point of trusting that response, because in the beginning we had this agreement that we would never not say anything to spare the other person's feelings."

Dorris, who has his own novel forthcoming next spring (*A Yellow Raft in Blue Water*), admits that "daily" stalemates are not uncommon. "The critic usually wins," agrees Erdrich. "I hold onto something because I like the sheer language of it; you [to Dorris] hold onto sentimental things. You just have to let go at some point. And then—absolutely, it always happens—I think, thank God, I didn't give in to my impulse."

Erdrich says the two feel equally committed to one another's fiction. "There's not a credit line available to reflect what we do," says Dorris. "I mean, it is not accurate to have both our names on it at this time, because we don't write it equally. But there just isn't a way of citation."

Of course, literary relationships of this intensity aren't without their precedent. But Erdrich's is the name on the work—on *Love Medicine* and *The Beet Queen*, anyway—and even a collaboration as fluid as this one must have suffered its share of ego challenges. Dorris and Erdrich nonetheless discuss their joint effort with equal candor, whether in unison or alone, often speaking in the first-person-plural even when the other is out of the room. Erdrich does admit that, in the early writing of *Love Medicine*, "it was still at the stage where with every chapter it was a test of wills.

"I think we're used to the other person being as harsh as possible, and there's this assurance that—even though it's quite painful to listen with an open mind—that it is for the best. That happens very slowly. I'd say that now it's less painful," she laughs, "and we do it more readily."

"It used to be harder, because my instinct was that if I talked about something, I would never write it. But that wasn't true. Talking about it clarified it in a way that usually didn't happen until the second or third draft. I don't think I could do that with anyone else. We had to set precedents for a long time. It's a feeling of safety, or trust, and we're very careful not to violate it by falsely praising anything.

"There's this whole romantic idea of the artist as the lone sufferer. You know, there are times when no amount of being together with someone can save you from that blank page. But I'm sure it's much easier because we have each other."

Certainly this collaboration might seem stranger than its fictional

product if the latter didn't ring so true. But the consistent power of
Erdrich's novels lies in their authenticity—in dialogue conveyed so
matter-of-factly that you half-expect to find the characters seated at their
creators' kitchen table. Often the skewed internal viewpoints seem
rendered from a blend of mysticism and verse. In *The Beet Queen*, a
woman's hallucinatory breakdown is described so vividly that her
purgatorial vision feels as real as yesterday's rainstorm:

"Then I went down to the tree where my silver was hung. Bracelets
and rings and old coins of it. I put my hands out. The leaves moved
over me, gleaming and sharpened, with tarnished edges. They fell off in
mounds. The air was a glittering dry rain. While I was down there I said
many things.

". . . I described the tree in detail. It bore the leaves of my betrayal.
The roots reached under everything. Everywhere I walked I had to step
on the dead, who lay tangled and cradled, waiting for the trumpet, for
the voice on the bullhorn, for the little book to open that held a million
names."

Erdrich's work is full of such silken imagery: still-lit candles flying
by in tornado winds, ironic Christian visions, visits from the other side.
While she claims that the flying candle comes from North Dakota
tornado stories, she's conscious of incorporating the elements of oral
tradition, allegory and myth in her fiction.

"You learn from the people you read, but you also learn from people
that you listen to, or we do. We have lots of relatives who tell stories,
and the stories people tell around the table are exaggerated, coincidental, you'll-never-believe-this kinds of stories. And they're always
couched in the most prosaic of worlds, but they're about the strange
things that happen to them. There's some remark that Gabriel Garcia
Marquez made: Someone asked him, 'How could you have written this?
It seems so real,' when Marquez' priest levitates. He levitates while
drinking a cup of hot chocolate. And Marquez said, 'It's the cup of hot
chocolate that makes this real.'

"It's the object, or grounding reality, that makes the unreal seem
plausible."

Beyond the quiet poise and generous interaction with Dorris, what
comes through in conversation with Erdrich is an acute literary intelligence that roams from Faulkner to Flannery O'Connor ("That's one of
the reasons I love O'Connor: Everything is so Catholic and bizarre at

the same time.") She received a strong dose of postmodernist fiction while at Johns Hopkins, which—given the warmth and abundance of her own work—seems peculiar if not antithetical.

"Hopkins had this very postmodernist slant. You couldn't help but be really influenced by this emphasis on the text, on experimental texts. People were fascinated with Robert Coover and Thomas Pynchon, and John Barth was there, and the focus was on that, which I found very helpful. I certainly went through this whole phase where I did nothing but read postmodernist stuff and try to write it, you know. It's probably in there somewhere.

"I think the emphasis on pure technique and language is a dead end. But that's not to say I don't admire their work, because I do love the texture—the sheer explosiveness of reading something in some form you didn't expect."

That shattering of expectations may be the primary legacy she received from the postmoderns, for one of the veins of Erdrich's compassionate writing is its defiance of Native American stereotypes. "There's this great sterotype about Native Americans as being very inarticulate," she says. "People who've had tribal language as their first language are going to be much more complicated in their own language . . . The way around it is to invent characters who have an articulateness that does not hinge on education. These people are very articulate about their lives, but they're not using literary references."

Not often, though Nector Kashpaw, in *Love Medicine*, is one exception. He takes comfort in *Moby Dick,* the sole book taught in his Catholic high school on the reservation:

"'You're always reading that book,' my mother said once. 'What's in it?'

"'The story of the great white whale.'

"She could not believe it. After a while, she said, 'What do they got to wail about, those whites?'"

"It never really happened," says Erdrich now about the "great white wail," "but I just laughed out loud. It's what this woman would say, because there's such a sense of humor and irony in Native American life, in tribal life. I mean, that's one of the things that does not get portrayed often enough—that there's such an irony and humor."

Still, there's plenty of each in Erdrich's novels, though her characters have also seen their share of wickedness and folly. But more than anything there's a sense of celestial decency to the work—an amorphous rectitude that justifies its characters' ends, even when they go the way of aimless suffering or death.

"In different tribal religions," says Erdrich (who, like Dorris, was raised Catholic), "the way they use spirit is as a living thing that animates everything. It's not good; it's not bad; it's not this guy with a beard. But it's this livingness, and that, I think, is to be revered."

For all their hardknocks and gritty consequences of fate, both *Love Medicine* and *The Beet Queen* spill over with livingness, a cast of characters with so many emotional and genealogical bloodlines that it's difficult to keep track of them all. The Erdrich-Dorris household has a touch of that unrestrained energy, with four of the five children—Abel, Sava, Madeline, Persia and Pallas, in descending order—bursting in by the end of the day. But even when Persia and Pallas arrive from the baby-sitter, the infants settle in a silent heap at their mother's feet.

Erdrich and Dorris remain sprawled in two rocking chairs, talking and laughing about the scheduled return appearance of some of their favorite characters. "It's almost like we're listening to them," says Dorris. "There was the Greek sculptor who had a theory that the statue reposed within the marble, and what sculpting was all about was just knocking off the excess." He laughs. "Certainly with all the cuts we do, there's a lot of knocking off."

Her long legs wrapped around the chair, Louise Erdrich seems certain of this larger vision. She smiles at her husband across the room. "It's almost like the story is all done," she says. "And we have to live long enough to be receptive to it."

Belles Lettres Interview: Louise Erdrich

Nan Nowick/1986

From *Belles Lettres*, 2.2 (November/December 1986), 9. Reprinted by permission.

Louise Erdrich's readers may be misled when they turn to her newly released novel, *The Beet Queen*, and see the names of Eli and June Kashpaw, vivid Native American characters from *Love Medicine*. This time around Erdrich is featuring not her Chippewa ancestry but the people she knew through her German-born father. While for me no character in this new book has a voice as sweetly comic as Lipsha's or as fierce as Marie's, these people are wonderful fictional creations, poignantly cursed and blessed with their powers to remember and to love.

During an April reading at Denison University and again more recently during a phone interview, Erdrich discussed an overall plan for her fiction. Her first two closely related novels are part of a proposed tetralogy or quartet. Each novel is made up of narratives that can be and have been excerpted as short stories (some are winners of major prizes), but the stories work together to form a whole, each novel representing one of the four elements. In *Love Medicine* the element is water, a whirling and dangerous element to a Chippewa. In *The Beet Queen*, the story of people living in the small North Dakota town of Argus, the element is air—both plot and imagery reinforce the theme of flying, and sounds of the rushing air in storms on the Dakota plains act as leitmotif. Furthermore, the novel's elegant dedication to Erdrich's husband reinforces air-as-element: "To Michael/ Complice in every word, essential/ as air."

Erdrich says it was only after several of the *Love Medicine* stories were written that she realized she had the makings of a novel. Then her anthropologist-novelist husband Michael Dorris, with whom she works in close collaboration, introduced the notion of kinship trees. Later she added the water element and the dates and bridges between stories that would give the first novel its coherence and chronology.

In *The Beet Queen* Erdrich has used a similar though more linear method of composition, and this time she concentrates on people of Po-

lish, Irish, or German descent, characters who are less self-destructive
and impoverished than the Chippewa, though no less driven or subject
to loss. They try to make their way: as traveling salesmen, models in
small-town department stores, or owners of small businesses like the
House of Meats. Argus, North Dakota, is the town that brings them
together and gives the novel its center; sense of place is important, both
to the characters and to Erdrich, who has said that a writer must have a
place "to love and be irritated with. One must experience the local
blights, hear the proverbs, endure the radio commercials . . . . Loca-
tion, whether it is to abandon or draw it sharply, is where we start"
(*New York Times Book Review,* July 28, 1985). Like two of her favorite
contemporary writers, Marilynne Robinson (*Housekeeping*) and Joan
Chase (*During the Reign of the Queen of Persia*), Erdrich is committed
to evoking the spirit of place.

At first reading the cast of characters seems very large. Once the plot
ensures that all of the chief actors find their way to Argus, however, we
begin to see complex connections building, and five or six characters
tell most of the stories, most of which are dramatic monologues. The
people who speak—the regulars—are all interrelated, either by blood or
by other intense and often passionate kinships.

Though one does not need to know the first novel to enjoy the
second, one of *Love Medicine*'s stories, "Scales," introduces us to Dot,
the epicenter of *The Beet Queen.* In "Scales," the pregnant Dot, wife
of fugitive Gerry Nanapush, gives birth as he is chased by Officer
Lovchik. What we saw in "Scales" is Dot's future; what Erdrich gives
us in *The Beet Queen* is a kind of Bildungsroman writ backwards. We
meet Dot's biological parents, her aunts, and her putative uncle as she
moves through her difficult childhood. Though Erdrich has no physical
resemblance to Dot, she strongly identifies with her: "I gave her some
of my jobs—selling popcorn and working in a weigh shack. And I
remembered how hard it was to be told what to do."

The novel builds to the day Dot is to become Beet Queen. The Argus
economy has been saved by the planting and processing of sugar beets,
and the Beet Festival provides the occasion for bringing these interrelated people together again. Dot has only one chapter in her own
voice, the last, and although her conception, birth, and maturation
provide the structure for the novel, she is not the heroine or even—by
far—the most attractive of the characters.

In fact, one of the interesting features of this work is that although several of the characters are compelling, few are attractive. Some are profoundly selfish or self-absorbed. Some are gullible. Erdrich's humor is sometimes based on people's capacity for self-deception, and the Catholic Church continues to be one of her favorite targets. One of the best sections of the novel deals with the Manifestation at Argus, a parody of the Shroud of Turin, a veil upon which Jesus supposedly left the imprint of his face as he wiped off his sweat while walking the road to Calvary. During her first winter in Argus, 11-year-old Mary Adare barrels head-first down an ice-covered playground slide at St. Catherine's grade school, leaving in the splintered ice below the slide a likeness of Jesus: "Christ's face formed in the ice as surely as on Veronica's veil," says the parish priest. The more skeptical Celestine says that shouting "miracle" in a convent "is like shouting fire in a crowded movie. They all rush down suddenly, an avalanche of black wool." Sister Leopolda sets up a tripod and photographs the "manifestation" for the textbooks. Later the face of Christ was "cordoned off and farmers drove for miles to kneel by the cyclone fence."

Those characters who are not gullible are often bitter, perverse, and unbalanced. Sita's destructive behavior parallel that of her aunt Adelaide, and Mary and her niece Dot are both lifelong bullies (aunts and nieces figure prominently in Erdrich's fiction). Time frequently "collapses" for these characters, and they vividly relive the "terrible small moments" of their youth, times of jealousy, grief, and desire for revenge. Mary, for example, never forgives her mother's preference for her brother Karl and her subsequent abandonment of them both. Mary writes her a postcard saying, "All three of your children starved dead." This is a novel about memory and its retrieval, a novel about wounds survived but never forgotten or completely healed.

Yet the bitterness is never Erdrich's, perhaps because she is so fascinated by tales of the human condition. "I loved my parents' stories," she says. "I was hungry for knowledge about their lives before I knew them." In *The Beet Queen* she understands the complexity of her characters, and her special combination of compassion and humor is becoming her trademark.

What happens to the characters is often grim, frequently outrageous, yet is told with a distinctive matter-of-factness. In 1932 at an orphan's picnic, the aforementioned Adelaide, mother of three illegitimate children impulsively takes off in a plane with The Great Omar, Aeronaut Extraordinaire. She never returns. On the same day, the youngest of her now-orphaned children is kidnapped by a man whose own infant son has just died. With these unlikely happenings, Erdrich introduced the key themes of the book: flight (literal and metaphorical), abandonment, and a dark necessity that guides certain characters to act as substitute parents for other people's children. "Informal adoption is common in Native American cultures," says Erdrich, "and being temporary parents can be very painful." In this novel she demonstrates by extension how all parenting is temporary, and painful, and often rewarding beyond expectation.

The plot of *The Beet Queen* is woven with sudden, inexplicable behavior that gives an edge of surrealism to the novel; the narratives have the suggestiveness of fairy tales—in the stories of the stolen baby, of the kidnapped bride, of the child born during the snowstorm, of the ubiquitous necklace with the red stones which gleam "sharp as malice." Furthermore, the novel is peppered with maladies and deaths: strokes, heart attacks, mental "episodes," rigor mortis, a corpse, and a near-corpse who ride in the Beet Festival parade. This novel reminds me of one written by another contemporary novelist, Toni Morrison's *Song of Solomon*. Both novels begin and end with flight themes and imagery; both novelists employ surrealism, fairy tales, and the grotesque. Both seem to have found their personal voices through a compelling and unconventional use of family legend elevated to myth.

One of *The Beet Queen*'s characters says, "I did not choose solitude. Who would? It came on me like a kind of vocation." Versions of solitude are especially well treated in six chapters called "Nights," times of epiphany for six of the characters. In "Karl's Night" a boy of 13 offers love and gets sexual rejection in return. In "Mary's Night" she has a vision of the baby Celestine will have. In Russell's chapter he loses his speech through a stroke; in Sita's she regains speech lost to her for months. Erdrich calls these haunting nights "moments of pure isolation" for her characters.

Erdrich prefers a first-person narrative, for both its immediacy and its expressiveness. Her skillful dramatic monologues are highly individualized, and she is as successful with male voices as with female. Sita and Mary are fixed personalities who do not change as they mature— they only become "more so." But Celestine, Karl, and Wallace are full of surprises, and Celestine's monologues in the present tense (so much a hallmark of fiction of the 1980s) are among the best in the book.

Erdrich's first two novels cover the years 1934–1984 and 1932–1972, respectively. The third, *Tracks* (in progress), treats the years 1920–1930 and backtracks to tell about the generation before *Love Medicine*. The fourth volume, *American Horse,* will deal with the future of the Albertine/Lipsha generation as well as return to characters such as Father Jude, left dangling in *The Beet Queen*. Erdrich has said that *Love Medicine* was her first attempt to write about her Indian background and that it was difficult to "speak in that voice" and to come to terms with that identity. She is not sure she would have done it if it were not for her husband, with his own mixed roots and his interest in hers. I read *The Beet Queen* with pleasure because of its intensity, lyricism, and mixture of humor and grief, and I look forward with even greater pleasure to the time when Erdrich returns to mine, once again, the Native American strain. I believe that, paradoxically, it is through writing about Native Americans that she will escape what she considers the danger of being labeled (and thus limited or dismissed) as an ethnic or a minority writer. It is in writing about a minority that she will gain acknowledgment as a mainstream American writer of unusual talent, one who specializes in a hybrid genre, fiction with the intensity and lyricism of poetry, short story sequences that transcend themselves to become novels.

Louise Erdrich

Nora Frenkiel/1986

From *Baltimore Sun*, 17 November 1986, 1B, 5B. Reprinted with permission of the Baltimore Sun Company.

The Garrett Room of the Eisenhower library on the Johns Hopkins campus on a chilly Thursday evening. Students in their I-don't-care garb, perfectly accessorized with Reeboks and orange knapsacks, file in for a reading by Louise Erdrich, author of *The Beet Queen*, No. 12 on the *New York Times* best-seller list, and *Love Medicine*, winner of the 1984 Book National Book Critics Circle Award. A few students, from the Contemporary American Letters course, have been requested to attend this reading. Or else.

Louise Erdrich (sounds a little like Earth-Rich) was a hopeful in rooms like this, a student in the Writing Seminars at Johns Hopkins in the late 1970s, grateful that she was accepted into the program, after Iowa and other schools discouraged her. She came to write poetry but switched to fiction. Living in a small apartment on Calvert Street, she befriended the elderly women who were her neighbors and had one goal: becoming a full-time writer. She didn't care much about a best-seller, or seeing her name on the list. She was just beginning then to find the courage to write about her background: Native American Chippewa on her mother's side, German-American on her father's. She was drawing on her rich background and creating the memorable characters, uncommon hard-working people with strange demons and passions. She was reaching into herself, deciphering a voice, as a poem she wrote during her days in Baltimore reveals:

Now shadows move freely within me as words.
These are eternal; these stunned, loosened verbs.
And I can't tell you yet
how truly I belong

to the hiss and shift of wind,
these slow, variable mouths
through which, at certain times, I speak in tongues.

As she reads a chapter from *The Beet Queen*, her soothing bedtime-story voice needs a microphone. Her eyes are brown, her hair a feathery light brown. She wears a gray vest over a plaid shirt, tucked into Levis and a leather belt that spells out "Montana" across its back. The French would describe her as a woman both beautiful and not. She is slightly embarrassed about wearing jeans for this reading, but at 32, still slender, she looks only a few years older than the students in the audience.

She has a dress back in a hotel room she wanted to wear but just flying in, delayed from Phoenix, there is little time to do more than mingle with the faculty, do her 50-minute reading, and answer questions. The students seem shy in this setting but gather around her informally when the evening breaks up. Fatigued, rubbing her eyes, she agrees to spend more time talking with the writing students before going to bed.

She's winding up a two-month book tour and is eager to return home to Cornish, N.H., where she lives with her husband-collaborator, Michael Dorris, an anthropology professor and author who also is of Native-American descent. The road has worn her down, but as she's traveled surprises have come her way. Such as finding *The Beet Queen* on the best-seller list.

"I still don't think of it as commercial writing and I still don't understand why people are purchasing enough of these books to make it a best-seller because I think it's not easy reading. Even people who buy the books, when I run into them on trips like this they say, 'I got through it,'" she says, laughing with sincere pleasure. "It's really surprising to me. It gives me hope that there are a lot of people out there who are willing to be challenged by a book in some way."

The Beet Queen spans 40 years, in the lives of Karl and Mary Adare, abandoned by their mother and left to drift, each ending up isolated and yet inexorably tangled up in relationships as complicated as a cat's cradle.

Michiko Kakutani, reviewing the novel in the *New York Times,* praised the "passages of shimmering poetic description: startling sequences of physical and emotional violence, and a cast of characters, at once ordinary and strange like eccentric folk-art figures."

Critical praise has come, as have awards and attention, much of it focused on Ms. Erdrich's heritage. While acknowledging "the bell curve of interest in minority writers," the author says, "When I was growing up, I didn't think about it a lot, and I took it for granted and I feel if I don't think about this too much I can keep writing."

Yet, in an article last year for the *New York Times Book Review* on a writer's sense of place, she wrote: "Contemporary Native American writers have therefore a task quite different . . . In the light of enormous loss, they must tell the stories of contemporary survivors while protecting and celebrating the cores of cultures left in the wake of the catastrophe . . . "

Born in Minnesota, she grew up in Wahpeton, N.D., where her parents taught at the North Dakota Indian Boarding School. Her grandfather headed the Turtle Mountain Chippewa reservation nearby, and she passed freely between both worlds. Her father, Ralph Erdrich, remembers his daughter, the eldest of seven, as a voracious reader. "She had memorized the Christmas story by the time she was 2½ years old," he says and although she loved making up stories and playing them out with her siblings, she also was a child of the outdoors.

"My clearest memory of growing up in North Dakota was the space and flatness," she says. "I remember the way things smelled and felt and tasted when I went back to Turtle Mountains. My grandfather was a great storyteller, a very colorful guy, a traditional Pow Wow dancer. He searched his fields for old stones used in tomahawks, and remade the entire beadwork."

On her father's side, she recalls, "It was very working-class, pragmatic, tenacious hard-headed German."

In 1972 she entered Dartmouth, admitted with the first class of women. After graduation she returned home, tried to write, and worked on a project teaching poetry in the schools. Feeling isolated, she realized she had to leave again to begin writing seriously. "I didn't have a lot of people around me doing the same thing," she says. "I was afraid to come out."

Yet at Hopkins she found a nurturing environment. "There was real caring among the students." While there was "honesty, fights and tiffs," she says, "I think that criticism was very valuable. I feel indebted to the other students and teachers here."

Cynthia MacDonald, a poet who had Ms. Erdrich as a student, recalls her as "a warm and lovely person. I would have picked her as one of the students to publish but certainly not *the* one."

After receiving her master of arts degree, Ms. Erdrich returned home and became absorbed with the Native American experience. "I had to go back," she says. "I worked with an urban Indian group and I did different things that made me a lot more part of the community and gave me a lot more confidence so that I could write about it. I had always been thinking I couldn't do it. It's too difficult, the problems are too complex, I don't know enough. And yet I didn't make a decision ever to really write about that specifically but finally let my subjects choose me. I finally let go enough to let it happen."

Her first book, *Love Medicine*, an interwoven collection of short stories told through multiple narrative perspective, was published in 1984 to great praise and won her the National Book Critics Circle Award. Not all the criticism was positive. Gene Lyons, writing in *Newsweek,* criticized the tales as "so self-consciously literary that they are a whole lot easier to admire than to read."

Certainly the lush language, the breathtaking set pieces, the descriptive richness of her work can be overwhelming. Ms. Erdrich responds to such criticism by saying, "I think that one of the things that surprised me was the fact that people who are not literary, people who have lived similar lives to the people in these books, people who live on reservations, say this is the way people talk and people think. People who are very educated think that people who aren't do not have as complex an inner world. I don't believe that, and that's why these [characters] have complicated thoughts and metaphysical thoughts. I think it's expressed poetically in a lot of places and I love language and I think people love reading it."

Rather than write directly about the Native American experience from a political or outside perspective, she chooses to dwell on the inner life. Although a character may occasionally bristle with anger:—"boom trash . . . to these types an Indian woman's nothing but an easy night"—the white world is not a crueler place than the world these characters create for themselves. Life is about loss and survival. And the search for love and tenderness.

Ms. Erdrich says she wrote most of *The Beet Queen* in between pregnancies, with a baby snuggled in her arms. In a scene from the novel, the mother Celestine James comforts her daughter Dot:

> "Her head falls heavy against me, salty, smelling of sour wool. Her shoulders rock, but I can't tell she's crying until the skirt sticks to my thighs damp, and she breathes out, harsh and deep.
> "It is so long before she draws another breath that I almost shake her

in alarm. But she is just asleep, and nothing will disturb her now. I don't leave, even though my arms go numb and Mary waits downstairs. I don't leave when she tosses in her first dream, throwing more weight against me. I sit perfectly still.

"Then her fingers uncurl, as if sand is trickling out, and she seems lighter. The radiator shudders in the corner. Dot's room smells like the nests of shoes and socks she has made this week. It smells of the mildewed stuffing of her battered and abandoned dolls and of the sawdust where her hamsters hide. It smells of oil that she puts on her softball glove, lilac water that she dumps on her hair. It smells of cold grit between the window and the sill. It smells of Dot, a clean and bitter smell, like new bark, that I'd know anywhere."

At her rambling farmhouse in New Hampshire, not far from the Dartmouth campus, five children are always snuggling into this rarely solitary writer's life. There is a sturdiness in Ms. Erdrich of a country woman with her good strong hands put to use. Although she misses her children when she's on the road, she admits to ambivalence about playing the role of parent, "driving all those miles in the country to appointments."

In the morning, after the children are off to baby sitters or schools, she and her husband stake out "opposite ends of the house to write." At regular intervals, they come together, sharing work and ideas in an unusual collaborative process. "It's different because I'm also in love with this editor, so I know the way I feel about his work is that I want to do the best thing for the work and I know he feels the same way," she says. "There's a lack of egos in this kind of thing and I wouldn't be able to let any other editor do this. There are times when it's very hard to hear something."

In the collaborative process the roles keep reversing. In March, Henry Holt and Company will publish Michael Dorris' novel, *A Yellow Raft in Blue Water*. So far, more attention has focused on her work.

She is at work on the third novel in a planned series of four that focus on the tumultuous lives and resilient dreams of the people from the world she knows. She says it will pick up the stories of the younger generation, trapped between the conflicts of the old and the uncertainty of the new. Yet she expresses reluctance to talk about it in detail. It is a story she began when she was a student in Baltimore, a story that has been a struggle to write. Yet so much seems to be coming full circle for her. She is going home.

A Novel Arrangement

Dan Cryer/1986

From *Newsday,* 30 November 1986, 19–23. A Newsday article reprinted by permission, Newsday, Inc. Copyright © 1986.

Sit down for an interview with novelist Louise Erdrich, and you will find another writer by her side, her husband, Michael Dorris. Ask her a question, and he is as likely to answer as she is.

Since Erdrich has written the current best-selling novel *The Beet Queen* and the award-winning *Love Medicine* of two years ago, she's been getting lots of requests for interviews. And *they* are giving them. If he steps in to finish her sentence, or vice versa, it's not surprising, since this is what they do for a living. They are a writing team, literary collaborators of a most unusual sort.

Though her name alone is on these novels, she gratefully acknowledges his help in conceiving and writing them. Though his first novel, *A Yellow Raft in Blue Water,* will be published next spring with only his byline, he wants the world to know that she was its co-creator.

Louise Erdrich, 32, is a tall, slim woman whose high-cheekboned face changes its look, without losing its beauty, with every tilt of her head. Brought up in Wahpeton, N.D., where her parents taught at a Bureau of Indian Affairs school, she is part Chippewa. Her books transform the lives of quite ordinary contemporary Native Americans (as many American Indians prefer to be called) and their white neighbors into extraordinary art.

Erdrich does not consider herself a spokeswoman for Native Americans. She is deliberate in choosing her words and rather shy. But she is well aware that her books, written in a poetic style rich in metaphor and rhythm, do give voice to people who have been out of sight and out of mind in the '80s.

"If art is one's first concern," she says, "whatever politics are behind it will be more effective. The art comes first. Otherwise, nobody's going to read it."

Critics who have read her work tend to shower it with praise. After reading her first novel, *Love Medicine*, Philip Roth pronounced Erdrich

80

"the most interesting new American novelist to have appeared in years."
Anne Tyler called the second book "a perfect—and perfectly wonderful—novel."

Not all critics, of course, have been so generous. Robert Towers in
The New York Review of Books liked *Love Medicine* but was put off by
its sometimes "overwrought" prose. And in several generally positive
notices, reviewers found the conclusion to *The Beet Queen* either flat or
unbelievable.

All the same, *The Beet Queen* is that rare combination, a best-seller
bearing the highest literary pedigree. *Love Medicine* also sold well
and was honored as best novel of 1984 by the National Book Critics
Circle and best first fiction by the American Academy and Institute
of Arts and Letters. (Erdrich is also author of a book of poems,
Jacklight.)

Both novels, set in North Dakota and Minnesota, follow a similar
pattern, with each chapter told in the first person by a single character
until eventually the reader is given a rich, multifaceted view of lives on
and off a Chippewa reservation. *Love Medicine* and *The Beet Queen*
make up the first two of what is intended to be a quartet of novels about
the same set of characters.

In these books we hear the stories of such memorable Native Americans as Marie Lazarre, a girl who longs to be a saint whom white nuns
would worship, and Nector Kashpaw a tribal patriarch reduced in old
age to playing a stereotyped role in a B-movie. Among the whites we
meet is Wallace Pfef, at once closet homosexual and the Babbitt of
Argus, N.D. Dot Adare, of mixed blood, is a feisty whirlwind of a girl
and unwilling queen of Argus' sugar beet festival.

Louise Erdrich's works draw heavily on her background, made up of
equal parts small-town West, Catholicism and modern Native American
life.

It is a milieu in which Native Americans live much like whites and
their lives mingle at every turn. Typically, her maternal grandfather,
who was tribal chairman of the Turtle Mountain Reservation, observed
both Catholicism and his traditional Chippewa religion and married a
woman who was part Chippewa and part French-American.

The writer's coming-of-age took place in the late '60s and early '70s,
but her years as a rebellious teenager were distinctly low-key. Her
disaffection, she says, "took the form of dressing funny [wearing her

father's castoff Army clothing] and listening to Joan Baez and keeping journals and reading poems and trying to be a little different."

But not too different. She also found time to be a cheerleader for the high school wrestling team.

Erdrich met Dorris, now 41, when she arrived as a freshman at Dartmouth in 1972, part of the first women's class at the Ivy League college and part of its renewed commitment to the education of Native Americans. (The school was founded in 1770 with that aim, but over the years, only 12 Native American students had been graduated.) Dorris was hired in 1972 to teach anthropology and Native American studies. (His mother is white; his father is Modoc, a tribe now found primarily in Oregon and Washington.) Erdrich, a creative-writing major, didn't take courses from Dorris until her junior year.

As an undergraduate, Erdrich "very definitely, very romantically" felt she was a writer. *Ms.* magazine published one of her poems when she was a senior, but after graduation, she went home to North Dakota and found work as a "poet-in-the-schools," a teaching job that took her, as she puts it, "to some of the seediest hotels in the state." For two years, she worked as a lifeguard, a waitress, a researcher for a TV movie and a writer-editor-photographer for a Native American newspaper in Boston.

All the while, she continued to write and send her work to magazines and she continued to get far more rejection slips than acceptances. In 1978, she enrolled in the graduate writing program at Johns Hopkins University and earned a master's degree. She returned to Dartmouth the next year as a writer-in-residence, and her acquaintance with Dorris blossomed into romance and then marriage.

She accepted the disappointments of the writing life as an inevitable phase of apprenticeship. "I was told you had to expect millions of rejection slips," she says. "I thought I'd give myself a certain amount of time and then I'd quit. And then I got married to Michael, and things changed because of our collaboration. It's no coincidence that my writing began to seem more interesting to magazines."

Love Medicine, Erdrich explains, "started with a story ["The World's Greatest Fishermen"] that was floating around in our heads and just got written one winter . . . I wrote it in the kitchen, and Michael was on his back on the floor there with a back problem. It was written in a great rush because we wanted to send it in for the Nelson Algren fiction prize.

The money was so attractive [$5,000], and so it was written very quickly."

Dorris continues: "We spent so much time talking about how it could be rewritten when it came back . . . and then, when we won the prize, we had all this material . . . and then, the characters really kind of took off by themselves."

Erdrich: "Michael had this ingenious way of seeing chunks that had to be filled with some kind of narrative. Michael was lying on the couch one day and he told me, 'I had this dream. The title of this part is "The Bees,"' and it was like turning the key. After that, there were almost no word changes. It was sort of like a quilt, where you don't really have a form that you're following."

Dorris: "We spent a year and a half thinking about these people day and night. We would take walks and imagine scenarios . . . We sat down one day and drew [the characters'] pictures. Just did anything that would help us get a hold of them . . . We would do a lot of plotting and just take notes. Whoever is writing the book writes a draft based upon that."

Erdrich: "There's always a shaping going on together."

Dorris: "It isn't necessarily a whole chunk. It could be a line or a paragraph."

Erdrich: "Like, 'Where does this scene go? Who is this character?' "

Dorris: "Each scene goes through six or seven drafts. They're always being revised. We read it aloud several times, the whole thing through, and then each separate chapter."

If this is the Erdrich-Dorris method for writing prize-winning novels, other literary observers are skeptical. Collaboration is certainly commonplace in the writing of nonfiction. But, as Peter Collier, who collaborated with David Horowitz in writing *The Rockefellers,* noted recently in *The Washington Post,* "the notion of more than one person writing a novel seems a contradiction in terms."

People do it, of course, but their efforts are usually blatantly commercial and without literary pretensions. As Abigail McCarthy, co-author with Jane Muskie of the political thriller *One Woman Lost,* puts it, "If I were going to write fiction that was deeply serious, I don't think I could collaborate with somebody. I would be so sensitive about anyone touching something I was creating." As it was, McCarthy and Muskie divided their chores this way: Muskie kept her hands off McCarthy's writing by restricting herself to doing research on terrorism, Washington folkways and such.

Among writers of serious fiction, collaboration as intense and close as that between Erdrich and Dorris is virtually unprecedented. Literary scholars believe, for example, that Leonard Woolf's aid was indispensable to Virginia Woolf's writing in this century and that of George Henry Lewes to George Eliot's writing in the 19th, but no one contends that either man figured so directly in what actually was set down on a page. Among contemporary writers, there seem to be no parallels. It is well-known, for instance, that Joan Didion and John Gregory Dunne co-author screenplays but write their novels separately.

The Erdrich-Dorris collaboration astounds an editor such as Jack Beatty, former literary editor at *The New Republic* and now senior editor at *The Atlantic*: "The whole thing [writing fiction] is an exercise in your own creativity, eccentricity, your own strangeness. I don't know how you can let anybody else in on that."

Michael Curtis, the editor who has published several of Erdrich's stories at *The Atlantic*, declared: "I have a hard time believing [the collaboration] can last for long. If it does they will certainly have set a world record for suppressed egos . . . Some couples work together and help each other, but none of them insist to such lengths and in such a firm way on their mutuality."

Erdrich and Dorris insist that their collaboration can survive any bruises to their egos. In writing *Love Medicine*, says Dorris, a lot of disagreements had to be sorted out, but with *The Beet Queen* and *Yellow Raft* they learned to rely on each other's judgment.

"If I gave Michael something and I knew he was pulling punches," says Erdrich, "I wouldn't trust him. It's certainly not easy to give something that you think is the best thing you ever wrote and then have the other person be ho-hum about it. But it's necessary."

The couple has used a joint byline on some nonfiction articles. Whether they will ever use it for their fiction is an open question.

Erdrich: "I think we will." Dorris: "Separate bylines work. We don't want to fool with it too much."

Dorris' next book of non-fiction, *The Broken Cord*, will come out next year under his own byline. It is to be an anthropologist's study of the tragic problem of fetal alcoholism among Native Americans. Dorris can joke about how he will feel if his novel is not well-received, but the alcoholism book clearly stirs up much more emotion. "This book, if we do it wrong," Dorris says "can cause harm."

Pregnant women who are alcoholics tend to have babies with gross physical deformities and brain damage that severely restricts abstract thinking. "By the turn of the century," Dorris says "it's estimated that on some reservations up to 50 percent of all the babies born will be impaired by fetal alcoholism . . . and those victims have more babies, so the problem grows geometrically with every generation."

Babies obviously mean a lot to Michael Dorris and Louise Erdrich. Dorris adopted three Native American babies of his own before his marriage to Erdrich: Abel, now 18; Saba, 14, and Madeline, 11. And the couple have had two children of their own since: Persia, 2, and Pallas, 1.

Erdrich and Dorris work in a world of professors and writers, and they live in a restored 18th-Century farmhouse in the New Hampshire town of Cornish. But the world of Native Americans is never far away. In their living room a Matisse print hangs on a wall near a cabinet filled with traditionally crafted Native American quill boxes. Family visits and research often take them back to the Dakotas.

New England is now home. But they keep in touch with another world that nourishes their spirits and their fiction. "One of the most amazing things about *Love Medicine*," says Dorris, "was the almost uniformly positive response of Indian people all over the country. From reservations where we had never been, people wrote and said, 'How did you know about my family?' . . . Our number one worry was how Indians would feel about it. Would it ring true? And it did."

That *Love Medicine* and now *The Beet Queen* ring true for Americans of all backgrounds is cause for celebration.

Something Ventured

Georgia Croft/1987

From (White River Junction, Vermont) *Valley News,* 28 April 1987, 1–2. Reprinted by permission.

CORNISH—The phone rings. It's Philip Roth.

The mail comes. It's John Updike.

Morning comes, and Michael Dorris wonders if he might wake up and find it's still 1983, that none of this has really happened.

So far, most of what has happened—the national press coverage, the literary award ceremonies, the book-and-author lunches—is because of the books written by his wife. Louise Erdrich.

But next month, Dorris' own novel, *A Yellow Raft in Blue Water,* will be issued and, for a while, at least, the focus will shift, then expand.

Already Dorris' book is inspiring glowing pre-publication reviews rarely accorded a first novelist.

Already, an Academy Award-winning team has optioned the film rights.

Already, the screenplay is nearly finished and star-quality names are being tossed around in casting discussions.

"But it's a long way between an option and when you buy your popcorn and go to the movies," Dorris says, pointing out that despite the option, there's no surety that the book will ever be made into a movie.

And the movie, whether it's made or isn't, is incidental. The book on its own is the thing.

Tight, gripping, poetic, risky, it cuts through all manner of distinctions to the bareboned links of human experience. Its three main characters are painted with a blunt compassion that depicts them as presences in other lives and then allows them to reveal their own complexities.

And it is a statement of survival, of acceptance, of the continuation of life generation to generation, burdened by the past, changed by the present, maybe not getting better, probably getting worse, but going on.

Dorris admits that he took enormous risks with the book. The first was deciding to write in a woman's voice—and not just one woman but

86

three, of different makeup, different ages, different experience levels, beginning with Rayona, a 15-year-old.

That was one of the things about the book that just happened, Dorris says.

"It didn't start that way. Rayona started out in the first four chapters as 'Raymond.' But I found the story was turning into a boy's coming-of-age, and that wasn't what I wanted to write."

Rayona was born on a trip West in the summer of '85 when he and Erdrich were discussing where he was with the book.

"Along about Indiana, one of us said, 'Wouldn't it be interesting if he were a girl?'"

And Dorris began rethinking the story from a female point of view. Writing in a woman's voice, he says, was not an alien struggle because of his background, an only child, raised by women after his father's death.

"I come from a family of strong women who had opinions and talked about their opinions all the time. I listened to them and understood how they thought.

"If you have to figure out anyone, you have to figure out your family first of all. They're the ones you have to live with.

"I just got comfortable once I started writing in a woman's voice."

By then he also knew his characters well and could anticipate their reactions in various situations.

"Once I had a character in mind, I would begin to develop her. If Louise and I were looking through a Sears catalogue, we would ask, 'What would this character pick out in clothes to buy?' When we went into a restaurant, we'd ask, 'What would this character order from this menu?'

"You get to know a character through that process. You try to get a kind of empathy with the character you've created and see the world through their eyes. Then you put them in different situations and see how they react.

"Sometimes they surprise you. They do things you don't expect, and that's how a story develops. Just like life—things don't happen in one, two, three order."

There was also the risk of ethnicity, of setting his characters apart by their Indian heritage.

Again Dorris' own background obviated any barriers between culture and commonality. Half Indian himself, he spend childhood vacations on reservations in Montana and Washington with his father's Modoc relatives, knowing them as people, not Indians.

Even Rayona, teenaged, half Black, half Indian, is more than her color, more than her age, more than her time.

"We're all human beings," Dorris says. "We're all Americans.

"The common denominator of being Americans crosses all ethnic lines.

"A person's ethnic group matters, but we all have so much in common that it's a bridge."

There was the risk of telling the story backwards, of starting out with the youngest character, the product of all the past, and going back to a point of beginning, revealing all the effects of family history but storing up the causes until the proper moments.

That meant sometimes retelling an incident from three points of view, without telling it to death and each time enriching it.

And there was the risk—averted by Dorris' sheer strength as a writer—of diminishing the initial impact by beginning the book in the present tense, so often too breezy and awkward to be taken seriously and sometimes too raw to allow sympathy.

But the flat present tense has a dual and legitimate effect. It gives Rayona depth beyond her years by placing her squarely in today, a product of past mysteries that continue to shape her life.

And it heightens the import while at the same time softening the shock of Christine's and Aunt Ida's stories, told in the more comfortable past tense to become incidents of history that have done their shaping and now serve to explain the present.

The use of the first person also gave Dorris much more room to develop his characters.

"Most of our characters," Dorris says, referring also to Erdrich's works, based on her own Indian heritage, "don't have much education. If we used the third person and just described them, it would not reveal much about them.

"But by doing this interior monologue, it shows they are much more complex in the way they think than in the way they speak.

"It shows especially with Aunt Ida. She uses very rich, complex language to express herself, and it is the kind of language people in a non-literate society have. People who don't have a written language have a much larger speaking vocabulary than others.

"They have to know and use all these words to explain exactly what they mean. There are no dictionaries in non-literate societies."

Yellow Raft is Dorris' first book-length work of fiction, although he says he feels "very much a part" of Erdrich's highly acclaimed *Love Medicine* and *Beet Queen*.

Yet, he says, neither he nor Erdrich would have ventured into fiction if they had not met and married, despite his early desire to be a novelist.

"In college, I desperately wanted to be a fiction writer," he says.

But both his confidence and desire were dashed after his first short story was published in a college paper and a student critic wrote, "This piece reads like bad *Mary Worth*."

"I was so embarrassed by that," he says, "that I didn't begin writing fiction again until 1980."

That was after he and Erdrich had resumed an acquaintance begun in 1972 and started collaborating on some short stories. Both had given up the idea of fiction—Erdrich for poetry, Dorris for scholarly works—but their success with fiction has today brought them to the point where writing could become their main income source in another year.

"We changed each other's professional lives as well as each other's personal lives," Dorris says.

Now in their sixth year of marriage, their work style would destroy anyone's romantic image of the lonely writer off in a garrett.

"We write at the kitchen table in the middle of five children. And we have to schedule our writing time because with five children and my teaching, there are so many other things to do.

"But one advantage of having very little time to write is that you don't have writer's block. You have writer's block on our schedule and you've lost your opportunity."

The collaboration that began in 1979 with their short stories is still their approach.

"We tell other writers we collaborate, and they say 'Mmmm' in a doubtful way," he says. "There's no actual name for it, I guess. But we both feel a part of all these books.

"We each write the book with our name on it. The initial idea comes from the person with his name on it."

But once the idea is born, the collaboration begins.

"Once you write the first sentence, the first paragraph, the first chapter, you give it to the other one, and they go over it with a red pencil, crossing out, writing in new words, making exclamation points for something good or a star, if you're lucky, or NO in big letters.

"You get back this savaged draft, and then the arguments begin. We find ourselves really fighting for our point of view, but now we fight with a sense that it's futile. The objecting person always wins.

"It's really hard, when you've got something you think is really good and you give it to the other person and get it back with words crossed out and NO all over it.

"But we've gotten to the point where we accept each other's suggestions completely."

The result of this kind of progress through a book is cartons of rejected, red-pencilled drafts.

"If anyone ever does a literary biography of either of us," Dorris says, "they'll find plenty of material on each of our books.

"We go through the entire book that way and eventually read the whole book out loud to each other. That's when we insert words, do the real fine-tuning.

"We both sort of know these books by heart. As a result, when they go to the publisher, almost no editing is needed.

"We are the toughest critics these books will ever see."

Dorris and Erdrich first met in 1972 when she came to Dartmouth as a student, he as an instructor in anthropology, his undergraduate work behind him at Georgetown and his graduate work at Yale.

A friendship developed that continued mildly over the years, through letters and occasional telephone calls until 1979 when Erdrich returned to give a poetry reading.

"I was blown away," Dorris says.

He, meanwhile, had advanced to professor and had founded the college's Native American studies department, serving as its first chairman.

"Half of me was assigned to the department," he says, "so I was chairman of half of myself. It was a real Gilbert and Sullivan situation.

"Now Native American Studies has become sort of establishment. That's because we were very scrupulous about making the courses hard and worthwhile."

Part of that was to prove the value of the course of study. Part was
Dorris' own respect for education.

"For me, going to college was the most wonderful thing imaginable,"
he says. "I always liked to read, and at last I was surrounded by other
people who read in a place where people were expected to read.

"I was the first person ever on either side of my family to go to college. I went on a scholarship. We were literally poor. We existed on my
father's pension.

"So I worked very hard. I wouldn't have dreamed of taking a year off
to 'find' myself or even missing a class."

It was during his anthropological field work in a Russian colony in
Alaska that Dorris collected some of the background for a tough section
of *Yellow Raft*—describing in Christine's voice the process of giving
birth to Rayona.

During Russian Easter, while all the villagers were involved in a
celebration at another end of the village, Dorris was the only person
around to assist when one woman who had stayed behind went into
active labor.

"I went over just to assist and ended up delivering the baby," he says.
"Until then, the closest I'd come to it was seeing a little on TV.

"The first thing she said to me when I came in was 'Boil water.'
I thought, 'This is a cliche. You can't say this.'

"But it was nothing to do with the birth. She was being hospitable,
offering me a cup of tea and telling me to boil the water for it.

"The child was enormous. I've never seen such a big child. There
was no way to tell what she weighed, but it was an enormous child.
I can still see it."

Since then he also participated in the births of his last two children,
Persia and Pallas, giving him an even more personal experience.

"At least, writing in a woman's voice, no one can look at this book as
a first novel and say, 'Oh, it's got to be autobiographical."

One incident, however, was drawn from an actual happening in
Dorris' youth when, like Rayona, he substituted at the last minute for a
cousin in a rodeo.

"I got thrown off the same horse three times at the Montana State
High School Rodeo, and just like Rayona, I thought if you get thrown
off, you get back on.

"But the outcome was different. The upshot for me was I decided I couldn't be a rodeo rider—until then I thought I could be—and I went off and took the SAT's."

Since Erdrich came back to Dartmouth for the poetry reading in 1979, Dorris' life has evolved almost like one of the characters in either of their books.

Their literary collaboration flowed almost without notice into marriage—"We had our first date on our six-month anniversary," he says. "That was the first time we went out for dinner and an evening alone"— and in between the writing and teaching, Dorris began to act as Erdrich's agent.

With her career firmly launched, the trip West in '85 gave Dorris a year to work on *Yellow Raft*. Another book now under way—a study of fetal alcohol syndrome titled *The Broken Cord*—will be published in the summer of 1988 and has already been contracted for serialization by the *Ladies Home Journal*—"With 20 million readers per issue," he points out.

The Broken Cord is the first extensive work to be published on fetal alcohol syndrome in humans. Dorris became involved in the study while he was doing some consulting work for the Bush Foundation in St. Paul, a philanthropic organization that conducts a number of projects on reservations and small communities in the West and Southwest.

"No one has done much research on the problem among humans, although a lot has been done with animals," Dorris says.

"I became interested when I saw young women on the reservations who were pregnant and drinking and the children that they had, then looking at the kids in a community and seeing what helps them survive."

Because fetal alcohol syndrome destroys the ability to think conceptually nine months ahead, the problem is progressive because its victims, when they grow up to become mothers, are unable to understand the damage that will be done to their child if they drink during pregnancy.

"It's a very complicated issue ethically and morally," Dorris says. "It has to do with fetal rights and parental responsibility.

"That's why it's called *The Broken Cord*. It's a rupture of the faith between mother and child, sometimes out of ignorance, sometimes out of disability, sometimes out of pure selfishness.

"There are all sorts of elements that enter into it—the number of previous pregnancies, the amount of alcohol consumed, the trimester of the pregnancy—but the only absolute guarantee that you will not have a child that is impaired is not to drink at all."

The first book on which Erdrich and Dorris began working—*Tracks*—now is the third book of the quartet begun by *Love Medicine* and is scheduled to be published in mid-fall of 1988. Dorris' next fiction novel, *The Cloud Chamber,* will follow two years from this summer.

Meanwhile there are articles for magazines, book reviews, promotion tours and ordinary life.

"I get up every morning at 5 and drive to Dartmouth to write from 6 until 9 when my first class begins," Dorris says. "The children go to a neighbor for three hours a day and that's when Louise writes.

"I'll teach through the summer then take a leave of absence, and who knows what will happen next."

Despite the seemingly pat publishing schedule and the successes so far, and despite having a partner who's always there and whose taste can be trusted absolutely, Dorris says there is nothing safe or predictable about starting in on another book.

"Anyone who sits down and tries to write a book and feels confident about it, I would suspect would not produce a very good book.

"You need that edge of anxiety. Every day has surprises. That's the way life works, and that's the way a story develops."

But when the characters have become real, the ideas are solid and the words seem right, there is a time when the writer becomes almost an instrument, Dorris says.

"When you're actually writing, it's almost as if you're hypnotized. It's almost as if you're listening and writing the words down.

"I don't want to sound mystical or as if we are hearing voices or anything, but we are becoming convinced that the stories are all there and we are listening to them and writing them down.

"It's as if they have an integrity, like the sculptor who believed the sculpture resided in the marble and he just had to figure out what to chip away to reveal it.

"It's there, and we just have to pare it down and get it out."

Whatever Is Really Yours: An Interview with Louise Erdrich

Joseph Bruchac/1987

From *Survival This Way: Interviews with American Indian Poets,*
ed. Joseph Bruchac (Tucson: University of Arizona Press, 1987),
73–86. Reprinted by permission.

It was a sunny day in New Hampshire when Louise Erdrich
and her younger sister, Heid Erdrich, a student in Creative
Writing at Dartmouth, met me at the airport. We drove to the
house her sister was subletting from Cleopatra Mathis, a poet
and teacher at Dartmouth. Louise and I sat out on the back
deck above a field where apple trees were swelling toward
blossom, two horses moved lazily about their corral, and we
could see the hills stretching off to the east. Louise is a
striking woman, slender with long brown hair. She is surprisingly modest—even a bit shy—for one whose early
accomplishments are so impressive: a powerful first book of
poetry from a major publisher, a first novel which won
critical acclaim, a National Book Critics Circle Prize, and the
Los Angeles Times Book Prize in 1985. But as we spoke, her
voice was clear and her convictions as strong as those of any
of the complex white, Indian, and mixed-blood characters
who populate her work and her memories.

> *Indian Boarding School: The Runaways*
> Home's the place we head for in our sleep.
> Boxcars stumbling north in dreams
> don't wait for us. We catch them on the run.
> The rails, old lacerations that we love,
> shoot parallel across the face and break
> just under Turtle Mountains. Riding scars
> you can't get lost. Home is the place they cross.
>
> The lame guard strikes a match and makes the dark
> less tolerant. We watch through cracks in boards
> as the land starts rolling, rolling till it hurts
> to be here, cold in regulation clothes.

We know the sheriff's waiting at midrun
to take us back. His car is dumb and warm.
The highway doesn't rock, it only hums
like a wing of long insults. The worn-down welts
of ancient punishments lead back and forth.

All runaways wear dresses, long green ones,
the color you would think shame was. We scrub
the sidewalks down because it's shameful work.
Our brushes cut the stone in watered arcs
and in the soak frail outlines shiver clear
a moment, things us kids pressed on the dark
face before it hardened, pale, remembering
delicate old injuries, the spines of names and leaves.

—Louise Erdrich

JB: That poem is among the ones I like best of yours. It does two things I see as characteristic of your work—juxtaposes the two worlds and also hints at a natural unity which is broken yet hovering somewhere in the background. Why did you choose to read that particular poem?

Erdrich: It might be something as simple as that the rhythm is something I like. Probably I chose it because I've been thinking about it on the way over here because it's the one I knew by heart and it started me back on remembering when it was written and the place where I grew up.

JB: I like the rhythm, but the subject matter, too, has a special meaning.

Erdrich: It does, even though I never ran away. I was too chicken, too docile as a kid, but lots of other kids did. This, though, is a particular type of running away. It's running home; it's not running away from home. The kids who are talking in this poem are children who've been removed from their homes, their cultures, by the Bureau of Indian Affairs or by any sort of residential school or church school. Many kinds of schools were set up to take Indian children away from their culture and parents and loved ones and re-acculturate them. So, it is about the hopelessness of a child in that kind of situation. There is no escape. The sheriff is always waiting at mid-run to take you back. It's a refrain and it's certainly the way things were for a long time. I guess now that the boarding schools have finally started serving a positive purpose, the current Administration wants to cut them. They're finally schools that can take in children who have nowhere else to go. They do serve some purpose, but naturally they are threatened. It's just a damn shame.

JB: It seems to me, too, to be a metaphor for the things that are happening with American Indian writing and culture in general. People have been dragged into the twentieth century, European/American culture and frame of mind and running away from that means running not away, but back.

Erdrich: Yes, running home. That's true. I have a very mixed background and *my* culture is certainly one that includes German and French and Chippewa. When I look back, running home might be going back to the butcher shop. I really don't control the subject matter, it just takes me. I believe that a poet or a fiction writer is something like a medium at a seance who lets the voices speak. Of course, a person has to study and develop technical expertise. But a writer can't control subject and background. If he or she is true to what's happening, the story will take over. It was, in fact, hard for me to do that when stories started being written that had to do with the Chippewa side of the family because I just didn't feel comfortable with it for a long time. I didn't know what to make of it being so strong. It took a while to be comfortable and just say, "I'm not going to fight it." "Runaways" is one of the first poems that came out of letting go and just letting my own background or dreams surface on the page.

JB: In my own case, being of mixed ancestry, I'm sometimes surprised how strongly those voices speak from that small percentage of my ancestry which is American Indian. That seems to be true of many other mixed-blood writers of your age and my age, that for some reason that's the strongest and most insistent voice.

Erdrich: I think that's because that is the part of you that is culturally different. When you live in the mainstream and you know that you're not quite, not really there, you listen for a voice to direct you. I think, besides that, you also are a member of another nation. It gives you a strange feeling, this dual citizenship. So, in a way it isn't surprising that's so strong. As a kid I grew up not thinking twice about it, everybody knowing you were a mixed-blood in town. You would go to the reservation to visit sometimes and sometimes you'd go to your other family. It really was the kind of thing you just took for granted.

JB: One reason I like *Jacklight* so much is that it does deal with both sides of your family—the sections in the butcher shop are very real.

They're no less strong than the sections which take place on the Turtle Mountain Reservation. When did you first begin to write, to write poetry or to write anything?

Erdrich: Well, my Dad used to pay me. Ever so often he'd pay me a nickel for a story. So I started a long time ago. Both my Mom and Dad were encouraging, incredibly encouraging. I had that kind of childhood where I didn't feel art was something strange. I felt that it was good for you to do it. I kept it up little by little until I got out of college and decided, this great romantic urge, that I was going to be a writer no matter what it cost. I told myself I would sacrifice all to be a writer. I really didn't sacrifice a lot, though. (laughs) I took a lot of weird jobs which were good for the writing. I worked at anything I could get and just tried to keep going until I could support myself through writing or get some kind of grant. Just live off this or that as you go along. I think I turned out to be tremendously lucky. Once I married Michael, we began to work together on fiction. Then it began to be a full-time job. It's a great thing, a miracle for a writer to be able to just *write*.

JB: That's something seldom talked about, those persons who enable you to be a writer. It's very hard when you're on your own to devote yourself completely to writing, even part-time.

Erdrich: Michael and I are truly collaborators in all aspects of writing and life. It's very hard to separate the writing and the family life and Michael and I as people. He's also a novelist and has just finished his first novel. It's called *A Yellow Raft in Blue Water* and it's in the voices of three women; a young girl, her mother, and the grandmother speak. Very beautiful—and unusual, intriguing, interesting for a man to write in women's voices. I think it is because he was raised only by women.

JB: The male voices in *Love Medicine* are very strong and legitimate. The book ends with a male voice.

Erdrich: Yes. I don't know why that is, but they just seem to be. You don't choose this. It just comes and grabs and you have to follow it.

JB: In one of your poems, *Turtle Mountain Reservation,* I notice how strong your grandfather is, how strong his voice is. A storytelling voice, a voice connected to the past in such ways that some people may think him a little crazy—in the poem Ira thinks he is nuts. I wonder if that voice of your grandfather's has made you appreciate more and relate more to the voices of your male characters?

Erdrich: He's kind of a legend in our family. He is funny, he's charming, he's interesting. He, for many years, was a very strong figure in my life. I guess I idolized him. A very intelligent man. He was a Wobbly and worked up and down the wheat fields in North Dakota and Kansas. He saw a lot of the world. He did a lot of things in his life and was always very outspoken. Politically he was kind of a right-winger sometimes, people might say. I think he gave Tricia Nixon an Anishinabe name, for publicity. I always loved him and when you love someone you try to listen to them. Their voice then comes through.

JB: His voice is a combination of voices, too. He can both be in the Bingo Parlor and then speaking old Chippewa words that no one but he remembers.

Erdrich: I think this is true of a lot of our older people. People who aren't familiar with Indians go out to visit and they can't believe that there's somebody sitting in a lawn chair who's an Indian. It's kind of incomprehensible that there's this ability to take in non-Indian culture and be comfortable in both worlds. I recently came from Manitoulin Island, a beautiful place. People are quite traditional and keep a lot of the old, particularly the very old crafts. There is a great quill-work revival. I don't know if you're familiar with the kind of quill-working done up in Ontario, but this is really the center for it. But people live, even there, incorporating any sort of non-Indian thing into their lives to live comfortably. That's one of the strengths of Indian culture, that you pick and choose and keep and discard. But it is sometimes hard because you want some of the security of the way things were. It's not as easy to find the old as it is to find the new.

JB: In the poem "Whooping Cranes," legend-time and modern times come together, when an abandoned boy turns into a whooping crane. There's a sort of cross-fertilization of past and present in legend.

Erdrich: And natural history. The cranes cross over the Turtle Mountains on their way down to Aransas, Texas. We always used to hear how they'd see the cranes pass over. No more, though. I don't know if they still fly that way or not.

JB: In some of Leslie Silko's work you see that mixing of times. Someone may go out in a pickup truck and meet a figure out of myth.

Erdrich: Don't you, when you go on Indian land, feel that there's more possiblity, that there is a whole other world besides the one you can see and that you're very close to it?

JB: Very definitely. Crossing the border of a reservation is always entering another world, an older and more complicated world. How do you feel when you go back to Turtle Mountain?

Erdrich: I feel so comfortable. I really do. I even feel that way being in North Dakota. I really like that openness. But there's a kind of feeling at Turtle Mountain—I guess just *comfortable* is the word to describe it. There are also places there which are very mysterious to me. I don't know why. I feel they must have some significance. Turtle Mountain is an interesting place. It hasn't been continuously inhabited by the Turtle Mountain Band. It was one of those nice grassy, game-rich places that everybody wanted. So it was Sioux, it was Mitchiff, it was Chippewa. There are a soft, rolling group of hills, not very high, little hills—not like these (gestures toward mountains)—and there were parts that my grandfather would point out. The shapes were called this or that because they resembled a beaver or whatever kind of animal. He even incorporated the highways into the shapes because some of them got their tails cut off. (laughs) Even that people can deal with. Not always, though. There are many places that are certainly of religious significance that can never be restored or replaced, so I don't want to make light of it.

JB: As in the Four Corners area.

Erdrich: Yes, I was thinking of Black Mesa. In the case of those hills at Turtle Mountain, there was that resilience because they were places which had a name, but not places—such as Black Mesa—much more vital to a culture and a religion. Catholicism is very important up there at Turtle Mountain. When you go up there, you go to Church! My grandfather has had a real mixture of old time and church religion—which is another way of incorporating. He would do pipe ceremonies for ordinations and things like that. He just had a grasp on both realities, in both religions.

JB: I see that very much in your work. A lake may have a mytho-logical being in it which still affects people's lives while the Catholic Church up on the hill is affecting them in a totally different way. Or you may have someone worrying about being drafted into the army at the same time he's trying to figure out how to make up love medicine—in a time when old ways of doing things have been forgotten. It seems similar, in a way, to Leslie Silko's *Ceremony,* where there is a need to make up new ceremonies because the old ones aren't working for the new problems, incorporating all kinds of things like phone books from different cities.

Erdrich: You may be right. I never thought about the similarity. This "love medicine" is all through the book, but it backfires on the boy who tries it out because he's kind of inept. It's funny what happens until it becomes tragic. But, if there is *any* ceremony which goes across the board and is practiced by lots and lots of tribal people, it is having a sense of humor about things and laughing. But that's not really what you're saying.

JB: Maybe—maybe no.

Erdrich: Who knows? (laughs) Anyway, I don't deal much with religion except Catholicism. Although Ojibway traditional religion is flourishing, I don't feel comfortable discussing it. I guess I have my beefs about Catholicism. Although you never change once you're raised a Catholic—you've got that. You've got that symbolism, that guilt, you've got the whole works and you can't really change that. That's easy to talk about because you have to exorcise it somehow. That's why there's a lot of Catholicism in both books.

JB: The second poem in *Jacklight* is called "A Love Medicine."

Erdrich: I was sort of making that poem up as a love medicine, as a sort of healing love poem. So, I suppose there are all kinds of love and ways to use poetry and that was what I tried to do with it.

JB: There are several things I see in *Jacklight*. One is an urge toward healing, a desire to ameliorate the pain, create something more balanced, even if it means facing difficult realities. Was that a conscious theme?

Erdrich: I don't think any of it was very conscious. Poetry is a different process for me than writing fiction. Very little of what happens in poetry is conscious, it's a great surprise. I don't write poetry anymore. I've in some ways lost that ability. I've made my unconscious so conscious through repeated writing of stories that I don't seem to have this urge to let certain feelings build until they turn into a poem.

JB: Another theme I see strongly in *Jacklight,* and in all of your writing, is the theme of strong women who become more than what they seem to be. Transformations take place—in some cases, mythic transformations.

Erdrich: That is true of women I have known. We are taught to present a demure face to the world and yet there is a kind of wild energy behind it in many women that *is* transformational energy, and not only transforming to them but to other people. When, in some of the poems, it takes the form of becoming an animal, that I feel is a symbolic transformation, the moment when a woman allows herself to act out of her own power. The one I'm thinking of is the bear poem.

JB: That's a really wonderful four-part poem.

Erdrich: Oh, I'm so glad! But, you know, she's realizing her power. She's realizing she can say "No," which is something women are not taught to do, and that she can hit the sky like a truck if she wants. Yes, it's transformational. It goes through all of the work I've been doing lately. Part of it is having three daughters, I think, and having sisters. I have an urgent reason for thinking about women attuned to their power and their honest nature, not the socialized nature and the embarrassed nature and the nature that says, "I can't possibly accomplish this." Whatever happens to many young girls. It happens to boys, too. It happens to men, no question. In the book there are men—maybe not so much in the poetry, but in the fiction—like Lipsha, who begin to realize that they are truly strong and touch into their own strength. I think it's a process of knowing who you are. There's a quest for one's own background in a lot of this work. It's hard not to realize what you're doing. And you say, "Funny thing, I have so many characters who are trying to seach out their true background. What can this mean?" One of the characteristics of being a mixed-blood is searching. You look back and say, "Who am I from?" You must question. You must make certain choices. You're able to. And it's a blessing and it's a curse. All of our searches involve trying to discover where we are from.

JB: It makes me think of Jim Welch's wonderful scene in *Winter in the Blood* when that old man turns out to be his true grandfather.

Erdrich: Oh yes, yes. Certainly.

JB: In that same light, there's a similarity there with Leslie Silko, though I don't mean to imply that you've copied anything of hers.

Erdrich: No, no, that didn't even enter my head. She's working out of a whole different tribal background. She was a discovery for me in a particular way I don't think any other writer will ever be. I'm very attached to her work.

JB: You don't write poetry now because you feel the conscious effort of writing prose makes it less available?

Erdrich: It sands away the unconscious. (laughs) You know, there's

really not much down there. But what really sands aways the unconscious is getting up in the middle of night to rock your baby to sleep.
When you live in isolation—I notice this whenever I leave—I dream
poems. But when you get up at all hours feeding babies, you just don't
have that kind of experience, you're just not able to let your unconscious work for you. However, I don't miss it. I'd rather have the kids
than the tortured unconscious. Also, I have a very practical way of
working. I just sit down and Michael works in one room and I work in
the other and we just sit there as long as we can. I really have got more
and more mundane about my work habits. There are times when I'm up
at 4:30 and I feel like something extremely strange is about to happen—
whether it's writing or not. Maybe I'm just crazy. But I sit down and, if
something is there, it will be written. Usually, though, after the kids are
taken care of, I try to write and very few poems come that way. Almost
none. I maybe have three now since *Jacklight*, which I don't think I'll
ever publish. Those poems now seem *so personal*. I just don't know if I
can put them in a book again! (laughs)

JB: I think you're tapping, though, the same sources for your prose
that you've tapped for your poetry, even though the method may be
different. I think the depth of experience, the types of metaphor, and the
direction it goes are all on the same road.

Erdrich: I'm connected to the poems because you feel so protective
toward your first outpourings. You want them to have some kind of
continuity in their life. I think that is probably true. You can see the
themes that were being worked with in *Jacklight* go on into the writing
in other ways. The poem you mentioned, "Family Reunion," turns into
part of "Crown of Thorns" once it goes into the fiction. A lot of them do
that. The next book, which is *The Beet Queen*, takes place in that sort of
butcher shop world and incorporates people who are and are not in those
poems. It's a very different book but also one which I think flows
naturally out of both *Jacklight* and *Love Medicine*.

JB: What years did you write the poems in *Jacklight*?

Erdrich: All through '77 and '78. Then, once it was accepted to be
published I wrote a few extra ones. I was so thrilled to be finally
published. The manuscript went everywhere and I thought it would
never be published. Then it was, and I was given this great boost. So I
wrote some of the ones I really like, like the one about the bear and
about living with Michael and the children, because I was so happy. I

guess it was surprising. I thought I would live my whole life without being published and I wouldn't care, but as it turned out I was *really* happy.

JB: When did you begin writing with Michael?

Erdrich: Once we were married. In '81. We began by just talking about the work, back and forth, reading it. He always—right at first before I got to know him—was the person I would go to with problems. I'd say, "Michael, should I get into teaching, should I quit writing? What should I do?" And he said to me, "Look, there's only one thing to do. Throw yourself into your work. Don't take any more jobs." And I did it. I just tried what he said. (laughs) At times I found myself in some unpleasant monetary predicaments. But I've been lucky. I think it is because we started working together. He had ideas for the whole structure of *Love Medicine* that became the book. We worked on it very intensely and closely, and I do the same with his work. We exchange this role of being the . . . there isn't even a word for it. We're collaborators, but we're also individual writers. One person sits down and writes the drafts. I sit down and write it by myself or he does, but there's so much more that bears on the crucial moment of writing. You know it, you've talked the plot over, you've discussed the characters. You've really come to some kind of an understanding that you wouldn't have done alone. I really think neither of us would write what we do unless we were together.

JB: Didn't the genesis of *Love Medicine*, "The World's Greatest Fishermen," come about that way. Michael saw the announcement of the Chicago Prize . . .

Erdrich: Yes. Michael was flat on his back, sick, and he said, "Look, you've got to enter this! Get in there, write it!" And I did, brought it in and out to him, changed it around, together we finished it.

JB: You have such a strong narrative line in all your work and stories seem so important to you, stories told by your characters in the poems, the stories of the poems themselves and then the structure of story in *Love Medicine*, which is, in fact, many stories linked together. What is story to you?

Erdrich: Everybody in my whole family is a storyteller, whether a liar or a storyteller (laughs)—whatever. When I think what's a story, I can hear somebody in my family, my Dad or my Mom or my Grandma, telling it. There's something particularly strong about a *told story*. You know your listener's right there, you've got to keep him hooked—or her. So, you use all those little lures: "And then . . . " "So the next day . . . ," etc. There are some very nuts-and-bolts things about storytelling. It also is something you can't really put your finger on. Why do you follow it? I know if there is a story. Then I just can't wait to get back to it and write it. Sometimes there isn't one, and I just don't want to sit down and force it. You must find that, too, because you tell a lot of stories.

JB: Yes, there's something about a story that tells itself.

Erdrich: The story starts to take over if it is good. You begin telling, you get a bunch of situation characters, everything together, but if it's good, you let the story tell itself. You don't control the story.

On Native Ground: An Interview
with Louise Erdrich and Michael Dorris
Sharon White and Glenda Burnside/1988

From *The Bloomsbury Review*, 8.4 (July/August 1988), 16–18.
Reprinted by permission.

The highly acclaimed novels of Louise Erdrich and Michael
Dorris—among them Erdrich's *Love Medicine* (Holt, 1984)
and *The Beet Queen* (Holt, 1986) and Dorris's *A Yellow Raft
in Blue Water* (Holt, 1987)—reflect both the spiritual richness of Native American ways of life and the harshness of
everyday existence on the edge of material poverty and
cultural displacement. Both writers are of mixed American
Indian and Euro-American ancestry, and their writings dis-
play the diversity of both worlds, extending the vital tradition
and universality of contemporary Native American literature
to countless readers here and abroad.

Erdrich, of German and Turtle Mountain Chippewa de-
scent, was born in Minnesota in 1952. She grew up in North
Dakota and studied writing at Dartmouth College and Johns
Hopkins University. Dorris, born in 1945 into the Modoc
tribe, grew up in Washington state, and he went on to study
theater and anthropology at Georgetown University and Yale
University and to teach anthropology to college students.
The two married in the late 1970s and settled in rural New
Hampshire, where they are caring for their five children,
teaching, and writing, each editing, criticizing, and collabo-
rating with the other.

This interview began in New Hampshire in December of
1987 and carried over into February of 1988, after Erdrich
and Dorris had returned from a promotional tour in Europe.
Erdrich's forthcoming novel, *Tracks,* a "prequel" to her first
two novels, will be published in September of this year by
Holt.

The Bloomsbury Review: How did you set out to become writers?

Louise Erdrich: I think that we both have always written, really. We
kept journals or diaries, wrote poems and that kind of thing, or at least

I wrote a lot of poetry before writing fiction. I'm from a small town. I don't think either of us had fantastic educations, but in my family there was an eccentric collection of reading material around all the time—Shakespeare and *Marjorie Morningstar* and Classic Comics.

Michael Dorris: We had *Good Housekeeping* at mine. When I came home from college I used to read all the short stories in *Good Housekeeping* because they were all one bath's worth apiece. We didn't have a shower, so I'd get into the tub and read three short stories and be clean.

TBR: Did you have a traditional upbringing?

LE: It was a very mixed upbringing, an awareness of family on both sides. When I grew up, my mother and father worked for the Bureau of Indian Affairs, and we lived on campus in a small town. It was German and Norwegian, and quite a few people who had Indian backgrounds came down there to work at the school. It was the kind of background you take for granted until you look back and see that there was something really quite different about it.

MD: My background was slightly more schizophrenic. My father died when I was fairly young, and so I spent part of my time living with an extended family on his side and part of my time with my mother's side of the family, which is not Indian. They're from Kentucky. My parents met at a USO dance at Fort Knox during World War II. It was a jolt to go from one family to the other. They were in very different settings, but eventually you resolve such things. I mean, most mixed-blood people have experiences of this type. We're a kind of tribe in and of itself, almost.

TBR: Did you plan early on to go to college and to study writing?

LE: No. Michael didn't either.

MD: No, I didn't. Nobody on either side of my family had ever finished high school, so that was a great aspiration, to graduate. I thought I was going to be a rodeo star, like Rayona in *Yellow Raft*. She got thrown off the horse and won a hard-luck belt buckle, and she persisted in trying to make sense of her life. Me, I went off and took the SAT exam.

TBR: Do you regret that?

MD: No, but it was a very strange experience, because I went off to college with a totally stereotyped idea of what life would be like in the East. I went to Georgetown, because I'd gone to a high school where

Jesuits taught. I studied Greek. I went off to college in the late 1960s
with the idea that people in the East wore suits all the time, and so I left
all my clothes, blue jeans and stuff, which would have been absolutely
appropriate, at home, and I brought along one tan suit with little silver
threads all through it. My roommate took one look at it in the closet and
burst into hysterical laughter, and I never went out for three years.

My family was very supportive of my going to school, but they
weren't certain about what was going to happen afterwards. When I was
a sophomore, I got the idea that I would go on to Operation Crossroads
Africa, which I think is a program still in existence, but in those days it
meant basically going off to Mali and building basketball or volleyball
courts. I needed a scholarship to go, but the funding ran out. My family
was willing to mortgage the house so that I could go. I never did, but
that's the kind of support I had. Louise's family is the same way.
Louise went to Dartmouth after her mother read about their winter
carnival in *National Geographic*.

LE: Yes, my mother and father were very supportive. Once I had
made it clear that I wanted to go, they helped me with all sorts of
things.

TBR: How do you affect each other's writing?

MD: It's hard to draw distinctions, even with such things as plotting,
because there's so much give and take. I think Louise was a much more
professional writer, more aware of herself as a writer than I was, even
though I'd written a couple of books by the time we started working
together. But now the process of everything that goes out, from book
reviews to magazine articles to novels, is a give and take. I think we're
so familiar with each other's critiques and pet peeves that even when the
other person isn't actually in the room, he or she is kind of perched on
the other's shoulder. I now know, for example, that I often have a
tendency to overstate and overexplain, and Louise keeps me honest with
that and reminds me that what I'm trying to get at is perfectly clear
without beating people over the head with it.

TBR: Louise, has Michael's understanding of anthropology brought
you a greater understanding of your characters?

LE: Yes, certainly. The kinship network, for instance, is very complex. It's sort of ludicrous when we start dissecting it. Michael is trained
to think about it in a very organized way, and that's been useful to both
of us. We have this kinship chart for our characters in our minds, but if

we wanted to, we could write it down, and Michael would know how to structure it. There is an organized mind behind the chaos.

MD: Doing ethnography in a small community is very much like puzzling out characters, which we do before we start writing. You're confronted initially with what looks like chaos, and gradually you get to know things and realize with time that you haven't understood what the basis of relationships really was. I did my fieldwork in an Alaskan village, and I was there nineteen months altogether and was constantly trying to figure out who was who and what was going on. I don't know if I ever succeeded, but that was the process.

TBR: What has Louise's mastery of fiction taught you about anthropology?

LE: That's an interesting question. I wonder if that would help you in any way, Michael?

MD: It is an interesting question. Whereas fiction and anthropology are contributory, I'm not sure that it works in the opposite way, because in fiction you ultimately have control over the characters and the situation, and what you're bound by most of all is the consistency at the core of your characters, throughout their lives, in various situations. In fieldwork, intuition is very important, but when you are writing about people who are disenfranchised, you can't afford to speculate. You can only write about what is absolutely, unequivocally true and agreed upon on all sides. That's a responsible way to do anthropology, but I don't think it's the best way to do fiction. So I think that the work Louise does and what I try to do, in terms of figuring out characters and speaking in different voices and putting ourselves into the heads of imaginary people, would have to be left behind if I should do more ethnography. It's just too dangerous when you're dealing with real people. There are too many cases in the history of anthropology where scholars have said, "These are my people, and only I really understand them, and only I can interpret them to the rest of the world," and they've been dead wrong. Many people have suffered from the presumptuousness of someone doing just that.

TBR: How much can non-Indian social workers, spiritual leaders, and so forth do to help Indians' causes, especially when they cannot make that leap of understanding?

MD: The most important thing, in a reservation situation, is for the government to honor its treaties. There are over two hundred existing treaties between federally recognized Indian tribes and the United States, and every one of them has been kept by those tribes, while not a one of them has been kept to the letter by the government. If those agreements were honored, it would create a much stronger economic and political base for the tribes and would provide a great deal more autonomy and sovereignty—and the right not only to control one's destiny, but also to make mistakes and learn from them.

One of the problems with American policy historically has been its treating all tribes as if they were the same, with uniform policies that deal with Indians as Indians, rather than as Chippewas, as Hopis, each tribe in terms of its particular history and treaty. Following the law would be the first thing that people could do.

The second is to allow a long period for reacclimation, so that the tribes might achieve self-sufficiency. Beyond that, there is a need to be candid and unromantic in criticizing things that are wrong. A willingness to take positions which might be construed as embarrassing to others is occasionally necessary, whether one is Indian or white.

TBR: Who would you say is the more critical of the two of you?

MD: I guess we both are.

LE: I think we're both pretty merciless.

TBR: In your own work, you don't end up kicking each other in the shins when the other one comes along and says, "This is terrible! This doesn't work"?

LE: I think it's harder to be the one who has to say those critical things. You know how hard it is to hear something critical.

MD: You don't want to bump into someone who's on a run, doing something they've finally been able to start, just because one word or sentence seems out of whack.

LE: Michael's very tackful.

TBR: Who—or what—influences your work?

MD: Well, Louise, primarily. I mean, I would not be writing if I were not working with her. Your previous work influences what you're doing. I read Barbara Pym for instruction, and for lots of different things. I don't think for me there's one particular source, except for the fact that I apprenticed with Louise.

TBR: Are the stories you write and the people you write about the ones you grew up with?

LE: No, we invent them out of our own heads. Every so often, though, there's something that comes from something that happened, or is suggested by something that happened.

MD: There are some writers who really do autobiography in the form of novels. We're not like that.

LE: It's not that we haven't tried. It was just so hard, and it turns into something else. That's one reason to admire, say, Philip Roth's novels. They seem to be autobiographical, but if you read what he writes as autobiography, you realize that these are so different and so constructed and invented that it's really a special art to make novels that play with real life.

TBR: So you didn't grow up, say, with people like the characters in *Love Medicine*.

LE: Not so that you'd recognize anyone. You know, you have to grow up with people who may say the kind of things those characters would say, or with some of those settings—especially the landscapes, which are as accurate as we could make them.

MD: Certainly we grew up in the contexts that we write about, but there is not someone particular who matches this character, someone who matches that character.

TBR: Are you breaking secrets?

MD: Well, we're making up the secrets. We would be violating only our own imaginations. None of our novels is based on real people. They are made of pure, dreamed-up characters and situations.

LE: But one of the oddest and most wonderful things that happens is that someone from a reservation we've never set foot in says, "How did you know that this was the way with my family?" or something like that. It may not be a particular incident, but the way in which the family interacts that reminds them.

MD: I think the greatest secret of all that we violate about Indians is that Indians don't have humor. The one thing that Indian people have said about our books, and the greatest relief to us, is that they find them very funny. Many literary reviewers read *Love Medicine* and saw it as a book about plight and despair and poverty and tragedy, all of which is there too. Many Indian readers saw the survival humor and the kind, odd, self-deprecating humor that Indians have.

LE: Indians have had mainly good responses to our books. Michael says that if people have bad responses, they've been kind enough not to say so.

TBR: How about the critics?

LE: We've been tremendously fortunate. There will always be some bad reviews that stick in your mind forever, but the response has far surpassed anything we could have hoped for.

MD: It's been a pleasant surprise, too, because you write a book in the privacy of your home and your thoughts and your shared feelings, and it all seems so very particular. It's such a surprise, because all of those books now have or soon will have lots of foreign editions, and the thought of people overseas reading them and finding things with which to identify in them is amazing and quite wonderful.

TBR: Do you think of yourselves as Native American writers, or as writers who happen to be Native American who happen to be writing about Native Americans?

LE: I don't know if we've made a decision about that. At least I haven't. Being Indian is something we're terribly proud of. On the other hand, I suppose that in a general sense I would rather that Native American writing be seen as American writing, that all of the best writing of any ethnic group here would be included in American writing. These are university-inspired divisions so that people can have courses and concentrate on certain areas.

MD: James Welch should not be taught only in Native American literature courses. He should be taught in contemporary American and World literature courses. To pigeonhole him is to deny access to him. To lump all Indians into one literary category just because their ancestors were here before the Europeans is hard to justify.

TBR: What are you working on right now?

MD: Well, the next book out is Louise's *Tracks,* which will be out in the fall of 1988. It takes place before the action of *The Beet Queen* and *Love Medicine* and involves some of the same characters. My next book is *The Broken Cord,* about fetal alcohol syndrome, a major problem in the Soviet Union, Scandinavia, Japan, Canada, and the U.S. It's a condition that occurs to an infant when the mother drinks during her pregnancy. It depends on a lot of factors to what extent the baby will be affected: her age, stress level, diet, metabolism, and so forth, what trimester she drinks in, all these things. But there is in some communities an enormous crisis with this situation, because one of the complications of FAS is that the part of the brain that deals with abstraction is not developed, so for a person who herself is the victim of FAS, it is almost impossible to counsel her not to drink during her pregnancy. And in some communities, in one in particular I'm thinking of, it's estimated that by the turn of the century, if things progress as they have, 50 percent of the kids born will be impaired.

It's a book about a big problem. I did so many personal interviews, and it's a situation that in a familial way we're both familiar with, so it's turning out to be a more personal book than we first envisioned. There are some scholarly books on this, but it's being published as a book for a mass audience rather than a scholarly book. It's a hard book to write because it's such a serious and such a sad problem, because there's no cure except prevention. Once it's occurred, there's no magic solution that's going to get that part of the brain to develop. It's something that has only been identified since the mid-seventies, very tentatively, and except for the occasional ad in a bar or something that says don't drink if you're pregnant, it's still not widely understood. In fact, there are still doctors who prescribe for people to drink a beer a night or drink a glass of wine and so forth, and that can be a very dangerous thing. There are women for whom that can be all right, but you don't know in advance whether or not you're one of them.

LE: The Surgeon General has said since 1981 that there is no safe level. It's like saying, well, what's a safe level of thalidomide. We know there is a miniscule level that might not affect the child, but what is that? Who would ever take the chance, and who should ever take a chance with alcohol? It's really the leading cause of birth defects in this country, and people don't even think about it or know about it.

TBR: One of your books is being filmed, isn't it?

MD: *A Yellow Raft in Blue Water* is optioned for the movies. It has not yet gone into production. The screenwriters wrote *American Graffiti* for George Lucas, as well as a number of other films, and Sidney Pollack optioned it for his production company. There's a long distance between optioning and writing the script and actual production. They have to find the cast and convince themselves that there's an audience for this kind of stuff.

TBR: And that it will make money.

MD: They've "costed it"—there's a whole new vocabulary one has to learn—and it would be a moderately priced film to make. It's just that they're not sure that people want to see movies about Indians in the United States.

TBR: Is living in New Hampshire an obstacle to writing about your home in the West?

LE: No. I mean, in some ways you're fueled by nostalgia to set your story in, say, part of Montana. I can remember thinking, "Where did you come up with the 'pearl sky'?" When you go out there and look, it would be that way. I think that with memories you try so hard to re-create the landscape that things happen that are probably more interesting than what you'd expect. But I miss it. And when I was out West, I missed the woods here.

TBR: Is *Tracks* constructed in the same way as the other novels?

LE: It's more like *Yellow Raft* because it has two narrators who tell the same stories in different ways.

MD: The narrators are a young girl and an old man. *Tracks* is after *Love Medicine* and *The Beet Queen*, so there's a set. Louise's next novel is tentatively entitled *American Horse*. The novel I've started, *Cloud Chamber*, is not in the first person at the moment, though it may go back. First-person stuff reads so much better in public than third-person. It's so much more dramatic and involving, and since we read these books out loud to each other so much, I think maybe that will have something to do with changing it.

TBR: With a houseful of children, how do you portion out your day so that you have time to write?

LE: We have a woman who babysits, and our older children are in school.

MD: It's fairly simple, really, except that there are so many days on which the ideal does not materialize. There are dental appointments and school vacations, this and that. One thing that keeps us going is that we always feel so lucky to be able to have a day of quiet just to sit and write.

TBR: What aspects of your work would you especially like your readers to understand?

MD: Well, there's a political aspect to it that I think is kind of interesting and subtle. We got a wonderful note in a Christmas card from Vine Deloria in which he said that one of the functions of people like us is to remind each successive generation that Indians exist. And he said that it's unfortunate that we, as Indians, rarely get past that thing of just reminding people that we exist. You know, some day we're going to have to deal with this. We certainly don't write polemics; we write about communities of people who happen to be Indians, but in the current political climate—in the past two presidential terms, the amount of money for Indian health care, for welfare and legal expenses has declined dramatically. The number of Indians in college and graduate school has declined because the funding has evaporated. The problems of the one and half million Indians in this country have become abstract to the population at large. If people read what we have written and identify with the characters as people like themselves, people with needs and desires and wants, that's political. That's something that we're very grateful to be able to do.

Marriage for Better or Words

Charles Trueheart/1988

From *The Washington Post,* 19 October 1988, B1, B8–B9. © 1988, *The Washington Post.* Reprinted with permission.

HANOVER, N.H.—Before there was Louise Erdrich, and before there was Michael Dorris, estimable writers each, there was Milou North. Under that synthetic byline, seven years ago, Erdrich and Dorris collaborated on a series of domestic tales, and a popular British magazine called *Woman* couldn't get enough of them.

"It got to the point where on every cover of the magazine they had 'Another Tender Story by Milou North,'" Dorris says. The English editors would occasionally tinker with their language—a story about the Bicentennial became a story about the Jubilee, and sometimes the characters turned up in the magazine with new names, like Nigel.

"They're not terribly deep," Dorris says of these stories, looking up with a giggle in his eye, "but they're uplifting."

He loves telling this; his wife loves to listen. "It's always about a young woman in stress who resolves her issue affirmatively," he goes on. "Very *definitely* affirmatively," Erdrich agrees. "Any sort of domestic crisis that came up we would make into 'another tender story,'" he says. "We found a crack in the bathroom wall one day and we couldn't afford to have it fixed, sooo . . ." Michael and Louise join in the refrain: ". . . Another Tender Story by Milou North!"

Sitting down to lunch at a restaurant in Hanover (they live 30 miles down the road, in the village of Cornish, with their five children), Dorris and Erdrich talk about Milou North with affection, and even some respect. "I don't think writing to spec in your formative years as a writer is a bad thing at all," Erdrich says, her voice just this side of a whisper. "I do think it's good practice."

It has been for them, in any case—not just writing to spec, but writing together. For Erdrich and Dorris, authorship is a dimension of matrimony: They can be married to their muses without risk of infidelity.

Dorris is 43, a chipper fellow with a Wally Cleaver grin and Ronald Reagan pompadour, notwithstanding which he is a handsome man. He

115

adopted their three oldest children during the 1970s, when he was a bachelor. Erdrich is 34, dark-eyed and soft-skinned, more wholesome looking than her exotic jacket photographs suggest. Even before they have unfolded their napkins, Michael announces that Louise is expecting another baby.

All this, and five books between them too.

Erdrich is the better-known writter. When *Love Medicine*, her first novel, was published four years ago, the critics swooned at their discovery, and her literary elders lined up to blurb their respects. "The most interesting new American novelist to have appeared in years," observed Philip Roth, a man not easily impressed. There was no second-book slump. When *The Beet Queen* appeared in 1986, Gail Godwin called Erdrich "a sorceress with language," and the public, so beguiled, made it a bestseller. This fall came *Tracks*, also a bestseller, the third book and not the last in what turns out to be an interrelated series of Native American stories.

Each novel cites her husband as her "collaborator," and this is not the usual author's curtsy to a patient helpmeet. Michael, she explains, is "a spiritual guide, a therapist, someone who allows you to go down to where you just exist and where you are in contact with those very powerful feelings that you had in your childhood." He organizes her work, he deploys a blue pencil on her manuscripts. He is, by her account, indispensable.

"You may feel threatened," she says of this unnerving dependence, "but you have to let your ego fall back, and let the work come first."

Lest this seem a picture out of balance, Dorris says that as a writer, he is "Louise's student." After a humiliating start as an undergraduate at Georgetown University, when a cruel fellow-student likened Dorris' first published story to an episode of "Mary Worth," "I didn't write another word of fiction for 15 years." Last year, he published a startlingly fine novel called *A Yellow Raft in Blue Water*.

Louise knew Michael was a writer all along, she says, he just needed the confidence. These sound like words he might have said as easily, and as truthfully, about her.

"We give each other presents of experience," she says.

Dartmouth College gave them the first present, of each other. "There's no place else we could have met," says Dorris, and this is not as peculiar a notion as it may sound. Dartmouth was founded in 1769 "for the education of Indian youth and others," according to the college charter, but somehow by the fall of 1972 others had outnumbered Indians by tens of thousands to exactly 12.

So theirs was a meeting made in penance: Dorris, a young anthropologist of part Modoc ancestry, was hired that year to run the new Native American studies department ("I was chairman of half of myself," he quips). And Erdrich, whose mother is a member of the Turtle Mountain Band of Chippewa, was in the first wave of Indian students recruited, better late than never, to fulfill their terms of the Dartmouth charter.

The difference in their years mattered then. "I mean, Michael was a professor." She laughs. "And I didn't have much to do with him. He was in a different world."

She graduated, and he stayed behind in Cornish. She worked as a waitress, she waved a flag on a construction crew in North Dakota, she wrote textbooks for an educational publishing company. She attended the Johns Hopkins University's graduate writing program in poetry. They wrote letters to each other, a "cagey correspondence" platonic on its surface but full of "veiled references," Louise begins, about "breaking up with former relationships," Michael finishes.

They returned to Hanover on the same day in 1980, "not knowing what to expect," Michael says. They were married in October 1981.

A further fusion, a merger of their styles and identities, is in the works. Until now—since Milou North was retired—each has had "the final say" (Louise's term) over the books that carry their names. Next they will collaborate in earnest on a huge novel, huge in ambition and huge in theme, about Christopher Columbus, scheduled to appear by 1992.

The discovery of the New World by the Europeans will be celebrated that year, and other novelists may glom on to the theme—Carlos Fuentes is already writing a Columbus novel, and James Michener undoubtedly will. The Erdrich-Dorris conceit is that a woman scholar at Dartmouth—Vivian Twostar, she's called, part Indian, single and pregnant—discovers what purport to be the lost diaries of the discoverer, and finds him not to be the man she had thought.

"It's revisionist history," Dorris proposes. "She has a very stereotypic view of the inevitability of European and Indian contact . . . And when she goes back and discovers that it could have been different but for a few chance happenings, she and Columbus almost form a relationship—but not," he says hopefully, "in a hokey kind of way."

Michael and Louise had the brainstorm for the book, tentatively titled

The Crown of Columbus, as they drove across Saskatchewan three summers ago. "We started talking about it as we left Alberta and when we got to Manitoba we were finished. It took us about a day," Dorris remembers. "That was, in fact, the famous five-page outline that we turned in." He seems almost embarrassed by the reference; the outline is famous for having brought them $1.5 million from Harper & Row, the winning publisher in a brief but intense round of bidding.

Louise began the book by writing the first 20 pages. She gave it to Michael. "It was just too much material. It was just moving too fast," he says. He took her draft with him to the vet's office one day and began to flesh out what she'd written, drawing the story out. Looking at her 20 pages, "Michael said this a hundred pages," Louise recalls. "It is very hard for me particularly to write long scenes. I've gotten out of the habit."

If the coauthors are intimidated by this deeper collaboration, they do not let on. After all, as Dorris says, "The more we've done this, the more we write alike."

One would expect as much. But if the books that bear their different names are a reliable measure of individual style, they don't write indistinguishably. Michael's narratives seem carefully invented and then set down, one foot before the other; Louise's stories seem received from the ether, and allowed to pass through her onto the page. Dorris is vernacular, Erdrich is oracular.

"People make a distinction between our work," Dorris says, and he sounds like he gets a trifle impatient when they do: "Fleur [of Erdrich's *Tracks*] is mythic and so forth and Rayona [of Dorris' *Yellow Raft*] is very contemporary. But they're also different people . . . I think that Louise could write in the voice of Rayona or Christine or Ida [his other characters] and they would sound very much as they do when I write about them."

In any case, the authors' power over their characters has its limits. "We don't pretend to know what's happening in our books," Louise says. "They're stories that are just irresistible . . . Much as we try to shape them we don't control them." For the newcomer to the world of *Love Medicine* and *The Beet Queen*, this imagined world can be hard to penetrate, the associations and kinships among families and across generations frustrating to parse.

"Our idea," Louise says, "was that it would be like stepping into the

community for anyone. It didn't make it easy for the reader, it's true.
But stepping into another culture or another community is never easy.
And in a way it doesn't matter how people are related so much as how
people treat each other."

Be that as it may, the Danish publishers of *Love Medicine* thought it
wise to prepare an unofficial diagram of its characters' family tree.
Then, with the publication four years later of *Tracks*, whose characters
are antecedents to those in Erdrich's previous two novels, the authors'
friend and publicist Blanche Brann persuaded them to assist addled book
reviewers with a not-for-publication cheat sheet, a more comprehensive
version of the Danes' family tree.

The genealogy of their characters, the authors say, is forever becoming clear to them—and even being revised as they go along. They
didn't realize until Louise was well into the writing of *Tracks*, for
instance, that its characters were related to the characters in the other
Erdrich novels. So a few appropriate details were added to make the
connections. "And after all four books are published, or however many
books there are," Dorris says, "there may be some changes made in the
text of *Love Medicine* or *The Beet Queen* to reflect what we know now."

"I think so, yeah . . ." Erdrich says.

Before they can devote their full attention to *The Crown of Columbus*,
Michael (with Louise's help, of course) is busy finishing *The Broken
Cord*, his nonfiction book on fetal alcohol syndrome—the lasting,
crippling damage, to brain and body, that drinking mothers inflict on
their unborn.

On one level, the illness has resonance to them because it is a scourge
on Indian reservations. But the affliction is by no means particular to
Native Americans. The new wisdom about abstention from alcohol
during pregnancy, they point out, is far from universal. What's more,
it's imperfectly understood even by the educated few: The one-glass-of-
wine-a-day permissiveness of first-time yuppie mothers is still sufficient
to cause brain damage in the fetus. As Louise points out, "The unborn
baby has no way to metabolize the liquor."

Though Dorris has been researching his book on trips to Indian reservations, he has been facing the illness at home for most of his adult life.
When he was 22, he adopted a child afflicted with FAS. Abel, now 20,
has severe learning dysfunctions. He has seizures. He will always suffer
from an inability to think abstractly—to appreciate and retain relation-

ships of cause and effect, for instance. Dorris has decided, in midstream, to write the book in the first person. He realized, Louise says,
"that he couldn't write about it as though it hadn't happened to him."

A portion of what Michael calls Harper & Row's "largess" will go to
establish a fund for school systems and community health organizations
to encourage experiments to deal with FAS children. Dorris and Erdrich
are publicly advocating measures in various state legislatures to label
liquor bottles with warnings to pregnant mothers. They also mention
another warning—a tribal statute on the Pine Ridge reservation in South
Dakota—that qualifies as Draconian: Mothers with FAS children who
become pregnant again and continue to drink are thrown in jail.

"The only way you can understand this law," Dorris says in a
measured voice, "is if you go into a classroom in Pine Ridge and see
half of the kids there clearly fetal alcohol-afflicted or impaired, and you
have lived, as we have for 17 years, with somebody who sees the world
through this very narrow focus. Then you think: Nobody has a right to
do that to anyone else.

"This is not a law that says a woman has to carry to term. This is not
a law that says she cannot opt for birth control, abortion or whatever. It
is a law that says if you're going to carry to term you may not condemn
this child to a half-life—Ruben Snake, who is past chairman of the
National Congress of American Indians, said we're raising a generation
of idiots. We have to stop this. We have to recognize this. We have to
stop this . . .

"These are crisis measures," he says, "that make nobody happy."

The Broken Cord is one piece of evidence that Dorris and Erdrich feel
a special responsibility to act politically, to lend their names and voices
to support Native American issues. "I don't know that we feel pressure," Louise says, "except pressure from within to respond to certain
things, more than pressure from anyone else."

To this, Michael carefully adds, "There are 300 different tribes and
there's no way we should, or could, be spokespersons for all of them.
Plus we're mixed-bloods . . . So it would be presumptuous to pretend to
be more than we are. We can only speak for ourselves."

When Erdrich excuses herself from the table after lunch, Dorris is
asked what he might be writing—or if he would be writing—if fate had
not brought them together.

"I don't think I'd be writing fiction. I would not have the courage. I went into writing fiction very much as Louise's student. She had studied it in college and graduate school; she had done it; she had already compiled her huge list of rejection slips. I came in basically as a suggester—very tangential—and in the course of time became more involved and more confident. But I don't think it ever would have happened without her."

After lunch, when Dorris heads down the street to mail some letters, Erdrich is asked the same question, and she begins by speculating on how her husband answered it.

"I bet he said he wouldn't be writing," she says, leaning forward so her dry whisper can be heard. "I bet he would, too. He's got something that would have eventually taken over."

She recalls when he first began to show her pieces of the novel that would become *Yellow Raft*.

"I had been there, saying 'You are a writer,' just the way he's done with me. I knew he was a writer, but I didn't know he had this *voice* . . . I was just blown off my feet. He's just the best writer going. It's just astonishing."

Whatever it is that he gives her in return, "I'm completely dependent on it . . . It's frightening, but it's the kind of writer I am. It's what's good for the work. You know, what the hell? Ego be damned, I'll keep working like this because it's really good."

Would she go on without him?

She considers the question.

"I don't think I would. I don't know that I'd feel the same urgency anymore. I always thought before that I'd be a writer no matter what, but . . ."

She shakes her head from side to side, staring at the floor.

". . . It's like that Mahalia Jackson song, 'Dig a Little Deeper.' I never would have dreamed I could dig that deep if it hadn't been for him."

Two Native American Voices

Michael Huey/1989

From *The Christian Science Monitor*, 2 March 1989. Reprinted by permission from *The Christian Science Monitor* 1989. The Christian Science Publishing Society. All rights reserved.

Louise Erdrich is an enrolled member of the Turtle Mountain Band of Chippewa. She is also a widely reviewed and respected novelist whose first work of fiction, *Love Medicine*, won numerous prizes including the 1984 National Book Critics Circle Award. It and her two succeeding novels *The Beet Queen* and *Tracks* delineate characters she might have known growing up on and near an Indian reservation in North Dakota.

Michael Dorris, of Modoc background, recently published *A Yellow Raft in Blue Water*, a novel about three generations of Indian women, set in the Pacific Northwest and on Montana reservation. (At the time of contact with settlers the Modocs lived near the Klamath Lakes on the Oregon-California border.) The novel is told by three narrators, the youngest of them a 15-year-old girl of mixed black and Indian parentage. Dorris is also a professor at Dartmouth College's Native American Studies Department where he and Erdrich met. He has also written several non-fiction works.

The Erdrich-Dorris marriage is a literary as well as a social partnership. Each gets involved in the development of the other's writing, a process they discuss in the accompanying interview with Michael Huey.

During long walks on their New Hampshire farm, Louise Erdrich and Michael Dorris together come up with the characters and story lines of the novels they write.

The two met in the early '70s at Dartmouth College, where Dorris was a young professor in the Native American Studies Department and Erdrich was a student. Erdrich graduated, left, and returned as visiting writer, and then " . . . suddenly we just fell in love" and married. They have six children.

Now they collaborate on all their writing, although each book appears
as the work of its "primary" author.

In a telephone interview, the two share their thoughts on the difficult
choices involved in writing about the American Indian condition.

*In LOVE MEDICINE there is a sentence that reads: "Power travels
in the blood-lines, handed out before birth." What is your responsibility
to the heritage that empowers you?*

Erdrich: That's a question we are always wrestling with. Right now
we're working on a manuscript that is about very grave problems on
American Indian reservations, but also about grave social problems in
the world at large. [Sometimes] we're working on fiction and involved
in storytelling because it's a good story and it's something that has to be
told, and another time we feel compelled to work on something that
deals with a cause. When you feel a compulsion you go with it. But
I can't say that I have any statement that makes absolute and ultimate
sense of personal or artistic responsibility.

Dorris: We write editorials sometimes. We write nonfiction articles.
In those cases it's pretty straightforward about being political. But it's
difficult to be self-consciously political in fiction and still have it be
good fiction.

The characters are rooted in a social context, but if you program them
to be [political], unless you're much more skillful than we, it appears
artificial and polemic and thoroughly unconvincing.

Tracks, for instance, is not a story of "good Indians" and "bad non-
Indians." It's a very complicated story of people within a community
who are trying to figure out what's going on in a time of great change.
Each person has his or her own perspective and destiny in that context.

In *Yellow Raft* the problem that Rayona [one of the characters] encounters is that she's the wrong color on an Indian reservation, although
culturally and linguistically she fits in. [Half Indian, half black] she
finds that there's a good deal of discrimination against her there that she
has to overcome the same as she did in the city.

Who knows what traditional values are? There's a lot of talk about
them. You recognize them when they hit you and when you experience
them. Our characters float in and out of that realization like regular
people do.

Is it legitimate to say that there is a native American voice, that it had been lost, and is now refound in writers like yourselves?

Erdrich: Native Americans haven't lost their voices. It's just that there's a curve in interest in native Americans and sometimes there's more interest, sometimes there's less.

People have been carrying on oral traditions in their own tribes and writing as long as people have been writing in the country. There's not a blanket "native American" voice. There are voices from different tribes.

Dorris: Exactly. "Native American" is a misnomer. There are traditions of expressions, humor, and mythology for each of the couple hundred tribes that are viable today. The traditions out of which we might write about the Indian experience would [probably not] be the same as those that Leslie Silko or others might write about, because they come from a different region of the country, they have a different contact experience.

There are things in common, of course, about living on a reservation and about dealing with federal Indian policy, but the way people see the world is very discrete from one tribe to another, and that distinction is preserved in the literature.

It's hard to say what is a native American perspective. But you can, I think, get closer to something like a Chippewa perspective or a Pueblo or Lakota perspective that combines the particular ingredients of a history and a contemporary reality in a way different than any other ethnic group in the United States might.

What about other contemporary authors who write about native Americans but aren't Indians themselves? Jim Harrison, for example, in his book DALVA.

Erdrich: I reviewed that book, I thought the diaries were very moving, and the retelling of Lakota history. I know he has emotional ties to everything he was writing about. I could tell that he was really internalizing a lot.

Dorris: I think the impact of your question is whether or not somebody who is not him or herself steeped in tribal tradition can write about Indians and have it be part of native American literature.

It all goes back to what your initial definition is. Is it "anything written by an Indian"? Is *The Beet Queen* native American literature even though it is not primarily about Indians? Is *Dalva* native American literature because it's about Indians though not by an Indian?

To say that nobody except an Indian can write about Indians, I think, is a mistake. But it's an equal mistake to think that anything written by an Indian about Indians is authoritative.

A real distinction has to be drawn between fiction and nonfiction, because nonfiction can be judged by fact and fiction has to be judged by impact. There's a book called *Nobody Loves a Drunken Indian*.

When I was growing up, it was the most popular book on the reservation. Everybody loved that book. On reservations all over the country everybody loved it because they said, "At last somebody's really got Indian humor down." But the author is not an Indian.

Let's talk about your collaboration. I've heard that it even includes "negotiating" parts in and out of each other's books. Is that true? How do you work?

Dorris: Before either of us starts writing we talk out the beginning of a story—the shape of the characters, some of the idiosyncrasies, and so forth. Then whoever is going to be the primary author of the piece will sit down in isolation, confront the blank page, and create some words that get passed back.

The other partner goes over them, makes comments about word changes and even about where the plot will go after this section— what's missing, or what possiblities are suggested by it. And then it goes back to the person who wrote it. Lately we've taken almost all [each other's] suggestions, I think.

The negotiations are friendly, then?
Erdrich: Definitely.
Dorris: What we're doing right now with *The Broken Cord,* for instance, is reading it aloud and talking about any word that strikes either of us as problematic or . . . not right. Eventually, in all the books, we agree upon all the words.

To the point of saying, "So and so wouldn't do such a thing—it's out of character"?
Dorris: Especially things like that.
Erdrich: Sure, that's very important. Sometimes the other person can tell better than the person who originally wrote down the words. We

both are involved with the characters and have an idea of who they are, how they talk, what they'd say, what they'd know.

Dorris: We know the characters. We set them into situations and watch them react, consonant to who they are. It does take both of us. Because we have a much wider knowledge of them than what appears in the book. We have talked about them in lots of situations that don't appear, and that gives us a three-dimentional impression. You can hear something that sounds wrong almost better than you can hear something that sounds right.

Relationships between your characters get rather complicated. I'd think you would need genealogical charts to keep them all straight— who's related to whom. Especially since TRACKS, the first book chronologically in Louise Erdrich's series, appeared after the other two.

Erdrich: We have them in our heads. We have the relationships worked out.

Dorris: And they've evolved, too. We started with one core set of characters and then the family expanded. In a review somebody very astutely said that characters in our books were met the way people in real life are met.

That is, you meet them and then you start knowing who their family is and what their background is. That is an impression we have about the characters as well, although, in fact, *Tracks* was the first book worked on. We didn't realize that it was related to the other books at the time.

Are you ever surprised by how your characters evolve? For instance, when Pauline becomes Leopolda in TRACKS. Was that planned?

Erdrich: That evolved.

Dorris: That has happened in each of the books. It happened with Dot Adare in *The Beet Queen*. We get to a certain point toward the end of a manuscript and we're trying to figure out who characters are. We think of how old they are and what their personality traits are.

Suddenly it occurs to us that they are a match to somebody in another book. Then we go back and check to see whether it really works and whether they really do seem like a younger or older version of the same person. And are amazed, delighted.

Do the stories you tell come from stories you were once told?

Dorris: No. They're really made up. One would hope that they tap into a spirit of storytelling and an approach to the world that has a resonance, but we dream up the characters and the particular incidents on long walks. Although we get a lot of letters from people who say, "Where did you hear this, because it is exactly what happened in my family," but that's just coincidence.

There's a part in LOVE MEDICINE where the character Albertine returns from college to the reservation. Would you care to comment about that passage in the book?

Erdrich: When I think of it I think of what it's like to go home, to go back onto the reservation where my mother was from. I think what it's like to get back on the plains.

There's a place on the drive across the country where one comes out of the hills of Minnesota onto a perfectly level, flat plain and you can just see on and on and on. And you keep going and you get up into the hills again.

It's a drive that we've made many, many times, and there's always a feeling of real happiness in returning. I think that's what she feels as she's driving her Mustang back home.

But home is also a difficult place to return to. It's difficult because once you're enmeshed in your family you're vulnerable again and you're part of a network of people you've loved and subject to all of the happiness and disaster that happens when people love each other very much.

Catharsis After Denial

Rebecca Bailey/1989

From (White River Junction, Vermont) *Valley News*, 28 July 1989.
Reprinted by permission.

An editor who worked on a magazine excerpt of Michael Dorris' new book *The Broken Cord,* was pregnant at the time. After the project was completed, she went into labor. It was late at night and her obstetrician told her to take a couple of stiff drinks and call him in the morning.

"Basically, what the obstetrician was suggesting is, 'Make your kid drunk, he'll pass out, stop activity and you won't go into labor until he sobers up,'" said Dorris, a Cornish resident and sometime Dartmouth College professor of anthropology.

"The question to ask anyone who says, 'Oh, a couple of drinks won't hurt' is, would you give your kid a couple of drinks a day after he or she was born?" said Dorris. "To everyone, it's patently obvious that you don't fill a baby's bottle with wine or beer or gin the day after birth and stick it in his mouth. But to do it the day before birth is somehow supposed to be OK."

Dorris' book, which will be available in bookstores Aug. 2, makes the case that it is very much not OK to drink during pregnancy. His book tells of raising his now-20-year-old adopted son, "Adam"—Dorris chose to not use his son's real name to protect the privacy of his son, who works and lives in the Upper Valley—whose natural mother drank heavily while carrying him.

The book describes Dorris' growing awareness of fetal alcohol effects (FAE) in our society, particularly among Native Americans, and his realization that Adam's slow physical development, his low intelligence, even his overriding personality traits—a superficial sweetness but a lack of apparent emotional depth—were caused by his mother's drinking.

Although not all children are harmed by prenatal exposure to alcohol and researchers haven't ruled out the possibility that it might be all right for a mother to imbibe occasionally, Dorris' own advice follows that of former U.S. Surgeon General C. Everett Koop and many other health

128

professionals: Don't drink if you're pregnant or think you might be, or are trying to become pregnant.

Having read Dorris' book the editor didn't follow her doctor's advice and went through labor and delivery without drinking.

Dorris hopes others will be similarly affected by his book, which includes a 15-page bibliography of reading material about fetal alcohol effects and fetal alcohol syndrome (FAS), a more pronounced and easily recognizable set of defects caused by a mother's drinking.

So far, it looks as if a great many people will read and be affected by *The Broken Cord*. An excerpt just appeared in *Ladies Home Journal*, other excerpts will appear in *Mother Jones* and possibly *Family Circle*. The book has been selected for Quality Paperbacks and Book of the Month Club, and will be published in at least eight foreign countries. A full-page editorial about it appeared recently in the *Chicago Tribune*, and articles will appear in the *New York Times* and the *Los Angeles Times*. Dorris also is touring 12 U.S. cities over the next three weeks and appearing on television via satellite in numerous other ones.

"I don't want to be the disease of the week—although there is an offer for a TV movie," Dorris said with a laugh. "But you're almost willing to do that if it puts it (the issue) in people's minds and if it stops somebody from drinking (during pregnancy)."

As *The Broken Cord* points out, fetal alcohol effects and syndrome are relatively new terms, coined in the early 1970s when studies of children of mothers who drank showed clear patterns of physical defects and stunted intellect. Although warnings against drinking during pregnancy go clear back to the Old Testament and ancient Greece and Rome; and British doctors started reporting in the 18th century that the offspring of drinking mothers were "weak, feeble and distempered," it was not until these early-1970s studies that modern health professionals started taking these warnings seriously.

Studies done in the past 10 years in U.S. cities place the incidence of FAS at between .04 and 3.3 per 1,000 live births. FAE involves many more children, but it is difficult to estimate how many because the manifestations are subtler and more difficult to diagnose. One 1981 study estimates that 5 percent of all birth defects can be attributed to prenatal alcohol exposure.

Dorris was drawn into the issue because of his son and also through his academic specialty, Native American anthropology. When he got the contract to do the book in 1984, he assumed he would write "a kind of scholarly book on fetal alcohol syndrome, with me as author being an omniscient narrator, and full of facts and figures and so forth," he said.

But after writing his first novel, the critically acclaimed *A Yellow Raft in Blue Water,* Dorris realized not only that he could write more than "heavily footnoted academic pieces," but that this book called for a richer style.

For one, it would have been dishonest to leave himself and his wife, poet and novelist Louise Erdrich, out of the story. "As I say in the book, I realized after so many people I had interviewed had been utterly candid and open with me, that it would have been hypocrisy to pretend that Louise and I, as authors"—the couple collaborate on their books although one or the other takes sole author's credit for each—"did not have very personal reasons for writing this," Dorris said.

They also wanted the book to help raise the public consciousness about FAS and FAE, so it had to be more readable than the average academic tract. But they wanted thoughtful, not pop, writing. "Because of the kind of writers we (he and Erdrich) aspire to be, this could not be simply an 'issue' book, or simply a health book, or simply a nutrition advisory book. . . . In order to sustain us as writers, it had to be a book that had merit as literature, or at least it had to aspire to that."

Meeting these different goals, said Dorris, "was a real challenge, because there's no easy category in which to fit something that aims at all those categories. It's up to the public and reviewers to decide whether (the book) succeeds, but that, at least, was the hope—that it would cross these boundaries that are not often crossed, even in ambition."

The result is a book that is likely to be widely read, which pleases Dorris because it will get the word out about the toll fetal alcohol syndrome is taking on children, particularly Native American children.

"Many of the people I talked to (in the book) . . . are right smack dab in the middle of a crisis. They don't have the luxury of standing back and considering the big picture. They are *in* the picture. And, to a degree, so are we, but we also have this luxury of trying to . . . catch it in historical perspective and social significance and implication.

"One of the things that surprised me is that the people I talked to in the book really liked that I had that role. They had the wisdom to see

that this (book) could make a contribution, too, as well as the really
hands-on, hard work that they do every single day. I hope that's true."

The book unfolds like a story, starting with Dorris' decision, as a
single man of 26, to adopt a Native American child. It quickly brings in
Adam and the many other people Dorris encounters as he raises the boy
and researches fetal alcohol syndrome among Native Americans.

Some emerge as near-heroes, such as social workers and educators
who were particularly caring and perceptive about Adam, and the researchers and health workers grappling with the immense, depressing
problems of alcohol-damaged kids on Indian reservations.

Others appear less admirable, such as an unnamed doctor in a small
New Hampshire hospital who was peevish and ignorant when the tod-
dler Adam suddenly began having seizures—a symptom, it turned out,
of FAE. When it came to the doctor and other unsympathetic characters
in the book, Dorris left out names and changed facts to make them
unidentifiable, but he recounted as accurately as possible the actual
conversation and encounters he had with them.

Most people in the book are named, however. Dorris sent each of
those named a copy of the completed manuscript, before publication,
and asked them to comment on the accuracy and tone. The only change
requested was from a Native American woman and FAS researcher
whose dignified mother Dorris described as having thin legs. Her
mother's legs are heavy, she informed Dorris.

As for those who are unnamed but might recognize themselves,
Dorris has no apologies. "I told the truth as best I could. And I really,
truly, tried to see things from perspectives other than my own. There is
nothing I would take back that is in the book. I thought very, very hard
about what to tell, and I think everything that is there that is necessary
to tell.

"For one thing, these things (the disappointments) are not just my
experiences. Other people have had similar expriences. For another, to
get from point A at the beginning of the book to point B at the end of
the book was a path that had to take a lot of turns, and the details of
those turns have to be recounted. If anything, the people who came off
sounding the worst, the ones who made the most mistakes, were Louise
and I." He added with a laugh, "I don't know—maybe we should sue
ourselves."

One particularly tough issue Dorris encountered on the reservation involved mothers who had given birth to not just one, but several children with fetal alcohol syndrome, even after being counseled not to drink during pregnancy.

Some of the people Dorris spoke with advocated that such women either be jailed during pregnancy to prevent them from drinking, or be given shots to make them infertile until they stopped drinking and committed themselves to remaining sober.

He surprised himself, he said, by finding sympathy for that outlook. "When I went into *The Broken Cord* research, like so many people who have a humanitarian prespective and think they know all the right ideas in terms of politics, I assumed that the limitation of individual rights was *ipso facto* wrong, that there was no ambiguity about that. And yet when you spend time listening to the perspective of women who work with other women who are the mothers of FAS victims . . . that easy assumption gets challenged.

"I wound up the book without an answer to that. . . . Rather, I reflected the answers women had come up with after years of internal debate and lots of experience."

As much as Dorris avoids casting himself as an FAS expert—"I'm the authority on one life, ours, and I don't even have all the answers for that," he said—women from around the country have been calling him for advice, most in reaction to the *Ladies Home Journal* excerpt.

Some have infants or toddlers and drank during their pregnancy, and ask him if the child has FAS; he tells them to talk to their doctors. Other calls—"the more horrible ones," he said—are from women who are pregnant and haven't been abstaining from alcohol, and ask him what they should do.

"And the answer of course is, stop drinking," he said. "But that isn't what they are asking. They are asking, 'Will my baby be all right?' and there's no test that certifies that and there is no answer except to say that to stop drinking increases the chances enormously the baby will be OK."

Dorris finished *The Broken Cord* in December. Since then he and Erdrich have been hard at work on their next novel, *The Crown of Columbus*, the first one that will credit them both as authors.

He is through with nonfiction for a while, he said. "I am so glad to be back to fiction, I cannot tell you—to have some control over the ending."

PW Interviews: Michael Dorris

Dulcy Brainard/1989

From *Publishers Weekly,* 4 August 1989, 73–74. Reprinted by permission.

Surrounded by family, Michael Dorris is in his element. In the living room of his aunt's New York apartment where he meets *PW* one recent summer morning, he sits with his wife, writer Louise Erdrich, and their four- and five-year-old daughters, Pallas and Persia. Faint street sounds mingle with voices from the fairy tale on the turned-low TV, as the girls quietly crayon the pictures in coloring books. Dorris and Erdrich talk about the August publication of his book *The Broken Cord* (Nonfiction Forecasts, June 2), while in the next room, new baby Aza sleeps sweetly on a nest of quilts, oblivious to traffic noises, her siblings and pub dates.

The Broken Cord offers a dark and moving counterpoint to this tranquil domestic scene. Focusing on the profoundly debilitating effects of Fetal Alcohol Syndrome on the life of their eldest son, here called Adam, the book chronicles Dorris's struggles to understand and solve Adam's health and behavior problems. It is also a throughgoing study for the general reader of the causes and scope of FAS—and a compelling alert to the dangers of alcohol consumption during pregnancy.

About 20 years ago, as a young bachelor and anthropologist, Dorris was moved by a sudden, imperative urge to be a father, though he was not married at the time. One of the first, single men approved as adoptive fathers, he found himself a year later in a South Dakota State Welfare Office being introduced to a three-year-old Sioux Indian boy who looked up from his toy trucks and calmly said, "Hi Daddy." Dorris, as he says, fell in love, taking the trusting Adam to his heart and then home to New Hampshire, where he was beginning his full-time teaching career at Franconia College.

Small in size and late in development, Adam had a long history of medical problems easily ascribed to the abuse and neglect he had already suffered. But soon his developmental problems, such as an inability to master toilet training or to learn to count or make connections between related events, combined with the onset of severe seizures, indicated a deep-seated disorder beyond the reach of the love, care and intensive attention offered by Dorris and a network of teachers, social workers and medical professionals.

Dorris learned that Adam's biological mother had died of alcohol poisoning. He research yielded studies confirming the symptoms of Fetal Alcohol Syndrome, a dysfunction caused by alcohol consumption during pregnancy that destroys brain cells in the fetus. No longer able to look on Adam as a boy with a rough start who would one day catch up, Dorris began his own dogged investigation into the disease.

Part Indian himself (Modoc, on his father's side), Dorris visited reservations—"There are no other places I could go in this country and with so few steps be trusted"—in South Dakota and, on a grant from the Rockefeller Foundation, spent a year in Minnesota studying the afflic-tion—first formally identified in 1968, the year Adam was born.

FAS, he found, "has nothing to do with genetics. It has to do with habit, with alcohol intake. It's a problem that occurs in any culture with a history of male drinking and a change in women's drinking behavior. It exists in the Soviet Union, in Scandinavia, Japan, rural America, Canada, all over the world."

Dorris was then teaching anthropology at Dartmouth, where he'd established the department of Native American Studies, and his inten-tion in writing a book about his findings was at first scholarly. "I signed a contract with Harper & Row in 1984 for an academic book. I wrote the first 30 pages and then stopped for about two years. There were two stories going on—the proliferation of scientific research, which con-tinues, and the personal story of our family. I didn't know if I could ever get on top of the material."

During those years Dorris was also working on his first novel, *A Yellow Raft in Blue Water*, brought out by Holt in 1987 and now in its fifth printing in paperback from Warner. In writing fiction, he found the approach he wanted for the book about FAS and Adam, the book that had to be accurate, but "not so pedantic or preachy or academic, that nobody would read it."

With its clearly distilled reports of studies of the causes and symp-toms of FAS, sparingly laced with harrowing statistics about the num-bers of FAS children being born today and predictions for the future, *The Broken Cord*, in addition, draws its strength from another source. Deeply personal, at other times funny and sad, but always rigorously honest, the book describes a father's gradual acceptance of the shape of his child's life, a future radically different from the one anticipated. Detailing his hopes and denial, frustration, rage and helplessness, Dorris also reveals an iron-clad grip on a belief in the need to love, act and to keep trying, no matter the odds.

"I wouldn't have had the sense or the courage to write nonfiction this way without writing fiction first. I could never have written this book without having written *Yellow Raft,* and I couldn't have written *Yellow Raft* without having worked with Louise on *Love Medicine* and *The Beet Queen*," Dorris says.

Dorris and Erdrich are known to collaborate closely on their writing, a process that takes different forms for different projects. Dorris says, "The person whose name is on the book is the one who's done most of the primary writing. The other helps plan, reads it as it goes along, suggests changes in direction, in character and then acts as editor."

Erdrich describes a contribution beyond technique and editing. "Often one will pick up something that is under the surface in a scene or setting and say to the other, 'There's something more here. I don't know what it is, but get it out.' It is sometimes even a painful process because it often involves something that you didn't want to face in yourself or your character."

"Another side," Dorris adds, "is that you can take risks with a trusted co-worker that you couldn't otherwise. I think I'd be a much more conservative writer if I didn't know Louise was there to read and catch me if I fall. You gain freedom when you have someone who knows you and your writing well and who is going to be absolutely honest, even to the point of making you want never to write another sentence."

In a coffee shop nearby, where we've moved for quiet conversation, Dorris explains that collaboration has been central to his non-academic writing since he and Erdrich met. Although they knew each other slightly when she was a student at Dartmouth and he a teacher, they met again when she returned to give a reading and he was bowled over by her poetry. Soon after that, he left for a year's research in New Zealand, accompanied by his three children (he adopted Sava and Madeline a few years after Adam), and began to write poems and stories which he sent to Erdrich. They committed their writing to a regular exchange, continuing to do so when he returned to New Hampshire, where Erdrich settled also and where they were married in 1981.

In her foreword to *The Broken Cord,* Erdrich recalls that five people were married on that October day in 1981: "Michael, his three children, and I." A year later, she adopted Adam, Sava and Madeline officially. Describing the halting development of her relationship with Adam, she marvels at the patience exhibited by her husband in his years of being both mother and father to his three children.

Many of the experiences recounted in *The Broken Cord* relate to the daily kinds of housekeeping and parenting known more often to mothers than fathers. But such gender conventions didn't deter the young father, whose first novel, perhaps not incidentally, is narrated by a teenaged girl, her mother and her grandmother.

"I have this very rich background of grandmothers and aunts and a mother, a wonderful extended family who made nothing seem impossible or out of reach. We were poor when I was growing up, but I never felt it. They could kill me for telling this, but sometimes on Sunday afternoons, they'd lock the door to the house, everyone would dress up and we'd sit at the dining room table and have lunch. If it were later at night, they'd call it the Stork Club. Everything they did was wonderful. When you don't have a lot of things, every event becomes special, like The Adventure of Getting the Deep Fryer." Such an attitude can cast a long shadow: when Dorris baked a choo-choo train cake for Adam's nursery school birthday party, it was an occasion that, besides raising poignant themes of parental hubris and hopefulness, could surely be called The Adventure of the Best Birthday Cake Ever.

A woman narrator figures in his current project as well. *The Crown of Columbus,* "about half done," is a novel due out from Harper a year from this fall. About a "difficult, cranky and complicated," woman in her 40s who finds a fragment of the lost journal of Columbus, it will carry both Dorris's and Erdrich's names as authors, and exhibits yet another form of their collaboration.

"In the Columbus book, we're both writing 50–50, the way we've done in our nonfiction articles, basically handing the computer disk back and forth," Dorris says. "But I know we're not going to do this for following projects. Louise has a book of poems coming out in January, and after that will be a novel by Louise Erdrich and a novel by Michael Dorris."

Having relinquished tenure at Dartmouth to devote all his time to writing, Dorris also maintains a full schedule of readings and speeches. After participating in an AIDS benefit at Manhattan's 92nd Street

YMHA (one of the events that has brought them from their New Hampshire home), he and Erdrich and the three girls head West for readings at a four-state bicentennial celebration. Since the younger children accompany them whenever possible, readings and book tours become family events.

Right now, though, Dorris's major focus is on promotional plans for *The Broken Cord*. Highlighted in advance reviews, the book has already received significant media attention, and is a BOMC alternate. Dorris's summer itinerary includes a 10-city tour. "I've read from this book three or four times and in every place, afterwards, strangers have come up with shocked looks on their faces saying, 'You've just described our child.' Some of the kids are Scandinavian, some black, some Indian. These parents were having the same kind of epiphany I had when I first realized Adam's symptoms were identifiable. It's oddly consoling to know you're not alone, that others have gone through what you have."

Adam, whose 21st birthday marks the end of his father's account, now works as a dishwasher at a truck stop. Living in a state-approved home, 20 minutes from his parents' house and within walking distance of his job, he is cared for by a loving, tolerant couple and sees his family frequently. He is not able to live on his own.

Dorris believes that parents who know or suspect their children suffer from FAS will be the book's first buyers, but the audience he'd like most to reach is "everyone considering having a baby." *The Broken Cord* was "written for a lot of reasons, one of them political: it is a book that hopes to effect change." After the promotional efforts are completed, however, he'll return to fiction happily. "The hardest part of writing *The Broken Cord* was not being able to resolve it—for Adam, for me and the rest of the family."

Louise Erdrich and Michael Dorris

Bill Moyers/1989

From *A World of Ideas,* by Bill Moyers (New York: Doubleday, 1989), 460–69. Copyright © 1989 by Public Affairs Television, Inc. Used by permission of Doubleday, a division of Bantam Doubleday Dell Publishing Group, Inc.

Michael Dorris and Louise Erdrich collaborate in life, in love, and in art. Husband and wife, they attribute their beliefs in family, community, and place to their Native American heritage: she is half Chippewa, and he is half Modoc. They are currently working together on a novel about Christopher Columbus, whose arrival in 1492 changed forever the destiny of Native Americans. Erdrich's most recent book is *Love Medicine*; Dorris's is *A Yellow Raft in Blue Water*.

Moyers: So many of your characters are bonded across time and space by ties of kinship and community. In fact, it's very hard to single them out as separate from their community or from their extended family. What does kinship mean to you and to those characters?

Erdrich: I think it's being enmeshed and sometimes not being in control. The characters in the books are always trying to take control, and they're never succeeding.

Moyers: What spins the web of kinship?

Erdrich: Accident sometimes. Even when you plan to have a family, you never know who the person is going to be that you decide to become a parent to. We're accidentally born to our own parents.

Dorris: It's one of those things that's larger than the sum of its parts. For us as writers it's interesting because we are discovering stuff about our characters as we go along, and when one or the other of us is writing, we go to the other and say, "You'll never guess what so-and-so just did, or who so-and-so really is." We have the illusion that we know more about these people than they know about themselves. But we're discovering all the time, too.

Moyers: You said kinship is an accident in the sense that you don't choose the children you have, and that you will your love for them after they come.

Erdrich: Will? It's helplessness—you're in love.

Moyers: I've learned as a father that while I might have had certain expectations, they don't matter as long as I learn to love the person who once was my child.

Dorris: That's the struggle—and it's a struggle for our characters as well. Many of them don't even know who their parents are.

Moyers: Do you take real-life characters and invest them in the fiction?

Erdrich: No, they're all inventions. The people are invented between us in conversation. We're out here in the country, and we walk around, and we talk about these people.

Moyers: You really talk to each other about these people who come alive in your books?

Dorris: Oh, for months before the first word is written. We'll open a Sears catalog and figure out what they would choose from it, or we will pick out on a menu what they would eat. Once they exist, once they have a voice and a bit of a history, then they're in control more than we are. Our job as a writer is to put them in a situation and portray how they really would react rather than to manipulate them. There's kind of an inner bell that goes off and says, "Tilt" if they're saying or doing something they shouldn't. On the other hand, they've got to surprise us in those situations to be interesting to write about.

Erdrich: It's not that we go out and say, "We're going to write a book about this kind of person." It's as though the characters choose us. They come to us and present themselves and seem inevitable, as though they're necessities.

Dorris: We dream about them, you know, and draw their pictures.

Moyers: Michael said, "Our job as a writer"—singular. Do you realize how incredible that is? "Our job as a writer"—two people writing a novel, not one. We think of the literary act as such a solitary invention.

Erdrich: I know. I did when I first began. It was this romantic ego versus the world.

Dorris: You are a romantic ego.

Moyers: So that changed?

Erdrich: Before we were married, we began to talk about one particular manuscript, and at first it was very hard for me to be open about it because everything was a secret. I felt if I let anything go, it would never find its way into words. But as time went on, and we began to work together in a closer way, it changed. It's hard to go back and say how something like that could happen. I suppose it's a process of gaining trust and going through the rough times when one of us had to say, "This stinks," and the other person had to take it. It was rotten and rough, but after you let go of the self who has everything invested in that particular character or that piece of language, you realize that what's important is the work. We're not important, it's the work that's important. However we work together on it is not important, it's the work. If that's out there, and if it gets to somebody and makes them respond, I don't care how—even if they throw the book at the wall— then something's happened. So there's often those times of letting go of that pull from the ego.

Moyers: —The self that says I would like to be the only one in the picture.

Erdrich: Right.

Moyers: Do you realize that a lot of people would say that just can't happen? Two people cannot create a sentence because that's a solitary act of a struggling, creative soul. It's impossible to merge those two, no matter how good the marriage is.

Erdrich: There's more than creating a sentence. We both write in separate places. We've both got an individual relationship with a page. But there's so much more to it than sitting down and writing.

Moyers: All right, take the book you've just agreed to write on Columbus. Have you talked about how you're going to do it?

Erdrich: This will be jointly written.

Dorris: We've talked about it for years and years and years. We've started working on it, and we're greatly relieved that the main character sounds the same whether Louise is writing her voice or I'm writing her voice. She's got her own voice already, and we both hear it the same way.

Moyers: Why Columbus? He's not been the subject of many novels. History, yes, but novels, no.

Erdrich: We were inspired by the diary he wrote about his first voyage. We found it a revelation. Here was this truly openhearted man interacting with the natives, who were, of course, what he thought of as the East Indians. Terrible things happened afterward, but the first meeting was genuinely moving, and it intrigued us. Then because our backgrounds are partly Native American, the glorification of Columbus as a person seems so terribly ironic. Columbus only discovered that he was in some new place. He didn't discover America. There were incredibly complex indigenous cultures—

Dorris: —in addition to which, it's anthropologically so interesting what happened, because Europe compared to the rest of the world was a very homogeneous place. Almost everybody spoke Indo-European related languages and shared the same cosmological worldview and even the same general political system. Indians, on the other hand, were used to an enormous plurality—five hundred different cultures, seven different language families, four or five hundred languages spoken, and many different religions. Within a day's walk of any place, you would encounter another group of people who looked differently, spoke differently, and had a different view of men and women. When Europeans came to Indians at first, it was no big deal. You read account after account of Indians saying, "Oh yeah, and they came too—and they don't bathe." That was the other big thing that all the Indian accounts talk about. Whereas for Europeans, it changed everything. Whose child were Indians in the Adam and Eve scheme? Were they human beings or not? These questions were argued in Spanish universities for eighty years until the Pope said Indians had souls. It changed the European worldview.

Moyers: When Columbus arrived, how many Native Americans were there throughout the hemisphere?

Dorris: Over a hundred million. In the United States in the 1910 census, it was down to two hundred thousand people because of diseases. There were diseases that existed in Europe, Asia, and Africa that had never come to the Americas before. The first time a European, Asian, or African came over here and sneezed, these diseases and bacteria were introduced into the networks of the Americas, and most Indians were gone before the Europeans had any conception they were here.

Moyers: Entire cultures wiped out?

Dorris: Yes—a perverted form of germ warfare. In the nineteenth century it became intentional.

Erdrich: Blankets were traded that were deliberately infected with smallpox because it was obvious that this was a way of clearing the path.

Moyers: The whites would trade blankets with the Indians after deliberately infecting them with smallpox?

Erdrich: Oh yes. But what we want to do with the book we're writing now is not to have Americans feel more of that comfortable guilt that is felt over reading *Bury My Heart at Wounded Knee,* where you think about American Indians being treated horribly in past centuries. We would want to transfer that guilt into the present reader and say, "These Americans haven't vanished." The ordained push West was supposed to clear the land of the native inhabitants. They were supposed to vanish before progress. That never happened. There are over three hundred tribes surviving and somehow managing to keep together language, culture, and religion. These are not visible people.

Moyers: But the picture you draw in your books is of a people serving a life sentence—chronic poverty, chronic alcoholism, isolation. Indians have the highest teenage suicide rate and an enormous infant mortality rate. That is not a pretty picture.

Dorris: It isn't a pretty picture, but there's a different status for Indians in this country than for any other indigenous group anyplace else in the world, because there is a political status that comes from treaties. The reservations that exist in this country are the remainder of Indian North America. They were never given up, and, consequently, they are defined by the Supreme Court as domestic independent nations within their boundaries. There's a nation-to-nation relationship with the United States.

Moyers: But they're not treated as independent powers.

Dorris: That's the point exactly. None of the treaties was kept by the government to the letter of the law. Those treaties provided for a continuing political identity for Indian nations which has not been supported by the kinds of prerogatives that should have come as a result of treaties. So unlike any other ethnic group in the country, when Indians look at the government, they don't say change things. They say, keep the laws that were made in the nineteenth century, which were more advantageous to Indians than laws that you might make now. And consequently, Indians often make poor coalition members for other minority groups because they're not looking for social change. They're looking to uphold the laws that exist. When cases go to the Supreme Court, they are almost always decided in favor of Indians, because the cases are rooted in the Constitution.

Moyers: Are you saying Indians still have faith, despite the last hundred years, in the law and in the political process?

Dorris: What's the alternative?

Erdrich: What else is there?

Dorris: We're talking about one half of one percent of the American population, and goodwill and following the law are the only options.

Moyers: But isn't the alternative what you write about—alcoholism, poverty, and chronic despair?

Dorris: I don't think our characters have despair. I think they have grit. Now, I'm not defending poverty. Indians should have the ability, through treaties, to be competitive economically in every sphere and have much better educational and health opportunities. During this current administration, funding for Indian health has declined by almost fifty percent and education by more than a third. We're in a dreadful crisis right now, but on the other hand, there is not necessarily a poverty of spirit that follows.

Moyers: If you go to the reservations, you see American Indians honoring the flag of the white society that has desecrated them. One of your characters advises her brother to go fight in Vietnam. He goes to fight in Vietnam, and he's killed.

Dorris: But, you see, you have to believe in American ideals if you're an Indian, because those ideals set up treaties that recognized Indian sovereignty, and if ever Americans lived up to those ideals, it would be a good day for Indians.

Moyers: When you see the flag above the reservations, you're seeing people paying tribute to the ideal, not to the history.

Dorris: Yes, and to their personal history. A greater percentage of Indians fought in the world wars than almost any other group. They're honoring their own valor and courage and determination to fight for the ideals that other people have fought for.

Moyers: I can see that on the level of patriotism. Psychologically, it's a different kind of problem. You have a character, Marie, in *Love Medicine* who has a strange relationship with a Catholic nun who has scalded her and scarred her with a poker. "And yet," Marie says, "there are times when I want her heart in love and affection, and there are times when I want her heart on a black stick." Then at the end, Marie comes back as this elderly nun is dying and kneels like a child beside her bed and is drawn in affection toward the one who has been her tormentor. There is a psychological bonding that takes place between the victim and the wrongdoer. Is there something of that in the Native American psyche today?

Erdrich: There's more of an ironic survival humor between the victim and the oppressor.

Dorris: —and an understanding. It's much more necessary for the victim to understand the oppressor than for the oppressor to understand the victim. There have been five hundred years of study of European systems by Indian people, but very little reciprocity in that respect.

Erdrich: Vine Deloria, Jr., said that when Western Europeans came over, they possessed knowledge, while the people of the western hemisphere possessed wisdom.

Moyers: And they possessed humor, too. Many of your characters have a wry outlook on the world.

Erdrich: It may be that the one universal thing about Native Americans from tribe to tribe is survival humor—the humor that enables you to live with what you have to live with. You have to be able to poke fun at people who are dominating your life and family—

Dorris: —and to poke fun at yourself in being dominated.

Erdrich: We're a mixture of Chippewa and Modoc and German-American and French and Irish. All of these different backgrounds have aspects that are part of us. If we took ourselves too seriously in any way, we'd be overwhelmed.

Moyers: It'd probably be like sitting in the General Assembly of the UN all day.

Erdrich: Probably we don't take ourselves seriously enough even as writers, although that's the deepest thing in our lives. But the most serious things have to be jokes. Humor is the way we make our life worth living.

Moyers: Why did the Native American culture become a dominant one in your writing?

Erdrich: It's partly that once one is a citizen of both nations, it gives you a look at the world that's different. There is an edge of irony. If you have a Native American background, it's also a non-Western background in terms of religion, culture, and all the things that are important in your childhood. There's a certain amount of commitment because when you grow up and see your people living on a tiny pittance of land or living on the edge, surrounded by enormous wealth, you don't see the world as just.

Moyers: What are you telling your children about their identity?

Erdrich: We're doing just what I did when I was a child. I didn't grow up on a reservation but went back and forth. You get a view of what life is like in very different cultures, and, of course, you tell your child, "You should be proud of your tribal background. We are proud of our tribal background. We are proud of our relatives. These are our relatives. These are our people."

Moyers: There's a character in *A Yellow Raft*, the fifteen-year-old half-breed, who dreams of having a dog named Rascal and of two parents. When I read that, I thought, "Is he trying to say something there about the further subversion of Native American identity with the images that come constantly through television to the young Indian child, or is Rayona just an interesting character?"

Dorris: Rayona is a contemporary character. Her father is a black mail carrier from Oakland. Her mother is an Indian from eastern Montana. They met in what her mother describes as the wrong bar on the right night in Seattle. They love each other, but they can't live together.

Rayona grows up very much an urban, black, Indian kid in a northwest city. And then, suddenly, through a set of circumstances, she finds herself on a reservation where she's inappropriate in every respect. She's the wrong color, she's the wrong background, she doesn't speak the language well—all these complications. What she's looking for is some stable form of identity. Like all of us, she finds that from the movies and television. That is the media barrage she's been exposed to. Where do people go when they try to imagine Indians? They imagine Jeff Chandler and Sal Mineo. We had one guy come to dinner, and we cleaned our house and made a nice dinner, and he looks and says, kind of depressed, "do you always eat on the table?" Contemporary people are contemporary people.

Moyers: You tell the story about the boy scouts going out to be Iroquois.

Dorris: Yes, our mailman several years ago stopped by and said that he was a Scout leader, and his troop wanted to be absolutely authentic Iroquois, so they were going to go live in the woods for a week. What would I recommend that they take along? I said, "Their mothers"— because Iroquois were matrilineal, and these little fourteen-year-old kids wouldn't know what to do without their mothers telling them what to do. Well, that didn't work. They wanted hatchets or something.

Moyers: This seems to me to be a critical point with your children and everyone's children. Rayona in *A Yellow Raft* is on a search for her identity. She has to pick here and pluck there and put it together in her own right.

Dorris: I think that's a plus, though. I worry about people who find themselves and life too uncomplicated and don't have to struggle.

Moyers: Or the people who are trapped on that reservaion, mentally, psychologically, geographically.

Erdrich: I don't think people who are living on reservations or the half of American Indians who are urban Indians think of reservations as traps. They are homelands. They are places where the culture is strongest, where the family is, where the roots are—

Dorris: —where the language is spoken—

Erdrich: —and where the people around you understand you, and you understand them. Even if you are of mixed background, you feel comfortable on a reservation. The best way to celebrate Columbus's quincentennial would be to begin keeping over four hundred treaties that were made and never yet kept. That would mean returning some of the land back to Native American people. Over the years, award moneys have been given to people, since about half of the United States was bought for less than a dollar an acre, and the rest of it simply taken. If some of the treaties were kept, perhaps through returning some of the land from the public domain to Native American communities, that land itself would mean that standards of living would rise. It really comes down to the land. The federal government has refused to return land in almost every case that has come up before the Indian claims commission. And yet there is public-domain land adjacent to almost every reservation that could be returned without causing angst and fear to private landowners.

Moyers: You once quoted Chief Standing Bear, who says that America can be rejuvenated by recognizing a native school of thought. What do you mean by that?

Dorris: There is one common experience that Indian people across the hemisphere have and that Europeans, by and large, lack, and that is the experience of pluralism, of cultures that developed in an atmosphere in which they were surrounded by other cultures.

Moyers: We all are tribes?

Dorris: We are really like that, you know. There are people whose languages have a whole different set of assumptions. The language that I learned to speak doing field work does not have a singular pronoun—

no "I," "my," "me," "mine." Everything is collectively "we" or
"you"—the people do this, and the people do that. That gives you a
whole different worldview about ownership and about your responsibility to somebody else. If I say, "I punch you in the nose," it is
expressed in that language as "I punch myself in the nose." If you say it
that way, you don't do it all that often.

Moyers: But that flies in the face of the dominant American indi-
vidualism.

Dorris: Cooperation comes in the most secure cultures. I would hope
that we would move toward that kind of security.

Moyers: A skeptic listening to you might say, "Well, Indian cultures
shared those assumptions and honored those values, and look at them."

Dorris: And I would say, but for the accident of being exposed to
European germs, it might be a very different story. To use the accident
of biology as a justification for domination is exactly what happened
five hundred years ago. Europeans thought, "They must be weaker than
we because they're dying off. Our culture must be God-ordained because we're winning." But victory is not the only judge of a culture's
viability and wisdom.

Moyers: What do you think we would hear if we listened to these
Indian voices?

Erdrich: The first thing is that people want to be who they are.
People don't want to assume a kind of rippling identity that America
thinks makes it the envy of the rest of the world. Even within our own
borders there are three hundred different cultures who do not envy
Americans so much that they want to give up their tribal status.

Moyers: But being realistic, can people survive this way in a highly
individualistic, competitive—

Erdrich: —technological—

Moyers: —era?

Erdrich: Yes, and it becomes more and more imperative that people
do survive that way. Native American people are surviving tribally
within the borders of a dominant country. This should cause people to
think twice about how they're living, what their assumptions are, and
what their view of the world is. When we talk about the wisdom that
was here, we're talking about cultures who managed to survive very
well on the land without pushing it toward the brink of a serious
ecological crisis. We need to look at how people managed to do that.

Moyers: What happens to a people whose gods have been banished? Because it wasn't until 1934 that the federal government allowed—

Dorris: —1978—

Erdrich: Yes, the Indian Religious Freedom Act was passed in 1978.

Moyers: What happens to a people when for over a hundred years their gods have literally been outlawed?

Dorris: It's devastating. In the nineteenth century there was something called the Ghost Dance that was practiced in the Plains and in the Northwest. The land had been taken away, the natural subsistence base had been denied, and people were confined to reservations. The Ghost Dance was a desperate belief that this was all a test, that this had not really happened, and that if the people believed strongly enough, if they joined hands and wore Ghost Dance shirts and danced in a circle and denied this reality, that it would all go away. All the animals that had died and the buffalo and the people—everything would be restored the way it was.

This was a response of people who had no other power but faith. What happened was the first Wounded Knee. A group of people, old men and women and children, traveling in the dead of winter from one reservation in South Dakota to another to do a Ghost Dance, were surrounded and obliterated by Gatling guns. The Ghost Dance shirts didn't work—they didn't turn away bullets. It was the low moment.

Erdrich: It did convince the government that religious beliefs among Native Americans were really dangerous. Some Indian people joke and say, "When missionaries came here, all they had was the book, and we had the land. Now all we've got is the book, and they've got the land." In so many cases the missionaries were the first contact with European society. When the missionaries' religious zeal was followed up by government withholding of food, it was not, in many cases, a gentle kind of conversion. And who shouldn't believe, when people are dying of diseases, and you don't have a cure, that the god of some healthy people isn't a better god? Now people are religious according to what denomination was issued to what reservation.

Dorris: Under the Grant Administration—

Moyers: —the government would say, this is a Methodist reservation. The Methodists have the franchise here.

Dorris: —No competition, right.

Erdrich: You get this one.

Moyers: And the Presbyterians have the franchise there.

Erdrich: But those religions are very strong because in some places the greatest advocates for American Indians—

Dorris: —and social justice—

Erdrich: —are within the church. Since the Indian Religious Freedom Act, and during the revival of interest in native cultures in the sixties and seventies, there's been a lot of interest in traditional religion among younger people on reservations. It's a very positive thing. There are revivals of Sun Dances and of communal celebrations. And sometimes these things change with time. Native American people are adaptable within their own culture, too.

Dorris: And religion is not something that's segmented away from other aspects of the society. In the Northwest cultures in Vancouver Island, British Columbia, and Washington State, there's a revival in the economic system of potlatching, which is a system of exchange in which you have an enormous party. At the end of it, your hosts of the party put all of their worldly possessions down, and the guests carry them away. You've given a successful party if you're impoverished, if you have absolutely nothing left. Then you go all the way up on the status hierarchy and all the way down on the wealth hierarchy. But you know that eventually they're going to have a birth or a death or a marriage or something like that, and the expectation is that you will take away more than you gave, so it's a spur to production. This is a system that worked for a thousand years among Northwest peoples that always keep things going, but with a twist, as it were.

Moyers: Given what you know from the past, given what you've learned in your research, given what's happened since Columbus came—the treaties, the broken promises, the perfidy, the betrayals— how do you trust people any more?

Erdrich: Who said that we do? Maybe we don't. Maybe we are somewhat cynical.

Moyers: I don't get that in your books. I don't get that from talking with you.

Dorris: It's the same thing we were talking about before. Why do many Indians today have a sense of identification with the American government in spite of the example of its past history? The answer is: Because what choice do you have? What choice do we have as writers? What choice do we have as people who have children and want a future for them? You get angry. You become an activist. You don't just stop. You have to believe that somewhere there is something that can be appealed to that is common to human experience.

Moyers: What do you think that is?

Dorris: I think it's empathy. We all share certain experiences, like being a child and a parent and so forth. The prime directive for cultures the world over is to survive. When you look at the greenhouse effect and overpopulation and perfidy and war and nuclear disaster possibilities, unless we've collectively lost our minds, we still have somewhere that determination to survive. It's a matter of making it clear that this is the time to ask that question—that there's no luxury of time.

Erdrich: I think you're probably right in that if we truly were cynical, we wouldn't be writers. There's a great French writer who said that the purpose of a writer is to try to increase the sum total of freedom and responsibility in the world. We think of ourselves as citizens of two nations, as writers, and as parents, and we just keep trying to do the best we can. But that doesn't mean that we think everything is going to turn out for the best.

Things are more complicated. We'd like to believe, and probably most people would like to believe, that we can keep going the way we are, that things that we hear about in the future don't relate to things in history, that things from day to day won't change for us living in the United States. To me, that doesn't appear to be true. It appears that we're on a course that will cause us to have to reevaluate ourselves in the very near future. We have to start thinking, more than anything else, and trying to learn from whomever we can what our solutions are going to be. They're going to be technological, and they're going to be solutions of the spirit. We've grown technologically, but we haven't progressed as far spiritually. We're talking about knowledge coming from Europe—but we need wisdom about how to deal with so many of the problems that we're going to face. Not having a happy-ending mentality may be something that we need.

Louise Erdrich

Mickey Pearlman/1989

From *Inter/View: Talks with America's Writing Women*, ed.
Mickey Pearlman and Katherine Usher Henderson (Lexington: University Press of Kentucky, 1989), 143–48. Reprinted by permission.

My interview with Louise Erdrich took place while she was trying to
hold onto her "wonderful, healthy" *active* eight-month-old baby (ten and
a half pounds at birth!) in Cornish, New Hampshire, and I was trying,
in New Jersey, to hold onto my $1.99 rubber dart-gun gadget from
Radio Shack that allows you to both tape and talk to someone on the
telephone.

The baby, Aza Mirion, is the third child of Erdrich and Michael
Dorris, author of the much acclaimed nonfiction book on fetal alcohol
syndrome *The Broken Cord* (1989), and of *A Yellow Raft in Blue Water*
(1987). They also have three children who were adopted by Dorris before their marriage, one of whom suffers from fetal alcohol syndrome.

Erdrich is the author of *Love Medicine* (covering the years 1934–
1984), *The Beet Queen* (1934–1980), and *Tracks* (1912–1924), three
parts of a four-part backward spiral into the lives and lusts of the Kashpaws, Lamartines, and Morrisseys, characters and families who grew
mainly from the richness of her mixed Chippewa and German heritage.
No one who has read Erdrich will forget Eli Kashpaw, a loner who
"couldn't rub two words together and get a spark," or "stark and bony"
Pauline Puyat of *Tracks*. She tells the story of Fleur Pillager, "wild as a
filthy wolf," who "messed with evil." Fleur is a hysterical martyr who
wears potato sacking for underwear, her shoes on the wrong feet, and
betrays the Chippewa as part of her own misguided penance and self-destruction. With Erdrich's unique genius for creating a mythical space
called Argus, she has given the reader a mysterious, lusty, comical
world full of elders, shamans, and mystics who are both foreign and, at
the same time, familiar to the more culturally homogenized reader.

"I think," she said, "that if you believe in any sort of race memory,
I am getting a triple whammy from my background—in regard to place

and home and space." First of all, "The connection that is Chippewa is
a connection to a place and to a background, and to the comfort of
knowing, somehow, that you are connected here before *and before* the
first settler. Add to that the (I think) overblown German Romanticism
about place" inherited from her father's family. "Add into that that the
German part of my family is most probably converted Jews" and the
Jewish "search for place, and you have this 'awful' mix. A person can
only end up writing—in order to resolve it. You can even throw in the
French part of the background—the wanderers, the voyagers, which my
people also come from. There is just no way to get away from all this,
and the only way to resolve it, without going totally crazy looking
for a home, is to write about it." The "Germans have a word for it—
unziemliches Verlangen, unseemly longing,"—and it's the incorrect
kind of longing that you have. I always put [those people longing for
home] into this box and that's the label that I give it, the unseemly
longing that [Germans] have. It's really unfortunate. Someone said, 'I
don't know how the average person feels the pain of death and the pain
of longing and the joy—these great extremes—without art.' I feel that
I am very fortunate to have some place to put [these longings] because
otherwise they would become very destructive."

Erdrich said that she was "born and brought up in the flattest, most
open, exposed part of the United States. The Red River valley of North
Dakota hasn't a tree in it in certain places. I *love* imagining and thinking
back to those spaces, although I write [now] in a very enclosed place"
of "trees and coziness. That's what the landscape is about out here." But
there "*is* a certain freedom in and peace that comes from home, the
feeling of having a homeland."

I wanted to know whether the open spaces associated both with some
Native American nations, and with American fiction generally, remained true for the women in her fiction, or whether Erdrich's fictional
spaces, like the spaces of so many of the writers in this collection, were
closed. Adelaide (in *Beet Queen*), who flies off with Omar, Aeronoaut
Extraordinaire, leaves her children behind at the ironically designated
amusement park. Adelaide, and June Kashpaw, who, in a drunken
stupor, freezes to death in an endless expanse of snow, were two of the
characters I had in mind. These seemed to be two examples of women
in open, undefined space which becomes, in effect, closed, limiting,
and entrapping. Erdrich agreed that "it has a lot to do with where I grew

up. I set myself back in that pure, empty landscape whenever I am working on something . . . [because] there's nothing like it. . . . It's the place where everything comes from." These characters, she continued, "*were* out in that open space, but their destination was home. June headed out into that open space, she was going across it, but she was heading home. She was heading into that wonderful and difficult mixture of family and place that mysteriously works on a person, that is home."

She added that Dot, the non-Native American character in *The Beet Queen* who "is flying up in the cropduster's plane, up in pure space (which is the atmosphere), also makes a decision to come back, to come home, and to be at her home with her mother. The one person who doesn't make that decision is Adelaide, who gets into the plane and flies off into nothingness. And it is a nothingness of madness for her, as a character." She leaves her children mired in their own vulnerability and helplessness, in sharp contrast to the air images which are associated with her as the missing mother. "You see her later," said Erdrich, "unable to reconcile her longings—with her life—unable to ever get over the fact that she has abandoned her children for this space and for this freedom."

The freedom of open space "is there but it's nothing that someone stays in. People aren't 'lighting out for the territory.' The women in my books are lighting out for home." She added that "going home for most people is like trying to recapture childhood. It's an impossible task; you're not a child, and unless your parents have, by some grace of God, grown up with you, it's almost impossible to go back and stay and live. In extraordinary families there are people who can do this, but it's not done very much any more." The treks and journeys in her work, I suggested, are both a desire to leave and a longing to return. "I think it's both," said Erdrich. "And I don't think there's any judgment in that." She said that she "loves going back [home] and that it's a combination of true complexity [because I have] a very large extended family and there's a drama per minute. But it's also very comforting. . . . I have parents who really have become friends over the years."

I asked her if she ever had thought of moving back, of going home. "I think about it a lot, and I think it's quite impossible. I am probably an Easterner who mistakenly grew up in the Midwest. I never felt very accepted or at home in my hometown. There are terrific people there but

I found growing up there difficult because the emphasis is on conven-
tionality. You have to conform, because otherwise there is a lot of
psychic pain that you have to go through. My parents happen to be truly
intelligent, and my father is a little eccentric in his intelligence. And it
is only after years and years and years that he was able to find a niche
where he can be the person he is and be loved and accepted in the town.
That is terribly important, and as a child growing up I was subjected to
all sorts of pressures to 'be nice,' to conform, to be [a certain] sort of
person. . . . I found it extremely difficult. I have thought often about
going back but I don't think I would. I don't think I *want* to in the end.
I love being out here [in New Hampshire], really being ignored."

We talked at length about silences, about whether her fictional
women had made a tacit decision to be silent, as have many of the
fictional women created by the writers in this collection. I asked her
whether this was linked instead to the experience of the Native American woman. "It's very true that if I were writing about a traditional
Native American woman you would say, 'This is a woman that has been
silenced because she's not allowed to speak in her native language.'"
She mentioned Lulu Lamartine, who appears in all three novels (pro-
ducing eight sons along the way by eight different men) as "someone
who has an interesting background. This doesn't appear in the fiction,
but she is sent to a boarding school, and in government boarding
schools during the time she would have been going to school, children
would have been punished for speaking native languages. So she has a
very lyrical and very unconventional way of speaking." Lamartine
speaks "the way I would like to speak but can only do in fiction. But
she is someone who was never allowed to speak and is punished for
speaking the language of her childhood, so she grows up taking on
English and, because of her peculiarities" her language very much
reflects that. "You find this with a lot of native women of a certain
generation, having their own way with the language, using it in an
interesting way—and she does that." Like many people of various
cultures who were denied language and the subsequent ability to name
things, she is disempowered. Erdrich said that Lulu Lamartine was
"punished for [language], punished for being your most fluent and
absorbing and interesting self, because self and language are so much
the same." There is an inalienable bond between "what you express and
who you are" and the denial of Lulu's native language had to "have

been an act that destroyed the self. We really have very few people who talk a lot about what that was like. You read some people who have reflected a lot more thoroughly on what language deprivation does to a person. Although I am *not* making any comparisons here—I think of Primo Levi's reflection in *The Drowned and the Saved* on what it was like to be thrust into a concentration camp setting and not to have the language of survival, not to have German"—it is "a truly profound reflection on the entire idea of being silent. I am *not* making a connection between being a child in a boarding school and being in this other horrific holocaust." It is fair to say, however, that in both instances you lose the ability to be connected, to link with those forces that you perceive as protective.

Erdrich's three novels are also defined by her use of non-chronological time, and by the reappearance at various ages of the same characters. I asked her if these techniques, associated with Modernism, were related to the amorphous quality of what she has called "the insistent tug of memory." "It probably does have to do with that—the unreliability of memory at any given moment. The memory is so unfixed, so fluid, you never know what's going to surface. I have a hold on a certain number of characters, it seems, so when a story surfaces it is usual that one of the people is in the story. I can't really go to the source and say, 'Here's what I want' and 'I want it in a nice package.' There is no way to control what happens, or when, or when somebody comes up with a story." I related incidents told to me by Rosellen Brown and Francine Prose, about taking down, almost like stenographers, stories that were dictated by the characters. She said "there are moments like that, but it rarely happens. . . . I truly think that you can't go and stock your material, you have to leave the door open, and whatever *chooses* you, chooses *you*. You can't go and wrestle it to the ground. I've never been able to do that. There are times when I'm desperate to talk about something or write about something in particular, but it's never been my real choice." I asked her which characters keep coming back most often. "Right now, it's Dot and Marie [in *Beet Queen*] but at any given time it's someone else. Who knows why?"

Louise Erdrich told me that she "grew up with all the accepted truths [of Catholicism] but," she added, "I don't have a central metaphor for my life. I only have chaos. I now read that there is some kind of order even in chaos, and that's comforting." What seems more comforting for her readers is that she continues to reach back in to the not so deeply submerged fullness of her multilayered racial memory to produce fiction that is full of sexual and spiritual power, death, derangement, the miraculous and the mundane. Since it was praised so often by the other writers in this collection, who are of various ethnic, religious, and racial backgrounds, it is clear that from that chaos has come something universal and of inestimable value.

Tales from a Literary Marriage

Vince Passaro/1991

From *The New York Times Magazine* (21 April 1991), 34–36, 38–39, 42–43, 76. Reprinted by permission of Georges Borchardt, Inc. Copyright © 1991 by Vince Passaro.

Louise Erdrich and Michael Dorris don't get out much. They live deep in the New Hampshire countryside, in an old farmhouse in Cornish, where they have children to raise and books to write and not a lot of help from anybody. When I meet them for dinner one mild winter night in nearby Hanover, they have about them an air of intimacy and romance that even the presence of a New York reporter can't fully dispel.

Erdrich is 36, Dorris nine years older, but in the warm light of a fine restaurant they look like newlyweds, shy, happy with each other, a tinge embarrassed to be the center of attention. We talk for a while about their new book, *The Crown of Columbus*, the first they've written in complete collaboration, and then, after a pause, Erdrich turns to Dorris and says quietly (she says everything quietly), "Tell him about the birthday present I gave you last year."

He tells me the story: When they went out to dinner last spring for Dorris's birthday, Erdrich presented him with a new travel case. Inside, he found a copy of *The Ladies Home Journal* with a piece she'd written, one he hadn't known about, a rare occurrence in their usually collaborative writing lives. In the story, she announced that she'd be using her fee from the piece to pay for a surprise trip to France for her and her husband. At the bottom of the case, below the magazine, were the tickets.

The enterprise involved Erdrich enlisting the editors of the magazine, both sides of their families, the waiters in the restaurant, even the local magazine merchant, to keep Dorris from finding out what she was up to. They went to Paris shortly thereafter, their first nonfamily, non-professional trip together.

As Flannery O'Connor once noted, writers are difficult biographical subjects; her own life story, O'Connor said, consisted mostly of walking from the house to the barn and back again. Erdrich and Dorris have

planned, obviously, to remember the birthday story for this interview—
they know I'll need colorful anecdotes and want to help out. And while
the story is charming, it also illustrates a more important issue: the
profound connection between their marriage and their careers—the
possibility, even, that their most important messages for each other are
passed between them in what they write.

In the summer of 1988, HarperCollins, then known as Harper & Row,
announced it would pay $1.5 million for *The Crown of Columbus*, a
projected novel about two Dartmouth professors and their quest to
discover Columbus's lost diary. The payment schedule was rare: half
the advance was paid immediately. Promised on the basis of a five-page
proposal, it was an almost unheard-of advance for two literary writers,
even ones as successful as Dorris and Erdrich. They were by then the
authors of, between them, four popular and highly praised novels: *Love
Medicine*, *The Beet Queen* and *Tracks* by Erdrich and *A Yellow Raft in
Blue Water* by Dorris. (Dorris was at work on what would become his
much praised 1989 nonfiction book, *The Broken Cord*.) The new novel
had about it an extra bit of exotica—it would be published under both
their names.

Dorris and Erdrich are an unlikely set of candidates for fame and
riches. Both are of mixed American Indian descent. Dorris was raised
by three women, after his father was killed in World War II. He lived
for a time on a reservation in eastern Montana, but spent most of his
youth in Louisville, Ky., where his aunt worked for the city and his
mother took care of his elderly grandmother. Erdrich (pronounced er-
drick), the oldest of seven children, grew up near a Sioux Indian reservation in Wahpeton, N.D., where her parents taught at a Bureau of
Indian Affairs boarding school. The family lived on the school's small
campus.

They met in the 1970's at Dartmouth, where she was his student.
Their romantic relationship began a few years later, and they married in
1981. Dorris came late to literature, having built a career as an anthropologist and later as founder and head of Dartmouth's Native American
studies program. Erdrich achieved literary success at a younger age, but
as recently as a decade ago she and Dorris were collaborating for quick
cash on romantic stories that they published under the name Milou
North in magazines like *Redbook*.

You get the impression with Dorris and Erdrich of two writers who manage their careers avidly, shrewdly and almost entirely by themselves. Their agent, Charles Rembar, is actually a lawyer and represents only about a half-dozen authors. The couple are, for the most part, their own editors. After their HarperCollins editor left the business, when *The Crown of Columbus* was still in production, they worked with the company's publisher, William M. Shinker, whose background is in marketing. "Our books need very little line editing," Dorris says. "By the time they leave our house, we've worked on them extensively together and they've been through many, many revisions."

They reserve the right to approve the covers of American editions of their books, naturally concerned about the depictions of American Indians that might go out under their names. At one point Dorris shows me the covers of some European editions of Erdrich's books, depicting savage braves and voluptuous squaws. They seem to amuse Erdrich, but to Dorris they are unambiguously painful. "We absolutely have to control the images," he says—a statement that also sheds light on the strict regulations they have established governing the terms of our interview.

Erdrich and Dorris look comfortable together. Both are dark and slender and very still. Erdrich's face is more lively, more delicate and readable than her pictures show; Dorris in person is more nervous and slightly less dashing than in photos. They seem, on first meeting, to give off an air of quiet modesty and sadness, punctuated occasionally with a wry, self-deprecating humor.

Our meetings take place in a room at Dartmouth and in restaurants because Dorris and Erdrich do not wish to be interviewed at home; they want to direct the discussion away from their family life. Dorris, before he married Erdrich, was the single father of three adopted American Indian children, now grown or nearly so. His oldest child, Abel, has suffered severely from the effects of fetal exposure to alcohol, the difficulties of which were explored in *The Broken Cord*. The other two experienced learning disabilities. When they were married, Erdrich adopted Dorris's children and has since given birth to three daughters, now aged 7, 6 and 2, whom the couple also wish not to see written about or exposed.

Erdrich and Dorris do not seem so much guarded about their family as openly vulnerable. All the publicity attendant on the publication of a high-priced book comes at a time when they are trying to recover from the larger exposures of *The Broken Cord*. Because it was so personally

revealing, its success, while welcome, became an assault on their difficult and isolated private lives.

After the book's publication and Dorris's appearances on television,
he received almost 2,000 letters from readers who recognized in the
portrayal of his son, called Adam in the book, symptoms they'd seen in
their own children or relatives, but never understood. Dorris spent his
weekends over the next two years answering the letters. He and Erdrich
are in for another session in the spotlight this fall, when a television
movie based on *The Broken Cord* is scheduled to appear.

"The whole thing has made us more protective of our time and our
children," Erdrich says. "Of course, what is the pain of exposing yourself compared to the good you can do telling this story? This book and
the film will reach lots of people, some of whom won't do damage to
their babies as a result. Exposing yourself doesn't mean much next to
that." Then she laughs and holds up her hand. "But once is enough.
Never again."

The morning after our initial interview, Dorris gives a reading from
the new book at Kimball Union Academy, a prep school in Meriden,
down the road from Cornish, whose day-care center Dorris and Erdrich's youngest daughter attends. There is an air of excitement about
the reading, the unveiling of a major new work by a friend and neighbor
of the school.

A longtime teacher and well-traveled speaker, Dorris is practiced at
public presentations, and he has chosen a lively and funny scene in
which the pompous university professor, Roger, finds himself stuck in a
tropical airport with the sullen teenage son of his lover and colleague,
Vivian. None of his or Erdrich's previous writing has the overall light-
hearted quality, or the plenitude of quips and repartee, that they've
given this novel.

Afterward, Dorris takes questions. He talks about how he and Erdrich
collaborated: they worked out the plot and researched together, he says,
but each wrote the first draft of specific scenes alone. They then passed
the revisions back and forth, many times over. Although the book is
written in two voices, male and female, Dorris and Erdrich did not split
the writing along those lines.

He also tells the students that even though this is the first book to
feature both their names, their work has always been collaborative—
they've read and revised and argued out each other's scenes, word by

word if necessary, and read them aloud to each other over the kitchen table until each was satisfied. No work ever leaves their house until this process has been completed, Dorris explains, until they have a version on which they both agree. (Surprise birthday presents excepted.) Yet even these high-school students, neither sophisticated nor suspicious, wonder how fiction—an internal search for language, consciousness, history and dreams—works as a joint venture.

"Isn't it difficult for two people with different and unique styles to write together?" one student asks. It's a question at the heart of everyone's response to the book.

"I'm not sure we *do* have different and unique styles," Dorris answers today—a quick and almost instinctive answer that is, in fact, quite radical. It is impossible to imagine a collaboration that does not at times require making sacrifices in style, voice and even intention. But Dorris and Erdrich have always insisted on a conception of themselves that is far more romantic and defiant of convention, in which art and marriage are complementary mechanisms. The impression they have promoted is that they are attempting as artists to make themselves, by mutual consent, into one voice, one vision, one language. Theirs is an art, as well as a life, directed toward synthesis and unity.

For those who have read both of them, this remains difficult to accept. So far, Dorris has worked in an entirely realistic style, and the novel and the memoir are oriented around distinct social problems and contemporary political and social worlds. Erdrich's writing, on the other hand, has been called "a northern outpost of magical realism." Her books are filled with blood and death and anarchic sexuality, animated by a spiritual vibrancy that, in part, explains why so much of it has been set in the past. *The Crown of Columbus* appears to be closer to Dorris's style than to Erdrich's.

There comes a moment in the lives of most writers, as crucial for their development as any bench-mark story or book, when they gain the internal confidence and authority that allows them to think of themselves as writers; it is a moment both of found identity and sustaining determination. By all accounts, this moment came considerably earlier for Louise Erdrich than it did for Michael Dorris.

James Wright, a history professor at Dartmouth and now its dean of faculty, recalls working with Erdrich during the summer of 1977, when she was 23, on a public television documentary about the Northern

Plains Indians: "I remember quite well, at the end of the summer, driving her to the Trailways bus terminal in Lincoln, Neb., to put her on a bus back to North Dakota. I remember her telling me, 'I have to do this, I have to go back and try to be a writer.' Of course, I'm sure I said something very encouraging, but inside I was thinking, 'Yeah, sure kid. Pretty soon you'll discover you have to do something else.' I love to tell them that story now."

She was writing mostly poetry in those days, beginning to make forays into fiction, with success still far from sight. "I was always glad I'd been a waitress," she says. "I knew I'd have that to fall back on."

By the time her first novel, *Love Medicine* was completed, she was married to Dorris, who took over as her agent after the book met with nice letters but little enthusiasm on its initial rounds with publishers. "The Michael Dorris Agency was phenomenally successful," Dorris says. "It had two offers for the book in a matter of weeks."

Love Medicine, a mosaic of fictional Native American voices from the area of North Dakota where Erdrich grew up, was published in 1984 and won the National Book Critics Circle Award as well as a number of other prizes. Reviewers praised Erdrich's "fine poetic gift" and "the remarkable sensuousness and energy of her prose."

All three of Erdrich's novels, to one degree or another, rely on a technique of accumulated knowledge, of splicing together different dramatic voices in different times in a series of interrelated stories about the lives, spiritual triumphs and physical tragedies of her mythological North Dakota families. They involve love, death, tradition and no little amount of magic. And her characters, as in the novels and stories of Faulkner and Garcia Marquez, both of whom she acknowledges as influences, live on and refer to each other from book to book.

The novels have been criticized as being confusing at times, of lacking a central and unifying narrative form. And some readers have expressed reservations about the emotional calibration of Erdrich's prose, which is pitched high. Robert Towers, in *The New York Review of Books,* wrote of *Love Medicine*: "At times the language becomes overwrought to the point of hysteria or else so ecstatic that the reader may feel almost coerced into accepting a romanticized version of a situation—a version that the hard facts belie."

Still, this richness and emotional punch is exactly what most of Erdrich's loyal readers have craved. Her novels have sold enormously well, here and in Europe; in a period of disillusion with the pared-down narrative and plain prose styles of her generation of American novelists and story writers, Erdrich's full-bodied prose seems like a return to literature's epic possibilities (with, it should be noted, a leading and profoundly redemptive role for women).

"One must reach for names like Balzac and Faulkner to suggest the sweep of her three interlocking novels," wrote Thomas Disch, reviewing *Tracks* (1988), which moves back in time to before *Love Medicine* and with *The Beet Queen* (1986) forms a loose trilogy. The three books, Disch wrote, "already constitute a *comédie humaine* of some 800–plus pages, a North Dakota of the imagination that, like Faulkner's Yoknapatawpha County, unites the archetypal and the arcane, heartland America and borderline schizophrenia." At an age when even successful writers are still generally looked upon either as promising talents or marketing curiosities, Erdrich already holds a spot as one of the country's most important novelists. One senses in Erdrich the confidence, albeit a very quiet one, that such a position bestows.

Publicly though, Dorris is the talker, the spokesman for the collaboration. A graduate of Georgetown and Yale, he speaks energetically, in long, articulate sentences, and is not above jumping in when Erdrich is talking, to clarify or expand. It is not unusual for a magazine editor working on one of Erdrich's pieces to speak primarily to Dorris.

His first novel, *A Yellow Raft in Blue Water* (1987), weaves together the often painful stories of three women of Native American descent. Although it was not the ground-breaking performance of Erdrich's first book, it received almost universal praise. *The Broken Cord*, for which he got what he calls "a tiny advance," not only became a best seller but proved also to be a crucial portrait of the horrors of fetal alcohol syndrome, which had been a little-known and little-funded problem affecting hundreds of thousands of families. Like *Love Medicine*, it won the National Book Critics Circle Award, and, more importantly, helped prompt Senate action on fetal alcohol syndrome, especially as it affects American Indians.

Yet, for all that, there is a tentativeness about his sense of himself as a writer. He seems truly surprised and slightly awe-struck by his own success, speaking of his various film deals with obvious pleasure. He tells of having given up writing fiction for 15 years, after one of his stories was severely criticized in his college newspaper. One imagines

that he still takes criticism very much to heart. Where he internally
believes himself to be as a writer, even now, seems to be an issue.
Taking questions after the reading at Kimball Union, he tells the audience, "I'm really Louise's student," a position he repeats to me in front
of Erdrich and one that she dismisses with a trace of annoyance.

HarperCollins has gambled big money on *The Crown of Columbus*,
but even in these hard times the book stands a good chance of paying
out. It brings together a promising portfolio of commercial possibilities.
Erdrich and Dorris combine large, well-established audiences both here
and overseas. A movie option for *The Crown of Columbus* has already
been sold; the film is to be produced by Michelle Pfeiffer and Kate
Guinzburg.

William Shinker of HarperCollins calls the book "a wonderful entertainment," and Charles Rembar refers to it as "commercial . . . a real
page-turner." But in emphasizing the book's commercial qualities,
Shinker and Rembar are opening it up to a criticism that is already being
murmured in some quarters—that *The Crown of Columbus* is not up to
the standards of Dorris and Erdrich's earlier books, even that it is calculated to be a best seller rather than an important work of literature. It is
certainly well positioned in its timing, published on the verge of the
heavily promoted Columbus quincentenary. "We wrote it with the same
care and attention and commitment we've brought to all our other
books," Dorris says. "We very much intended this to be a serious
book."

The plot line is fueled by a classic love story, involving an unlikely
and likable couple of Dartmouth professors, Vivian Twostar and Roger
Williams, each exploring the myths of Columbus for different reasons.
Their relationship, physically potent though edgy and competitive, is the
main story of the book, but they also become involved in a cloak-and-
dagger adventure involving Columbus's long-lost diary, a page of which
Vivian believes she has turned up in the dusty files of Dartmouth's
alumni archives. The page seems to contain a key to finding a treasure,
a crown, that Columbus left in the Bahamas on his first voyage.

It was about 10 years ago that Dorris and Erdrich happened to read a
translation of Bartolomé de Las Casas's 16th-century edition of Columbus's lost diary. Shortly thereafter, they began thinking about doing a
novel together involving Columbus, but the book idea remained on the
back burner, they say, because of other projects.

A few years later, Erdrich says, "We had to take a long trip to Tacoma and we said, 'We'll plot this book on the way back.' The problem of the book was that we had to avoid too much explication about Columbus, the diary, the history. We wanted to pare it down to its essence, to the idea of personal discovery."

"One part of the issue of discovery comes out of the North American creation myths," Dorris says. "Vivian is part Navajo, and in the Navajo creation story, a first man and a first woman emerge from under ground to begin a new world, a new cycle. And that's what happens to Vivian and Roger at the end of the book. We were interested in that newness and freshness, the discovery of a lost thing, which is the basis for their relationship."

"The sense that the past is past and the future is possible," Erdrich says. "We try to grapple with time—the impact of history. What creates the present."

Although the setting and some circumstances of *The Crown of Columbus* are similar to apects of their own lives, the only real trace of autobiography in the book, Erdrich and Dorris say, is in the person of Violet, the baby girl whom Vivian bears near the beginning of the book and who ends up perilously abandoned and rediscovered at its end.

"We don't write autobiographically, but we did have a baby daughter, Aza, while we were writing this book," Dorris says. "And we knew early on she had to be in there because she was certainly making herself felt."

"A lot of times, one of us would write that the baby was crying," Erdrich confirms, "and the baby *was* crying."

The story of Columbus is of an ethnically confused man introducing ethnic confusion to a continent. In a way, this represents a deeper autobiographical theme. Vivian might be speaking for Erdrich when she says of her mixed heritage: "There are advantages to not being this or that. You have a million stories, one for every occasion, and in a way they're all lies and in another way they're all true. . . . There are times when I control who I'll be, and times when I let other people decide. I'm not all anything, but I'm a little bit of a lot. My roots spread in every direction, and if I water one set of them more often than others, it's because they need it more."

And the overall thematic conflict of the book—the question Dorris posed as "What do you do when you discover something you didn't expect to discover?"—flips back in an intriguing way on *The Broken Cord,* which is a narrative about Dorris's discovery of his son's problems, a discovery that ran counter to his expectations and that he strongly resisted. The issue of Dorris and Erdrich's relationship with their son is symbolically reconstructed in *The Crown of Columbus* in the person of Nash, Vivian's 16-year-old son by an earlier marriage. Roger's rage at Nash, a difficult and unkempt boy who exposes Roger in surprising ways, forms a subtle parallel with the father-son relationship Dorris described in *The Broken Cord.* Their union at the end of the novel is a fictional working out of a problem that in the earlier book was never fully resolved.

In all their books, both Dorris and Erdrich can be said to be bringing back news of a silenced nation, but the nation they are talking about is our own. They are the two most prominent writers of American Indian descent we have, two of the very few to have found a significant audience out in the large world. So that even if they aren't writing about themselves in the contemporary sense, as individuals, they are writing about themselves in the collective sense—they are writing about their people.

It is an enviable postion: How many American writers of this generation even know who their people are, much less have the authority to speak for them?

Their life since their marriage has been particularly intimate and strenuous. For them, one senses, the act of collaboration serves a vital, extra-literary function, perhaps as a fortification against an insinuating and inevitable competition. If every work that leaves their hands is in some sense a joint work, they can escape the awful consequences of one talent overshadowing another. Up in the country, with a house full of children, through years with little money and stressful careers, this would have been no small danger. The escaping gas of burning egos could have blown off the roof. As it turned out, they've both been successful, and the machine they've developed for working together has brought them closer rather than driven them apart.

Dorris and Erdrich met in 1972 at Dartmouth, where she was a member of the first class of the college to admit women. A mixed-blood Turtle Mountain Chippewa from North Dakota, she had never been away from home. He was a bachelor with three small children, who had come to Dartmouth that same year to help develop its new Native American studies program. They didn't become close until a few years after Erdrich had graduated, when she returned to Dartmouth to give a reading of her poetry.

After the reading, which made a deep impression on Dorris, they left a faculty reception together to sit and, out of shy nervousness, mostly not talk. After a while he drove her to where she was staying and they shook hands good night. As brief and silent as the evening had been, both admitted later to knowing this was the person they wanted to marry.

Unfortunately, Dorris was off the next week to New Zealand for seven months on a research fellowship. During that time, they wrote each other often. Since they'd met over literature, that's what they corresponded about. Spurred by Erdrich's example, Dorris put aside the pain of his early criticism and took up poetry and story-writing again. (Part of that college story was included in his first novel, Dorris says, at least in part to get back at his never forgotten critic, "who's probably selling insurance now.") When he and Erdrich were reunited at Dartmouth, where she had become a writer in residence, they stayed up late into the nights, talking "editorial fine points," until finally it was time to get married.

This intricate connection of the history of their relationship with their efforts to become writers may be the reason that talk of their collaboration fades almost without distinction into talk of their marriage. "The person who has an objection to what the other one has written takes pains as much as possible to be constructive, not hurtful," Dorris says. "Still, you come out with a page in your hand, still hot, and the other one reads it and is, like, well. . . . "

"That's an awful moment," Erdrich says.

And is it painful? "It's painful, yes, sure," she says. "It definitely is. But something about working with Michael gives me support and permission, too, a safe way of going beyond and beyond. Especially when it comes to sex. Growing up Catholic, there's a certain amount of repression." And then she brings the subject to what is, for her, its only and most natural conclusion. "I'm *glad* I know Michael," she says quietly, "It's a *relief* to know Michael. It's a good thing we got married."

Double Vision: An Interview with the Authors
Douglas Foster/1991

From *Mother Jones* 16.3 (May/June 1991), 26, 78–80. Reprinted by permission.

With dozens of short stories, four novels, and a nonfiction book between them, Michael Dorris (*A Yellow Raft in Blue Water* and *The Broken Cord*) and Louise Erdrich (*Love Medicine*, *The Beet Queen*, and *Tracks*) have now achieved the unthinkable: They produced a jointly written novel, *The Crown of Columbus*—a four-hundred-page opus about Native Americans, Columbus, and the idea of discovery—and their marriage has survived.

Parents of six, Erdrich and Dorris live with their three youngest children near the remote hamlet of Cornish, New Hampshire. With two-year-old daughter Aza down for a rare nap, they took time to reflect on the meaning of their new book and the unusual process of creating it.

MJ: This is a big book, a complicated book. There's a love story, a mystery and a killer, a shark—and through it all, Columbus keeps popping up.

Erdrich: There's a discovery made—

Dorris: Right.

Erdrich: Or the potential of a discovery.

Dorris: Vivian Twostar is a forty-year-old, divorced, abrupt, mixed-blood woman who is tired of being categorized by her ethnicity, but at the same time has been asked to write a puff piece, for the alumni magazine, about Columbus, because she happens to be part Indian. She is initially bored to death with this idea, but because she is at heart an intellectual, though she may not quite know it, she gets caught up in the notion of who Columbus was, and how complex a character and how complex a question this is. And she has begun a relationship, which she believes has no future, with, in some respects, her polar opposite—a very fastidious, self-protective, established English professor named

168

Roger Williams, who *People* magazine has said is working on a poem
about Columbus that's going to be important.

Erdrich: Which he takes completely with utter seriousness, that
this is going to be important. He's a terrible self-important person.
(Laughter)

Dorris: They have not a lot in common, except that they are incredibly attracted to each other physically, and they have a relationship. She
becomes pregnant, by choice, and decides that Roger is not good father
material, and so she basically lets him off the hook without him ever
knowing he was on the hook. She and Roger are trying to figure out
their relationship, they're trying to figure out shared parenthood, and all
the time they're trying to figure out who Columbus was, because Roger
is committed to the notion of the historical Columbus. He spent years
doing research on this guy, and he doesn't want this research to mean
nothing. He's got a big poem, and it's got to work. Vivian, on the other
hand, thinks that if she can discover a kind of revisionist Columbus, it's
going to mean something for Indian land rights or even for self-esteem:
they weren't "discovered" but rather were equals in the very beginning.

MJ: Do you think some readers will expect a critical treatment of
Columbus from you?

Erdrich: I think it's pretty critical. The book says, "Columbus was
the first European slave trader." If anyone got that in to a child's history
book, it would be an amazing fact to have there, and it would be a truth
about a history that is not said.

Dorris: But I think it's important to say that this book is not didactic.
We don't write didactic novels. I don't think we could. Columbus is a
metaphor. His name stands for a notion of encounter of the unexpected.
And what do you do with that encounter? Do you try and fit what you
find into a pre-existing structure, do you change your worldview as a
result of it? Columbus was static in many respects. And that may be his
tragedy.

Erdrich: What fascinated us was that there was this human being in
the excerpts of the [Columbus] journals who came across as someone
who was fascinated with this other culture. And then you see the next
step, the next voyage, in which he decides that the only way to make
[the venture] economically feasible was to send Indians back as slaves.
What happened to this man internally, mentally—what happened to that
small niche of openness that was there during those first encounters?

There was this sense that perhaps he had encountered some sort of golden age of humans left over from another age; and yet, within two years, he's trying desperately to ship these people back, and the Spanish monarchs are refusing. He's doing it even against the wishes of the king and queen! And he really sets, through that action, the paradigm for the destruction of these people during the next twenty years.

Dorris: It would be too simple to say that it was really all Columbus, though. I mean, Columbus was just one person. What Columbus represents and carries with him are the seeds of the problem: ethnocentrism; rigidity in the face of a dynamic world; the notion that might makes right; not seeing what was there but seeing what he expected to see. I mean, that is a legacy that in a sense our characters are constantly struggling with, to be open to possibility.

MJ: What was the biggest surprise for the two of you in doing this book, in terms of what you thought the book would be and what it became?

Erdrich: I thought we were just going to rewrite an original diary as though it was Columbus'. The other surprise was Roger. I sort of fell in love with him during the writing of this book.

Dorris: Roger started out as a foil to Vivian. We didn't even know if he was going to have his own voice. He was the "other," he was all that she was reacting against, and in a sense the book was much more simple then, because it was good and bad, and Vivian was triumphant. But I think what we discovered, as Roger got his voice, was that he was a kind of innocent.

MJ: I know you've collaborated for a long time. But this is the first piece of fiction that you're publishing with both your names on it. How did it work to write a work of imagination together?

Erdrich: We did it as we always do. We always talk, and so we talked talked talked talked talked about the book, and talked about the plot and the characters. We don't write in the same room or with one desk or with hooked-up computers. No, we do go off our own ways, so we wrote things separately. We sort of made the rules up as we went along. Michael could hand me something and say, "What's next?" I could do the same and say, "Plot that. . . ." I mean, we just meshed. If you could sort of take a writer out of both of us and mind-meld. Mind-meld! That's what it was! It was the Vulcan mind-meld.

MJ: You said that one of your surprises was that originally this was going to be a treatment of Columbus' story. What happened between that expectation and the novel you've ended up with? Did Roger and Vivian take it over?

Erdrich: Well, yeah, they did.

MJ: They had things *they* wanted to say?

Erdrich: The nerve! It became unworkable, sort of boring, to rewrite the diary. It just didn't work. So ours became more of a novel about the process of discovering than about the discovery itself.

MJ: This is a novel you collaborated on. It's partially about two people in a couple relationship, fighting with each other and then collaborating on a search together. Did you learn anything about each other that you didn't know when you started the novel?

Dorris: I think we learned that we could do it. We have different processes of working. Louise writes absolutely every day. I tend to write in bursts. I think when it started out, I was still finishing *The Broken Cord,* so Louise started working on this intensely first. I wrote one little bit of it at the Subaru dealership, two paragraphs.

Erdrich: It's an act of faith to believe that the other person [will come through]. Michael had to believe that, Yes, I really do have to just plod in there and work with desperate slowness. And I have to think, Oh yes, well, Michael really is going to get to it eventually. There were times when I was totally dry and had no ideas, and Michael was just going whammo, wham, whirrr.

Dorris: There was one magic moment in which I was absolutely stalled and I didn't know what to do, and I called Louise up [across the road] where she works, and I said, "What do I do?" and she said, "I've just started working out this one particular section," and it was actually Roger in an encounter with the shark, after he jumps overboard. And she said: "I will give this up, and you write this. Your assignment is to write Roger overboard, what happens to him." And it was just great to get an assignment. I hadn't gotten an assignment since college.

Erdrich: I always wanted to assign him homework.

Dorris: The dominatrix . . . (Laughter)

MJ: Was it such a successful collaboration that this is the way you'll both want to work from now on?

Erdrich: Right now we have two books in mind that are very much set in areas of our past experience, so we are working on those separately.

Dorris: Separate, but not separate. We've always worked collaboratively.

MJ: Does the fascination with this close collaboration surprise you?

Erdrich: Well, no. The idea that people have of a writer is someone who goes into a locked room and doesn't come out.

MJ: . . . and falls into an individual trance.

Erdrich: Yes, which is also the case. But we also have a collective trance.

Dorris: Well, but I think there's a lot more between the two extremes—us on one end and the solitary in the garret on the other. There's a lot in between that is unacknowledged. I mean, we have writer friends who never do other than, "I thank my spouse for his or her enduring patience while I worked on the book, or typing the manuscript, taking care of the kids, blah blah blah," who really worked much more closely together, we know, than is acknowledged.

Erdrich: Many, many writers have someone who is more than an editor, but it isn't something that is—I don't know why, but it isn't something writers like to talk about.

Dorris: Well, they don't talk about it because they get dumped on, like we did at first. There were articles after we started talking about working together in which people said: "Oh, it will never last. They both have strong egos and so this relationship will break up" and lovely things like that in print. So no wonder people don't say anything. But the thing is, it's not as calculated or unusual as it sounds. Over the last ten years of being married and living together, we evolved a way of collaborating that works for us, and that we've come to depend on and enjoy and find challenging and stretching. So it isn't like a little light bulb went on saying, "Hey, let's work together," but it just happened. And you can see where we live, there's not a lot of traffic. . . .

Erdrich: We don't get a lot of interaction with the world, no. (Laughter)

MJ: What are your biggest hopes and fears about the coming reaction to this novel?

Dorris: Our biggest hope, I think, is that people will read it, and take it seriously, and our—my—biggest fear is that people will say, "She ought to write by herself." (Laughter)

Erdrich: Mine, too, that one of them will say, "She did him in as a writer, he did her in as a writer." That kind of thing. I don't know. My biggest fear is always nasty reviews. I'm a real chicken.

Louise Erdrich and Michael Dorris: A Marriage of Minds

Michael Schumacher/1991

From *Writer's Digest*, (June 1991), 28–31, 59. Reprinted by permission.

Literary marriages are by no means rare. They range from poet Percy Shelley and *Frankenstein* creator Mary Wollstonecraft Shelley to, more recently, Stephen and Tabitha King. Louise Erdrich and Michael Dorris, however, have developed a style of matrimonial collaboration that may well be unique.

Between them, Erdrich and Dorris have written five novels and one nonfiction book. Erdrich's name has appeared on the cover of three of those (*Love Medicine, The Beet Queen* and *Tracks*), while Dorris's byline ran on *A Yellow Raft in Blue Water*, a novel, and *The Broken Cord*, an award-winning nonfiction study of fetal alcohol syndrome. Both names appear on their just-published novel, *The Crown of Columbus*.

This question of author identification is what makes their literary marriage a singular one: All of the above-mentioned books are collaborations in every respect, but on most only one author receives cover mention. In an era in which great discussion is devoted to whether a writer's name should appear above or below the title on a book's cover, it is virtually unheard of for an author (other than a ghostwriter) to *decline* cover credit for a book he or she collaborates on. These are not times in which egos are comfortable with anonymity.

Which brings us to the question of *how* these books are written. Who comes up with the ideas? Who does the actual writing? Are we talking more about a writer-editor relationship? And what of the occasional magazine article or essay—or the couple's current novel, for that matter—for which both authors are given byline credit? Is the writing process for these projects different than that which produced the other five books?

The answers to these questions begin to become apparent when you actually meet Erdrich and Dorris. They not only share similar interests, but at times their levels of interaction are almost uncanny. They will finish each other's thoughts, embellish or clarify ideas, banter back and forth—all in a way that makes their answers to a question seem to come from one person.

As we began this interview, Dorris had not yet arrived, and while Erdrich was both frank and generous in responding to my questions, I later found her to be more at ease talking about writing issues when her husband was present. (This isn't to say that Dorris is the dominant voice in the interview; if either one were to talk about craft without the other present, I'd bet that *something* would seem to be missing.)

Writer's Digest: You've written quite extensively about Native American themes, yet very little of your writing, until *Tracks,* seemed to carry openly political messages.

Erdrich: I think each of the books is political in its own way. I hope so. But *Tracks,* by virtue of its setting, was bound to be more political. There's no way to speak about Indian history without it being a political statement. You can't describe a people's suffering without implying that somebody's at fault. There's no way around it. You can't write a book about South Africa without it being political, and you really can't write a book about Native Americans without being political. Even writing about common, ordinary life is going to strike some people as a political statement.

WD: Wasn't it Pete Seeger who once said that any time you assemble a group of people, for whatever purpose, you have the body politic?

Erdrich: That's what people on reservations say. You know, everything's political. Getting your teeth fixed is political. There's no way around it. I just don't want to become *polemical.* That's the big difference.

WD: Your mother was a Chippewa Indian; your grandfather tribal chairman of the Turtle Mountain reservation. Yet you once mentioned that you had a difficult time writing about your Native American heritage, that it forced you to come to terms with who you are. Why was that so difficult?

Erdrich: It's really quite simple. I have a mixture of backgrounds [as does Dorris, whose father was a member of the Modoc tribe], and I didn't want to simply exploit the most exotic part of my past. I felt uncomfortable in setting out to write about Native American life, so I didn't for a long time. But it became impossible to deny. I mean, you can't deny your own background. I guess I also had to work out a sense of responsibility. After I got out of college, I kicked around a lot, and I finally ended up working for the Boston Indian Council. Settling into that job and becoming comfortable with an urban community—which is very different from the reservation community—gave me another reference point. There were lots of people with mixed blood, lots of people who had their own confusions. I realized that this was part of my life—it wasn't something that I was making up—and that it was something I *wanted* to write about. I wanted to tell it because it was something that should be told. I was *forced* to write about it. [laughs] I didn't choose the material; it chose me. It's not as though I set out to do it.

WD: One senses that urgency in your work. There's also a very real feeling of oral history in your novels, as if your characters are real people saying to your readers, "sit down, I'm going to tell you a story."

Erdrich: I love that "sit down and tell you a story" idea. It's what I read for. I want everything in a book—I want the language and the ideas—but I want the story, too. I'm hooked on narrative. I think Michael's the same way, because we've got more books in mind than we can ever get to, so sometimes we just have to talk about them. We don't have the fear of talking a book out and never writing it. There are even a few which I think we could stand to talk out and never write [laughs] because we find great pleasure in it.

Why is it that, as humans, we have to have narrative? I don't know, but we do. I suppose it goes back to before the Bible; that storytelling cycle is in oral traditions of *all* cultures. You tell certain tales at certain times in the year. It's certainly part of the native tradition to never let go of those characters. I think Michael and I are working with something like that here: For better or worse, we can't seem to get rid of our characters.

WD: Did you hear a lot of stories when you were young? Was this something that really enthralled you?

Erdrich: Sure. It wasn't something distinct from everyday life, though; there wasn't anything mystical about it. The people in our families make everything into a story. They love to tell a good story. People just sit and the stories start coming, one after another. You just sort of grab the tail end of the last person's story: It reminds you of something and you keep going on. I suppose that when you grow up constantly hearing the stories rise, break and fall, it gets into you somehow.

WD: Getting back to this whole oral history idea, I'm very interested in the episodic nature of your books. A reader gets the feeling that the narrator is coming forth with the important events of his or her life, but the details aren't necessarily presented in a linear manner. How do you design these episodes?

Erdrich: To answer that I'll have to touch on the whole issue of working with Michael. The writing doesn't start out and proceed chronologically. It never seems to start in the beginning. Rather, it's as though we're building something around a center, but that center can be anywhere.

There's something very conversational about it. Michael and I form a story between ourselves when talking. That's our connection to the oral history. When we make up a story, we're talking. When we spin it between ourselves, we're talking about it. And when one of us is struck on something and goes to the other person to talk about it, some block comes unblocked. There are people who are worried about the fact that Michael and I work so closely with each other. They try to figure out exactly how this works: *"Who does what?" "What happens?"* So much goes into it, but we are separate writers. We're both individually involved in the work, and we both have that all-important writer's angst. [laughs]

WD: I'd like to ask a couple more nuts and bolts type questions before Michael get here. For instance, *Tracks,* as an actual title, is one that you had on your mind for nearly a decade. It's as if you felt compelled to write a book with that title.

Erdrich: It's been that way with all of our titles. Michael had *A Yellow Raft in Blue Water* [before beginning the book] too. We both have title collections. I think a title is like a magnet: It begins to draw these scraps of experience or conversation or memory to it. Eventually, it collects a book.

WD: Often all those independent little filings are originally published as short stories and wind up being incorporated into the novels. Some of your chapters, such as the second chapter of *Tracks,* have even won prestigious awards as stories. How do you assemble these different stories into a novel?

Erdrich: Well, it's like collecting scraps of thought and material. I'll piece together memories, stories, bits of conversation—everything. The different thing about *Tracks* is that nothing in the book *started out* as a short story. In fact, "Fleur," which was later published as a short story,

was adapted from the original *Tracks* book manuscript dating back to
when Michael and I first met. I was in the dumps and Michael said, "Go
back to *Tracks* and see what you can do with it." I was in a ruthless
mood, so I compressed every bit of material I found worthwhile in those
300 pages of book into one story. That's why there's so much happening in it. Then we looked at it and knew it was now a part of what the
novel *could* be, and it eventually became the second chapter in the
book.

   At this point Michael Dorris joins the conversation.

   WD: Now that I have the two of you together, I'd like to discuss your
collaborative adventure. Let's start with the most obvious question:
How does it work?
   Erdrich: One person—the one whose name is to be on the book—
will write the draft, will actually be confronted with those blank pages.
But we have this continuing process of talking about the work: We get
ideas and discuss them, often before we write anything down.
   Dorris: It's like that all the way through. "Don't use this line." Or,
"How about if such and such happens?" Or, "How about if this word
comes in?" We go on a word-by-word basis. As we've worked on
more and more books together, it's become harder to separate one or
another's contributions. A long time ago, when we first started out, in
those very early drafts of *Tracks,* or while building *Love Medicine*, it
was much clearer where I was coming in. Over the course of the next
three or four books, though, whatever each of us individually contributed was always perched on the other one's shoulder, even when we
weren't physically there. I guess the point to make is that ours isn't just
an editing relationship. That's *part* of it, but we're both also involved in
the planning. In a way, these books are like our children. Our emphasis
is on the books, rather than the attribution, and as the book develops,
we get so involved in the characters and the story that the last thing we
think of is whose name is going to be on it. When the book comes out
and we get reviews and so forth, I think we read them with equally
proprietary eyes.
   Erdrich: I know I took the reviews of *Yellow Raft* personally. We
both feel like we're responsible for each other's work.
   WD: What happens when you have strong differences in opinion?
Who has the final say?
   Dorris: Theoretically, whoever has the name on the book would have

the final say, but that authority has never been exercised. I mean, if the other person really objects strongly, you know there's something wrong. It may be that what that person suggests isn't the right solution, but something else *is*. You'll sulk and regret that it's not perfect, and you're disappointed and everything like that, but we've both concluded, after many, many such experiences, that the objecting person, whether it's Louise or me, is always right; the book will always be better for the objections. And so as we do more and more collaborations, we sulk less and less. It's much harder, I think, to be the person who says, "This doesn't work" than it is to hear it, because you risk derailing a train of thought and you don't want to do that. On the other hand, if you really feel parental toward the book, you can't *not* say what you really believe.

Erdrich: It's terribly important to have someone who cares about the work as much as I do, who is involved in the same way. We're probably a lot harder on each other than other editors are with writers because we really have more at stake in each other's work. We each tend to be quite ruthless about our ideas for the direction of the other's books. That can be very difficult sometimes because it's very hard to tell someone, "This doesn't work."

WD: What's the key to reaching this understanding? All this sounds good on paper, but even the most professional of writers has a creative ego.

Dorris: You just learn to trust that the other person is right. It's like having children: The fictional characters belong to both of us, regardless of who's sort of trotting them out at any given time. I think we respect that. It's all give and take.

Erdrich: Right. Marriage is a process of coming to trust the other person over the years, and it's the same thing with our writing. I started out being very wary of collaboration and working together, but I trusted it and trusted it, and when I would have trouble with it, I would really look at the work and I'd realize that it was better for the efforts. In a lot of ways, I'd have to sacrifice the ego for the work, because it worked better to go back and forth and not resist changes. It's not easy—sometimes I want to hang onto something because it makes sense to me, and it seems as though it would be impossible to relinquish that control over it—but I know in my heart that Michael is right. It's been a humbling experience.

WD: Let's look at all this on a practical level, using *A Yellow Raft in*

Blue Water as an example. Michael, I assume that you had the original idea for the story.

Dorris: Yes.

WD: How was that idea developed into a book?

Dorris: Actually, it started out as a different story entirely. We were sitting in the living room, talking about seminal experiences, and I said I remembered that once, when I was a kid and went out to a state park with my family, I swam out to a raft and there was a man in his 40s sitting there. He was a Jewish-Polish man, a concentration camp survivor with numbers tattoed on his arm. For some reason, he talked to me as if I were an adult. I stayed there for about an hour and a half, and he talked to me about his experiences. As I was swimming back, I realized that I was a more serious person than I'd been when I swam out. I'd actually grown.

I said to Louise, "Even though it's been 25 years since that happened, I have a vivid visual memory of it, and it centers on that yellow raft in blue water." And she said, "You should write that as a memoir." So I went to the computer, right away that next minute, and wrote "A Yellow Raft in Blue Water" at the top of the page. Then I started writing something that had almost nothing in common with my memory: It was the section in which Rayona [one of the book's main characters] went out to the raft with Father Tom, except in that first draft the protagonist was Raymond, a male character. So I wrote about three chapters and we talked about it as it was going on. I kept thinking that somehow this concentration camp survivor would come in, but he never did, and while I certainly didn't have a sexual experience on the raft, like Raymond did, my character still swam out one way and came back changed.

Soon after I began writing we traveled to Minnesota. We were driving in the car, and I said, "You know, I'm really getting bored with this character." He was going off to the state park, and the book was about all of his relations with the counselors and the young girls and so forth; it was becoming a story of a boy's coming of age, and that's not what I wanted to write about. We kicked it back and forth and decided to try it with a female character, with Rayona. Suddenly it became a much more interesting book. Once we settled into the project, I'd write some and we'd talk about it; I'd write some more, take it to Louise, she'd like it or not like it, and she'd suggest where it should go next.

When I got to its final stages, Louise kept wanting me to rewrite the first part of the "Christine" section. At that point, I didn'tknow if the story ended after Christine or what; I hadn't even decided if there was going to be an "Ida" part [the section that now closes the book]. Louise went up to Manitoulin Island to visit some people and do some quilling. While she was gone, I wrote the first four or five pages of "Ida," and when she called from a phone booth on Manitoulin Island, I read it to her and she liked it and suggested a few changes.

By the time she came back, we were at the stage of doing the galleys of *The Beet Queen* and the final polishing of *Yellow Raft*. And we had a few arguments. For example, Louise wanted to leave in Ida's line, "I never grew up but I got old," which I was going to change—

WD: That's a great line.

Dorris: Well, you agree with her, then. [laughs] And there was a bit of dialogue in *The Beet Queen*, in which Celestine used a very flowery turn of phrase. It was a beautiful piece of writing, but I just didn't think that Celestine would say it; it didn't seem consistent with her. As it happened, an interviewer arrived while we were in the middle of this fight, so we just said, "Okay, I'll leave this in, you take that out." And that's the way it worked.

WD: It's hard to imagine *Yellow Raft* without the "Ida" section. That last segment of the novel ties together all the loose ends.

Dorris: See, I had no idea *what* Ida's story was when I got to that point of the book. I didn't know why she was called Aunt Ida. I didn't know why she treated Christine and Lee differently. I didn't know who Clara was. I didn't have the faintest idea.

WD: But all of that information is essential to everything that occurs earlier in the book.

Dorris: Well, I think we've both come to the point of trusting that there's always an explanation for any loose ends in the writing. We just have to look at the work closely enough and it will emerge.

WD: That's an interesting idea, especially in light of the detailed family tree that's been drawn up for Louise's books. It all looks so planned and orderly.

Erdrich: That family tree was all in our heads—

Dorris: Rather than having a plan beforehand, we figured out who people were afterward. Some reviewers talked about how they were sure that we had the fourth book in mind before *Tracks* was written, that we knew exactly how everything was going to be. They gave us all this credit for knowing what we were doing. [laughs] It's very kind, but not very true.

Erdrich: Absolutely not. If we'd known that these were going to be interrelated books, I suppose we would have started at the beginning.

Dorris: If we'd even known they were going to be *books* . . . I mean, *Love Medicine* started as a short story.

Erdrich: Right.

WD: How would you suggest these books be read? In what order?

Dorris: *Tracks, Beet Queen* and *Love Medicine* in that order. I mean, that's the way they will be if the famous boxed set is ever published. [laughs]

Erdrich: Yes, and we're supposed to have conceived of *that* from the very beginning, too!

Dorris: We're not even sure anymore that there won't be *more* books.

Erdrich: I wonder if there are more of these [points to *Yellow Raft*].

WD: Well?

Dorris: I don't know. We've talked about letting the male characters have their say, but it isn't in the immediate plan. We have some other books to finish before we get to something like that.

WD: I wanted to ask about that. You've signed a lucrative contract for the novel *The Crown of Columbus*. That book [published in May by HarperCollins], unlike your other works, bears both of your names. What can you tell me about that book and the way you collaborated in its writing?

Erdrich: It's about a contemporary woman discovering Columbus's previously unknown manuscripts and diaries. We worked on it in a different way. We both faced the blank page. I gave Michael what I'd written, he gave me what he'd written, and we were free to add scenes and play around with it a lot more than we've done with the other books. We've had a certain protocol in the past, but this project is especially interesting because we both wrote it. We tried to keep each other's words, though. We didn't cut so much as add.

Dorris: It's a book we've talked about for years. We'd been doing the historical and ethnographical research, reading everything we could get our hands on about Columbus and Spain and so forth. We actually plotted it while driving across Saskatchewan. We crossed the border of Saskatchewan going east, and if you've ever been there, you know it's

the *flattest* place one can imagine. There is nothing to interrupt it except
Regina, which is in the middle. It's the perfect drive for contemplation,
so we'd scheduled the Columbus book for Saskatchewan. [laughs] As
soon as we crossed the border, we started plotting it, and by the time we
got to Manitoba, we really had it right down. And the result was, in
effect, the proposal we submitted when we auctioned the book.

WD: And it's more or less about a contemporary Native American
who discovers Columbus through his papers?

Dorris: Right. The narrator is a woman who teaches Native American history, and she's an Indian herself. She's in her late 30s and is
pregnant, frustrated, and coming up for tenure. Her university's alumni
magazine assigns her to do an essay on Columbus from the Indian point
of view, which is the most boring thing that she can possibly imagine.

But she goes to the library and eventually gets hooked on the thing
because Columbus is such a weird character. She's a person who has
been disappointed continuously in her life, as Columbus was. He was an
uneducated but obsessive personality who discovered this notion that the
world was round when he was washed ashore in Portugal. Up to that
time, he hadn't really thought about it. He hadn't even learned to read
yet. All the intellectuals of his day thought the world was round, but
Columbus had the fanaticism of the convert.

Once he got the idea in his head, he just badgered and badgered and
badgered. But the odd thing was that he never, in his whole life, could
accept what he had actually found. He went to his grave trying to prove
that he'd been to India. In fact, he was taken back in chains from his
last voyage because he'd become so flipped out over this issue.

And the parallel is: Will this woman, whose name is Vivian Twostar,
be able to make her final leap of discovery, in terms of revisionist history, in terms of what might have been, in terms of who he was, or will
she be stuck the same way he was, in a kind of swamp of preconception?

WD: It sounds as if you both really thought out this character—or,
perhaps, *talked out* is the more appropriate description.

Erdrich: Well, every day, about 3, if it's nice and the kids are okay,
we go for a long walk out in the country, and a lot of times our conversations just start rolling on the characters we've been working on. We'll
start speculating about what could happen or what kind of physical
detail might lend itself to a bigger storyline or a twist in the storyline.
And then one of us will go back and write it down.

Dorris: Every time we look at a catalogue, we decide what each of our current characters would select. Or if we go to a restaurant, we decide what clothes they'd wear, what each of them would choose from the menu, what they would say to the waitress. When we go through an airport, we sort of pick out people who look like the characters. We're constantly trying to get a three-dimensional picture, and then we just put down a fraction of that when we actually write.

Dorris: Oh, we *dream* about these people. We wake up in the middle of the night and have new episodes for them. I'm serious. We really do.

Erdrich: We can't get rid of them.

An Interview with Michael Dorris

Allan Chavkin and Nancy Feyl Chavkin/1992

This interview was conducted by telephone on 28 October 1992.

Chavkin: Dave Brown in his Des Moines *Register* review of *A Yellow Raft in Blue Water* remarks, "Dorris writes as though he were born composing novels." When did you begin writing fiction? Are you able to write with ease?

Dorris: I wrote short stories when I was in college and wanted very much to be a writer. After I was subjected to some very nasty reviews by one of my peers in the school newspaper, I stopped writing fiction for almost ten years. Whether I write with ease or not, I can't say because I don't know how other people do it. But I do know that it's a lot of work. When the process is going on and I have time for it and I am into a character, it is entirely pleasurable. I could never say that it was painful—it is a pleasure—but I don't know if that's the same as "ease."

Chavkin: How many pages of fiction can you write on a typical day?

Dorris: I don't think there is a typical day, but certainly not many pages.

Chavkin: Do you ever suffer from writer's block?

Dorris: No, I usually am working on more than one project at a time and in different genres. For instance, next year I have a book of short stories and a book of essays coming out, and also a book of journalism based on a trip I took to Zimbabwe last summer. I'm working on a novel, a screen treatment, a play, and poetry. If one becomes blocked, I move on to something else.

Chavkin: Do you write on a word processor or in longhand?

Dorris: Both. I certainly edit on a word procesor, though.

Chavkin: Are there certain times of day when you work better than others?

Dorris: I get up early, sometimes at four o'clock. The best writing time for me almost always is from 4 A.M. to about 8 A.M.

Chavkin: Are there certain places where you work better than others?

Dorris: I think you get into a habit of being in the same place and

184

having everything stabilized so that there are constants in the environment, and your imagination becomes the variable.

Chavkin: Some writers, such as Bertolt Brecht and Jean Paul Sartre, could write in public places. But many other writers emphasize that they need complete isolation to write. What about you?

Dorris: I think you often come up with lines in public places. I sometimes will jot down a line on any available piece of paper while driving along in a car, but when I'm trying to reword a piece, perfect it, isolation is important and quiet is important. I take a lot of notes in public places, but I wouldn't say that I do much writing there.

Chavkin: Are you writing all the time? Do you take a "vacation" between major projects?

Dorris: No, I don't. With small children, you're never doing anything all the time. Louise and I share responsibility for various aspects of the kids, and we have large families and busy lives. Besides, writing isn't something I like to take a vacation from; it is something that, when there is time for it, it's so nice to be able to do. It is the fulfillment of a long ambition. It's work that feels like pleasure.

Chavkin: What's a typical working day like for you?

Dorris: Well, again, typical is a hard word. An ideal working day would be to get up very early and work for three hours or so on original stuff, get the kids off to school, have a cup of coffee with Louise and talk about what I've done in the morning, rework some of that stuff, take a long walk in the afternoon and talk about either what she's working on or what I'm working on, be on the telephone in the afternoon, pick the kids up from school, and read in the evening. That's the perfect day, rarely achieved.

Chavkin: Before beginning a novel, do you have a detailed outline of the plot, or do you discover the story as you write?

Dorris: Absolutely the latter. I would find it boring to work with an outline.

Chavkin: Have you ever tried to work from a very detailed outline, where essentially every scene is planned ahead of time?

Dorris: Never. If it doesn't surprise me line to line, there's something wrong with it as far as I'm concerned.

Chavkin: What prompts you to write—is it a situation, a character, an idea, a memory, an image, a feeling?

Dorris: It varies; sometimes it's a sentence that calls for expansion. I think once the process starts, you get interested in the character and you want to see what that character will do in various situations. I would say that it is more character driven than anything else. Even the nonfiction tends to be stories that revolve around characters who work out their personalities in the course of incidents.

Chavkin: When you write, do you ever use such things as charts, genealogies, maps, biographical dossiers of characters, or anything like that?

Dorris: No, Louise and I have generally talked about the characters extensively before and during the time of writing about them. We talk about their tastes, dress, style, looks, and all of that kind of stuff, though most of that is not ultimately included on the page.

Chavkin: When you compose a novel, do you find yourself moving scenes to different parts of the novel as you write the various drafts?

Dorris: It happens occasionally.

Chavkin: John Updike revised *Rabbit, Run* and John Fowles rewrote *The Magus* after their original publication. Do you ever feel the desire to substantially revise a novel after you publish it?

Dorris: No, I don't think so. It gets revised so much before it goes out of the house to the publisher that it takes on a life almost of its own. Louise is expanding *Love Medicine*; it's going to be reissued next year with about sixty additional pages. But that isn't so much a revision as it is including things that weren't there before. One of the short stories in my new collection is a kind of "pre-quel" to two characters in *A Yellow Raft in Blue Water* that I couldn't get out of my head, but it's not a revision.

Chavkin: How much do you revise before submitting your manuscript for publication?

Dorris: Tremendous amounts. Between the first draft and the twelfth draft, parts of sentences may survive, but not much more than that. Much of the revision involves cutting, and much of it is also the product of Louise's reactions, suggestions, and comments which are part of every round of revision. Again, I don't know what other people do, but it strikes me that revision is at least as important a part of the process as the initial creation of the draft.

Chavkin: Are your revisions mainly a matter of polishing the style or are there major changes in character, plot, setting, and so forth?

Dorris: Both. Some are very major—sometimes even changing the gender of a character.

Chavkin: As with *A Yellow Raft in Blue Water*?

Dorris: Yes.

Chavkin: If you get stuck at a certain part of a novel that you're working on, will you move on to another part?

Dorris: I've done that, yes. Sometimes there are incidents or scenes that you know are eventually going to happen, and I get impatient to work on them. And sometimes if that desire is strong enough, it probably shouldn't be denied, so a finished vignette floats out there until the rest of the novel catches up with it.

Chavkin: Is there any part of writing that you especially enjoy, and is there any part of the writing process that you find difficult to do, such as dialogue, setting up a scene, constructing a plot, that kind of thing?

Dorris: Well, let me see . . . I think the answer to your question is that one always enjoys what works, and if something is working on a particular day, whether it's the dialogue or the scene, it is enjoyable. If it's not working, it's terrible. But I wouldn't say that there's one thing more than another. The challenge is always in putting two words together in a way that seems fresh, at least at the time that you're doing it. I like the process of revision, although I often hate the reason for revision—and that is, if Louise tells me that a paragraph is terrible or it's not working or that I should change direction or drop a line I'm wedded to—it takes a while to get over that hump. However, in my experience, she's always right, so the lag time, the sulk time, is shorter than it used to be.

Chavkin: Has film influenced your writing?

Dorris: Do you mean the fact that some of my books are going to be made into films?

Chavkin: No, we were referring to the art of the cinema.

Dorris: I'm sure it has, but I've no idea how. I like movies, and I used to go to about six movies a week while I was in college. Georgetown was close to a movie theater that changed double features of forties and fifties and thirties movies four or five times a week, and it cost a dollar to get in, so I've seen a lot of movies—but I don't really know exactly how that has influenced my writing.

Chavkin: How do you know when a story or a novel is finished and ready to be sent out for publication?

Dorris: I think that when a piece has sat around for a month and is then reread and I don't see things to change. Almost always, until it is over, I will find parts that need to be revised. At times, I'm amazed that

I could have been so stupid as to have written this line or not written that line. But when I don't have that reaction, and after it has settled for a while, then I think it's ready to submit for publication.

Chavkin: How much influence on your work are such people as editors and publishers? Do they suggest substantial changes or is the book ready to be set in type when you send it out?

Dorris: It has so far been the case that *the* major influence is Louise, as I think I probably am on her work. We're so much tougher on each other's work than editors tend to be. We revise so much and rework so much before we send out a manuscript for an editor to see that by that time there is very little to revise, maybe a line here or a word there, certainly copyediting changes that are very helpful and made, but it has not been the case that a major alteration in the work has happened as a result of an editor's urging.

Chavkin: Looking at some of the proofs of Bellow's novels, one can see some significant revisions, but that is not the case with you, is it?

Dorris: Well, there are huge changes between Louise and me which you would see if you looked at the stacks of revisions of each draft—they're covered with writing and suggestions and comments and cross-outs and substitute words and all that kind of stuff. But by the time the copy leaves our house, the work is basically done. We continue that revision process when it comes back at the copyedited stage, making our revisions and suggesting revisions on each other's work—but, as I said, we are far more intrusive than editors, or least the editors with whom we've worked. We recognize what we want when it is done, so there hasn't been that much advice offered—nor has there been advice offered that has been rejected. That just hasn't been part of the process.

Chavkin: A lot of writers have suggested that in the process of writing, they are attempting to discover something they didn't know—is that your experience?

Dorris: Yes—what happens next—what X character will do in Y situation. Sometimes when I used to teach, I would discover something new by listening to myself ramble on about a subject. You have that same process in writing. Louise and I know that something is working when one of us goes to the other in the middle of a workday and says, "You'll never believe what this character just said!" If we're lucky, we're both surprised, but not so much so that we say, "Impossible."

Chavkin: Do you have a method for selecting the names of your characters?

Dorris: No, they suggest themselves. Titles always seem to precede our books, and sometimes the character's name precedes the character. But there is no particular method.

Chavkin: Henry Miller talks about feeling almost "possessed" at times while writing, almost as if his writing is being dictated to him and he just has to copy down what is being "given" to him. Did you ever have an experience such as this?

Dorris: Yes, but I don't think I would express it in quite that way. It sounds like Mrs. Yeats. I think that when you know characters very well, however, you get to a point where you are listening to them rather than putting words in their mouths. When you know them very well and you know a situation well and you put the two together, there are only certain things that they *could* say or certain reactions that they *could* have because they are unique individuals. You are listening for that correct, appropriate, possible interaction of setting and individual, and that's very exciting. That's when it is really going well.

Chavkin: Do you think that there is anything wrong with basing fictional characters on people you know?

Dorris: It would make me uncomfortable because in a sense you inevitably presume to know your fictional character better than we ever truly know another real person. And so I would tend to make mistakes if I based a character on a real individual, and those mistakes might be hurtful.

Chavkin: Some authors have suggested that when they write a novel, some of their characters become unmanageable or least go their own way despite the author's plans for them. Other authors, such as Nabokov, have insisted that their characters are their "slaves." What's your experience between these two extremes?

Dorris: Well, I never make plans for them, so basically I am along for the ride. For instance, in *Morning Girl* I didn't have any idea what the characters would say. I knew what Taino people ate, I knew what the weather was like, I knew that everybody knew each other's business because they lived on a small island, and I knew from Columbus that they were peaceful, but what particular incidents I would include, I had no idea. Then it occurred to me that mirrors were a big trade item, and I wondered why that was, and I came up with one story line about the fact that people didn't know what they themselves looked like. I knew also that in hunting and gathering societies a large percentage of babies didn't survive their first six months of life, and so I dealt with a miscarriage. Trying to imagine how that happened and how it was going to take place and how people were going to react, I basically learned along with my character, as hokey as that may sound.

Chavkin: Have you ever tried dictating your work into a tape recorder?

Dorris: I couldn't possibly do that. I can barely manage a tape recorder with correspondence. There's something palpable about seeing the words juxtaposed with each other that is all part of whatever gets generated.

Chavkin: That's interesting because one of the things that seems so marvelous about your work is your ability to capture the speaking voice, and we were wondering if on some occasions you spoke aloud before you wrote the passages down to actually hear how they sound.

Dorris: Sometimes I will orally try out a line, but it will just be me sitting at my desk. Everything of Louise's and mine gets read aloud to each other many times before it gets sent out, and there are a lot of aids that I think are helpful, especially with technology, in getting things perfected. For instance, to print out each draft in a different font makes it look fresh on a page and you can see inconsistencies or word repetitions, or something that you wouldn't notice if the text all looked the same every time it was printed out. I certainly use technology, but I've never worked successfully with a tape recorder. I always think that maybe I can, and I carry a cassette player along with me when I travel, and then I wind up jotting notes on napkins or something anyway. I use the tape recorder in interviews, when I was doing *The Broken Cord* for instance, and then transcribed all the tapes myself with a little machine, but I never manage to use one with original stuff.

Chavkin: Is writing therapeutic at all for you? Do you think that there is any truth to D.H. Lawrence's idea of casting off one's illnesses in books?

Dorris: I certainly have never thought of it in that way. I'm sure that there is some psychological drive that channels people into one artistic direction or means of expression as opposed to another, but basically when you're dealing with fictional characters, you just want to know them better. Whether that is your innermost self that you're knowing or somebody that is hypothetical, I can't say. Certainly none of these characters are autobiographical substitutes for me, at least in fiction. Perhaps my mother would disagree, though!

Chavkin: Should writers examine social issues in their fiction?

Dorris: That's a tough one. Let's put it this way—I think it usually doesn't work when it's self-conscious. Personally, I'm much more comfortable in doing the explicit examination of social issues in non-fiction. Fictional characters are part of a context that certainly involves social issues, but I don't think the writer can be any more aware of those issues than his or her characters are, and that's a product of their particular constellation of personality. Being oblivious to a social issue may in fact be part of who they are. I think that I have to make a con-scious decision sometimes not to let characters speak my words, but rather speak their own, and if the social issue is compelling enough, it will break through the whole work rather than in a kind of didactic statement. This is the exact opposite, for instance, of the Op-Ed pieces that I like to write or the journalism, the Zimbabwe reporting that I did this summer that's going to be published by Milkweed as a little book. In those cases, though I tell stories, they are stories told to emphasize a political point, and they are not fictional. They are true stories, though framed in a way that I hope engages the reader.

Chavkin: Do you think a writer has an obligation to become involved in politics?

Dorris: Let me put it a different way. I think that being a writer provides a wonderful opportunity to become involved in politics. One of the great benefits to me of having an audience through fiction is that some of those people will read my nonfiction and consider it seriously. Writing provides a forum that I find very valuable and very rewarding. If you feel strongly about something politically, then I believe you have an obligation to speak out, but one has to do so sparingly and conscientiously.

Chavkin: Why sparingly?

Dorris: Because you can't try to influence opinions on every subject. You have to select the issues that you care deeply enough about to put yourself on the line for in print and then work hard to inform yourself. You have a duty to people who are generous enough to read you not to go off half-cocked. When you write you should attempt to say some-thing that, in a sense, collapses your experience and makes it available for somebody else without them having to have lived that particular thing. That opportunity is a privilege, but it is also a responsibility.

Chavkin: You've had a tremendous influence on some severe social problems, such as the abuse of alcohol. You dramatically changed the way people perceive drinking and pregnancy. That would be one example of the kind of thing you're talking about.

Dorris: Well, I hope I have been of some help, but really it was simply the translation of my son's life. What compelled *The Broken Cord* was something about Abel that didn't work just on me but affected many people who knew him, that brought out a sense of indignation. I've known a lot of people who have disabilities, but there was something charismatic about Abel that inspired, that sustained, anger, and that was the basis for that book. Anger may not be the right word— "emotion" perhaps.

Chavkin: His autobiographical account at the end was a very moving part of that book. It was very powerful.

Dorris: Oh, it was an extraordinary accomplishment.

Chavkin: Some people argue that it is more difficult to write a good short story than a novel; do you believe that? Which do you prefer writing?

Dorris: When I was recently on a panel with Louisa Valenezuela in Seattle, she said something very wise: "Everything you write has its own time of day and its own appropriate length." I'm not usually a very good poet, and usually it's hard for me to write short stories. It's very difficult for me to write in the third person, to be an omniscient narrator. And so I naturally think that the most laudable genres in which to write are poetry and omniscient narrator short stories. One always seeks the thing that is most difficult as the challenge. But I'm not complaining. I find pleasure in working on whatever I'm working on. For fifteen years, I was a person who didn't even know that he was a frustrated writer, and now to suddenly be able to write full time is such a gift and a surprise in life that quite frankly I really don't have any gripes at all. I'm a very lucky person.

Chavkin: There are a number of writers—Conrad, Golding, and others—who started writing relatively late. Do you ever have any regrets for starting writing fiction relatively late?

Dorris: No, I don't. One of the tools that a writer has to have is material, and you gain material from experience. The greatest treasure a writer has is wide experience—and not self-conscious experience—so there is no part of my life before I became a full time writer that I would give up. You can go back and re-wish your life, but I am glad I *finally* got started in literature.

Chavkin: When you write, do you write for yourself, or a friend, an editor, or do you have an ideal reader in mind? Do you have a specific audience in mind?

Dorris: Louise is my ideal reader. Somebody asked me in Seattle recently if I would write even if I had no readers, and I pointed out to them that actually I had done precisely that for years. So I guess I have to say, I write for myself, but that having readers also is a lot more fulfilling than not. There is a human compulsion to communicate. I come from a family where everybody talks, and getting a word in edge-wise is one of the first skills I had to learn. And perhaps it's as simple as that being a writer, I can communicate without interruption. I'm temporarily in control of the conversation. But I don't know. I'm not a very self-reflective person. I don't think to myself, "Why am I doing what I'm doing?" or "How do I feel about what I'm doing?" I've basically gone through life following opportunities that present themselves and that method has usually presented a pleasant surprise or two. It's like working without an outline: being open to the next path that opens even though you don't know quite where it's headed. The pleasure of the unexpected. I rarely stand back and contemplate the process or my stance toward it.

Chavkin: Do you ever become annoyed at reviewers who fail to understand your work or something you've done in it?

Dorris: I guess I take responsibility if a serious reader fails to understand something I write. One of the things Louise taught me very early is that you can't be around to explain to somebody what you really meant with a line. It either has to speak for itself or it doesn't. The only times I have become annoyed with reviewers is when they don't read what's on the page or criticize something that isn't there, bring their own agenda to a review that in a sense manufactures a hypothetical flawed book and then attributes me as its author. The review that most annoyed me was one on *The Crown of Columbus* in the *Cleveland Plain Viewer* by the book review editor who asserted a number of things about the book and then criticized them. The problem was, her assertions weren't correct. For instance, she said that the book was predictable in terms of gender stereotyping because Vivian had to go to the grocery store and shop when she and Roger went to the Bahamas, but that's absolutely backwards. *Roger* went to the grocery store. The only actual letter I wrote to a reviewer of that book was in response to that review because I thought it was unfair.

Chavkin: Is it possible to discover new territory for fiction or do you believe, as some writers have said, there's nothing new under the sun?

Dorris: There are infinite new possibilities. For instance, take a writer like Barbara Pym, whose work I respect and from whom I always learn. She's writing about things that you would think have been done to death—small village life in England, with almost a drawing room cast of characters—and yet somehow by juxtaposing her words in a certain way, it's as if nobody has ever thought of the situation before. That's what it's all about.

Chavkin: And infinite amount of new to discover for both content and technique?

Dorris: I guess so. I never believe in altering technique simply for the sake of doing something different. The ultimate exploration is the complexity of human relationships. Technique shouldn't get in the way of that. So what I am after is the most unobtrusive technique possible, so that readers will forget they are in a book, forget that I'm out there dealing with characters, and have a very intimate experience where nothing calls attention to artifice. Some avant-garde techniques distract me—maybe I'm just not smart enough to figure them out—but I like a very unobtrusive style in which no word jars you out of your absorption in the story. There's this thin line between originality and cuteness that one has to avoid crossing.

Chavkin: Your comment reminds us of Arthur Miller's view of his writing. That is, he likes to think that everybody, from a professor to a grocery clerk can understand his work. In effect, he says, there's nothing wrong with being clear and being able to be understood by . . .

Dorris: Absolutely! There's probably not a lot of things I agree with Mr. Miller about, but that one I'm sure. Did you say Henry Miller or Arthur Miller?

Chavkin: Arthur Miller.

Dorris: Arthur Miller? Oh well, Arthur Miller I'll agree with. Henry Miller, I don't know. But I think that's true. I'd also add that *Morning Girl* is viewed not just as a children's book. Older people have read it, too. So, it isn't just the professor and the grocery clerk. It's the ten-

year-old and the sixty-year-old and the thirty-year-old all taking something different from the same text; each finds something in the piece
that's involving. When they re-read it at a different age, its going to be
a different experience. When I worked as an anthropologist in native
communities that are primarily oral, I loved to observe mixed audiences
listening to the same story. Often it was familiar to all, but variable
qualitatively and in terms of its content depending on who was listening.

Chavkin: Do you have any advice for beginning writers?

Dorris: Don't be discouraged by bad reviews. Find a perfect reader
and insist that this person be absolutely candid with you when he or she
assesses your work. Keep a journal. Write everyday. Never be satisfied.
And don't pen yourself into too small of an arena. Try lots of different
things. Don't get defined by a narrow category.

Chavkin: Are you ever afraid that some reviewers might do that to
you?

Dorris: I think that the frustration both Louise and I felt in the beginning was being identified as ethnic writers rather than as writers who
happened to be mixed bloods and sometimes wrote about American
Indians. There is a tendency to pigeonhole anybody who is not, shall we
say, mainstream, to be condescending and patronizing and place them in
some little corner of literature. And that isn't what our ambition was all
about. Our ambition was not to limit our subject or our readership or our
perspective beyond whatever it happened to be, what it might be.

Chavkin: Saul Bellow has been upset when reviewers would label
him "a Jewish writer" because he saw that as a way of suggesting that
somehow what he was doing was unimportant to the mainstream and
just involved a small group of people. I guess that's the kind of thing
you're talking about.

Dorris: It is. And it's also a matter of who certain papers or magazines may choose as a reviewer. If only someone happens to be from the
West is asked to comment on our books, if I'm asked to review only
books by or about other Indians, that is the kind of self-perpetuating
literary ghetto that's totally unnecessary and sometimes very insulting.
One of the reasons I think I write in so many different fields is because
I don't like to be defined or to fulfill expectations that are set apriori by
somebody else.

Chavkin: Are there any writers who would be good models for
young writers trying to learn their craft? When you were learning your

craft were there any key novels that taught you some important lessons about technique?

Dorris: Well, I have always read constantly. I read cereal boxes. I read *T.V. Guide.* I read two newspapers a day. I probably read five books a week. So I would say read everything and read a lot and learn how to accomplish certain things and how to avoid certain pitfalls from the books or articles or whatever you're reading. I read a lot of plays, for instance. I went to graduate school initially in History of the Theater, and I know that I learned about dialogue simply from reading plays and listening to plays. You learn from the classics, you learn from Shakespeare, you learn from Faulkner, you learn from very American writers like Eugene O'Neill and Sinclair Lewis and Tennessee Williams things about plot and the cadence of speech. But more than from anyone I've learned from Louise. She is the person who initially instructed me and still does—how to pace and how not to overstate, which is my biggest danger in writing. I think I've learned to spot it better now than I used to, but that's the perpetual flaw of my early drafts and possibly of my final product.

Chavkin: You've always read a great deal? Your comments remind us of that amusing anecdote you tell in "Life Stories" of how a man for whom you mowed lawns never seemed to have the change to pay you and suggested instead that you could select books from his library for payment for your work, and you stated that you kept mowing by day in hopes of turning pages by night.

Dorris: I always read. I was a very lonely kid. I didn't have brothers and sisters. I was not popular with other kids because I was very adult-oriented, but I was always very popular with librarians who used to give prizes for reading a book a day and writing book reviews during summer vacation. I did that with gusto. My aunt let me use her library card, and so I got to check out adult books. I'm the first person on either side of my family to go very far in school. And yet, stories about ancestors, about my grandfather whom I never knew, for instance, were my role models. After being a carpenter all day, apparently he would come home and lie on the floor and read Victorian poetry aloud. He went only as far as the sixth grade, but he loved books. We always had books in the house. One aunt aspired to work in the theater, another would often write letters to the editor of the newspaper. Communication by written word was very very important.

Chavkin: Today books seem threatened by television and film. In fact, Jerzy Kosinski has observed that reading serious novels is done not only by a small percentage of the enlightened public, and others have pointed out that the audience for the serious novel is decreasing. Some have predicted the situation of the novel may go the way of poetry, that is to say, to be read only in the university. Do you think this is a real possibility?

Dorris: I don't know. It is a unique pleasure to sit down with a book and basically populate it with your own imagination. Television or film are no substitutes for that experience. Certainly we need an educational system that introduces people when they're young to the joy of that experience. But to tell the truth, I always watched a lot of television, too. My mother and her sisters watch television for hours every night of their lives and always have since we got our first T.V. So, it isn't that I'm a snob about mass media, it's just apples and oranges. There's nothing, *nothing* like reading, just as there's nothing like music; it's its own thing. If there are fewer readers of serious novels, it's probably because the educational system hasn't prepared people to appreciate them or to enjoy them the way that it should. But that is not to say that the joy of reading has diminished, because even if the level is less impressive then it might be . . . I think that there is still . . . people go out and buy the *National Enquirer,* they read magazines, they read comic strips. The challenge is preparing people for the complexity and delight of a deeply complicated book.

Chavkin: So essentially the public schools need to make people better readers.

Dorris: They need to introduce reading earlier. It's important to offer each child that amazing experience that I remember having with *A Connecticut Yankee in King Arthur's Court,* the first book I read all night. I was so impressed with myself both for staying up and for being so involved in that story. I never quite got over it. I was in the fourth grade. It was a seminal experience.

Chavkin: For some writers, completing a work is a kind of psychological shock. You think of Faulkner, his going on a drinking binge after he finishes a novel. What's your experience?

Dorris: I miss the characters. I miss *being* that character for a certain number of hours a day. But these days with publishing, after you go through the copyediting phase and the galleys and the catalogue copy,

you're weary of the book and then there's a year between when you
finished the book and when the book appears, by which time, if you've
got any sense at all, you're working on something new so that you're
not preoccupied with the critical reaction. So, no, I think by the time
I'm finished with something I'm anxious to move on. Usually I've got
four or five things that I plan to do, and it's a question of which one
gets priority after a particular project is completed. Psychological shock
or post-partem depression are not problems. So far.

Chavkin: In your book, *Native Americans: Five Hundred Years
After,* you write: "There are many things Indian people are not," and,
"they are not represented by the stereotypes of Hollywood or most
fiction." Would it be correct to assume that in your fiction, one of your
goals is to undermine such stereotypes and present Native Americans as
individuals?

Dorris: Yes. Absolutely.

Chavkin: Were there other goals in writing *A Yellow Raft in Blue
Water*? Explore certain attitudes or ways of looking at the human condition? Challenge people's assumptions about some things?

Dorris: No, not a primary goal. That book had a curious evolution.
Louise and I were sitting in the living room one time talking about how
sometimes in the middle of an experience you *recognize* that you're in
the middle of an experience that's very important. I told her that one
time when I was a kid, in a state park, I swam out to a raft and there
was a man on the raft probably about forty or so, and for some reason
he talked to me. I was eleven, yet he talked to me as if I had a brain in
my head. He turned out to be a Jewish-Polish-concentration camp
survivor with a number tattooed on his arm. For about an hour and a
half he related some of his experiences, and then it was time for me to
leave. As I was swimming back I had this thought that the world was
changed, different for me, having heard him. I said to Louise, "I have
this very visceral memory of that experience, almost visual. I see this
yellow raft in blue water." She said, "You should write that as a memoir." I went in my office and wrote on a pad *A Yellow Raft in Blue
Water* and then instead of that factual story coming out, a little part of
what eventually turned into the book appeared. And so, I guess that's
what the novel is about: that sense of being self-aware during important
times every rare once-in-awhile. I guess that's the intent of the book.
But, again, I'm not very reflective—and so it's also a matter of simply

being interested in what happens to these people, and then something in the subconscious creates a kind of paradigm that has resonations and you don't see the whole picture until it's all done. If then.

Chavkin: How much time did it take you to write *A Yellow Raft in Blue Water*?

Dorris: Well, let's see. I was working on *The Broken Cord*, doing interviews while I was writing the fiction. But it was about a year and a half from the time I started until the time that the manuscript finally was set into type.

Chavkin: Were there any technical problems that you had to solve when you were writing the book?

Dorris: I wrote in a sort of time-backwards fashion and the question was, was that a problem? I didn't know how editors would react to it or how readers would feel about it. I finally decided to risk it. But otherwise, though of course there were certain parts that needed more rewrites than others, there was no particular problem.

Chavkin: So, if we understand you correctly, you knew from the very beginning that you were going to tell the story in reverse chronological order.

Dorris: No. I didn't know that it was anyone's story but the first narrator's. And I didn't even know when I got to the end of her section—where Rayona is outside and has been thrown off the horse again and the mother comes out and gives the story about the letter and the end of the world. I was all set to keep going on and see what happened to Rayona next, but it just suddenly occurred to me that her tale, for now, was over. Maybe it was a novella, but to put another word in her mouth would be wrong. It was enough. And so there I was faced with something that was too short for a book, yet questions remained, "Who was this mother and why was she so cranky? What's her story?" So I tried to figure that out. Then I thought it was all over with, except that there was this dangling weird character who insists upon being called "Aunt Ida," but was supposed to be Christine's mother. Why was she called Aunt Ida? I had no idea. It was just one of those details that gets inserted while you're writing, and at the time you don't think about why it's there. Louise was up in Manitoulin Island learning quill work, and I called her and said, "Do you think this book is done? Is there something missing?" She said, "I don't know, maybe." So I decided to see if I could get a bead on this old lady, and I wrote—you asked at the beginning of this interview "how many pages did you write in a day?"—I wrote the first five pages of Ida's section in one sitting. Louise called up from a phone booth freezing to death one night, and I read her those pages, and asked, "Is this a companion piece to the other two sections?" And she said, "Absolutely." And from that moment Ida's part virtually wrote itself, very fast. She had a lot to say. Somewhere in my brain the whole story must have existed in one piece without my knowing what I was doing.

Chavkin: Sometimes these things work themselves out unconsciously.

Dorris: It has been the case with Louise's work, too. We'll be reading something and think, "Well, why is that dangling detail there? What does it mean?" Then, pursuing that detail actually makes the book happen; it's quite a surprise. You don't know who a character is, and then suddenly you realize that they're not who you think they were, but actually somebody else who has appeared somewhere else in an other book, and you change them into that and then everything else works out. It's like fitting a puzzle together.

Chavkin: Does *A Yellow Raft in Blue Water* imply that we should not be quick to judge harshly because such a judgement will probably be based on inadequate knowledge? Ida's father seems to be an unpleasant man, but perhaps if we knew his past, his story in the kind of depth we know about Ida's, we would not judge him harshly. Was this conscious? Was part of your purpose to suggest that there is usually a reason that people act cruelly, if we could only understand it?

Dorris: When you do first person narrative, everybody gets their own defense. I'm sure if I told Clara's story, she would have a rationale. That doesn't mean that all self-justifications are equally valid or that I buy them all. I think that one can be persuaded by Christine, for instance, who buys her own publicity, without agreeing with her. One can be sympathetic and understand why she did what she did, why she left Rayona with Ida and so forth and so on, but that doesn't make it right or kind. I can be very frustrated with Ida for not telling Christine what Christine needs to know, but it doesn't make it wrong that she didn't tell her. So I think that there are two things going on here. Every speaker has a platform, but we don't know what voiceless character's excuses might be.

Chavkin: It seems to us in the novel that the church often disappoints

those that need its help. In fact, the church in various ways betrays all
three of the narrators, yet oddly enough, they don't judge the church
very harshly. Why is that?

Dorris: I don't think that "the church" is even that important—it's
individuals that matter. Father Hurlburt is a sad, lonely, but very decent
man who is Ida's strength, who is the one person who really understands her. Father Tom is a schmuck whether he is in church or not in
church; church is his defense and his hideout. The church is an institu-
tion that is out there floating, but it is the individuals who get involved
in it or use it in some way—the God Squad kids, have nothing to do
with the church, but it's their excuse for getting together. The hypocrisy
that's involved in that is interesting and perhaps even amusing. I don't
have a political axe to grind towards the church in my fiction that I'm
aware of.

Chavkin: Has the portrayal of the lustful priest in the novel upset
some people and provoked criticism?

Dorris: I'm sure it has, but I haven't heard it. I don't think anybody
would think that I was suggesting that he was either typical or con-
doned. He is a weak and a bad person, and it would be interesting to
hear his story to see if that could be made convincing or persuasive
or sympathetic. I'm sure he makes excuses for himself, but he is also
a man who does real damage. He's like several of the characters in
Louise's books who ultimately we don't like very much. That's odd to
say about characters that you make up, but we don't like them.

Chavkin: In the early stages of *A Yellow Raft in Blue Water*, you
wrote several chapters with a male protagonist named Raymond, but
then abandoned him for a female protagonist. How different from the
published version are those early chapters that you decided to abandon?
Did you plan to fundamentally change the novel when you decided to
abandon Raymond for Rayona?

Dorris: I wish I could say that I had a plan for the novel, but I didn't.
What happened is that it got to a certain point—and where the character
was standing, looking out over the lake, and seeing this attractive young
woman swimming and making an identification with her. When it was
Raymond, it suddenly turned into a boy's coming-of-age story, which
I didn't especially want to write. That wasn't what I thought the story
was about. Louise and I talked about it and came up with the idea of a
gender change. That altered that particular incident, and I think it really

did create the rest of the book because I had no notion at that point that there would be Christine's story or Ida's story. Those sections balanced the gender change. Incident for incident, the novel wasn't all that different between those first few draft chapters and what eventually was published with Rayona in a different gender, but in terms of the feel of the book, it was night and day.

Chavkin: How important is the setting in *A Yellow Raft in Blue Water*? Is it correct to assume that the setting is more than a realistic description of the landscape? It seems to take on a symbolic importance, revealing something about the characters. Is that a fair statement?

Dorris: I think so. It's kind of embarrassing not to know the answer to a question like that. I'm just not a self-conscious writer. What goes on the page, goes on the page, and then you work with it to try and make the balance right between description and dialogue and incident and character and all of that kind of stuff. But I never have a plan for it in advance—it's as though, once it's there, as if it were a bunch of clay, I shape the ingredients that are present on the page when I'm trying to perfect it, when I'm rewriting it, redrafting. But not with the kind of "stand back" perspective of what I want to achieve. I just know it when it's there. It's intuitive.

Chavkin: Images such as the braids and braiding that run throughout *A Yellow Raft in Blue Water* must have been conscious, right?

Dorris: Actually, it wasn't. The book was published for a year before someone pointed out to me that Christine was braiding Rayona's hair at the beginning and Ida was braiding her hair at the end. I was pretty impressed! I thought, obviously, of three strands, three stories, but all the little permutations of that were purely subconscious.

Chavkin: That's interesting that you say it was subconscious because when one reads the novel, braids and braiding seem to be such a deliberately planned pattern of imagery. You have Lee's braid, which symbolizes his political activism, and then later on Foxy has a braid, which suggests something quite different. But what you're saying is that this all worked out intuitively, not with a conscious plan.

Dorris: Yes, that's true. In fact one of the reviews criticized the book as being too self-conscious, and I had to laugh because that's one thing it isn't.

Chavkin: One reviewer, Austin MacCurtain, suggested that you betrayed, "to some degree, the integrity" of your characters by making them more verbally adept than they should be. He claims that, what he calls "the semi-literate, the confused, the willfully blind," do not "see themselves, or tell their stories" with the kind of verbal ability that you gave them. Do you feel that your first-person narrators are too intelligent, or too well educated?

Dorris: Well, no, obviously not. I think that when you do first-person narrators you have this wonderful ability to get into people's interior monologues, and those are always more articulate than their external presentations, especially if they don't have a lot of formal education. I tried to be very careful not to let people use any words that they wouldn't know, but the complexity of their thought in my experience is quite valid for people on reservations. The imagery that they use and the way they see the world is not a product of education, it's a result of being inherently intelligent. These are people who probably don't appear to the outside world as intelligent as they are because they're not adept at English, but when they have their own voice they can be whoever they are, and express any complex thought or emotion. I think there is a certain—and it's been true of Louise's books too—a certain stereotyping of Indians as stoic or laconic by reviewers. Then they read our characters and conclude, "They couldn't possibly be that way," but in fact one of the most reassuring comments that we've heard from Native American readers is, "At last you have characters who talk like Indians really talk, or think like Indians really think." So what may appear to other non-Indians as magical realism or art is in fact the style of people who are primarily oral, and who are part of an oral rather than a literate culture that values creating stories and dialogue and ideas— making stories out of things.

Chavkin: Would it be fair to say that *A Yellow Raft in Blue Water* despite all the pains and troubles the characters suffer is ultimately an affirmative, perhaps even an optimistic book?

Dorris: It depends on which character you identify with. Rayona is a very optimistic person who keeps getting up after being knocked down. But to me, the central and most important character in the book is Christine because she is a shallow person who has made a million mistakes in her life and then suddenly she has a limited amount of time to get certain important things straight. Despite her limitations, she succeeds. Of all the characters in the book she was the one I was most proud of because she didn't have as much to work with, yet she did accomplish the limited goals that were very important to her and, in a sense, she was able therefore to die happy.

Chavkin: *The Broken Cord* played a major role in changing people's attitudes about a serious social problem. Do you feel that *The Broken Cord* is therefore more important than *A Yellow Raft in Blue Water*?

Dorris: No. Not any more than I feel that one of my kids is more important than another.

Chavkin: Your intentions in the two books were different . . .

Dorris: They are completely different books. I don't mean to sound self-aggrandizing, but a lot of people come up to me and say that they've read *A Yellow Raft in Blue Water* and that it has had an important impact on their social relationships, say with their parents or their children. I think any book that succeeds has an impact on its readers. And, in fact, just today the woman who is the editor of *The Horn Book*, which is I think the premiere reviewing organ for children's books, told me that she really liked *Morning Girl*. I said to her, "If it's not too ingenuous to ask—because it is a new field for me—why?" She answered, "Because I was different when I finished the book than I was when I began it." I think that's the measure of success for a work of literature, that it changes the way a reader sees the world over the course of its pages. I don't know that you can measure the importance of that process by anything other than the individual impact.

Chavkin: How popular was *A Yellow Raft in Blue Water* compared to *The Broken Cord*?

Dorris: *A Yellow Raft in Blue Water* sold about 40,000 copies in hardback, and it's just passed the 300,000 mark in trade paperback. It's actually selling more now than it did in its first year in paper, which is pretty unusual. It's had a lot of college and senior high school course adoptions in recent years. It's about to be made into a movie, and I imagine that will give another life to the book. *The Broken Cord* sold about 90,000 in hardback, and it's in its ninth printing in trade paperback, probably up to around 250,000 copies. Both books have been translated into lots of foreign languages.

Chavkin: A movie will be made of *A Yellow Raft in Blue Water*?

Dorris: John Sayles has written a screenplay, and he seems to have the funding together, so he's going to direct it. I think that they are hoping to go into production next summer.

Chavkin: You decided not to write the screenplay?

Dorris: I don't know how to write a screenplay; I've never tried.
Besides, he's great at it.

Chavkin: How important is a knowledge of Native American cultures
in understanding your work?

Dorris: I think people who are in the inside of a tribal society, or are
themselves of Indian background, probably read the books differently.
They see a lot more humor, for instance, in *A Yellow Raft in Blue Water*
than someone without the insider's knowledge, because they can be
more relaxed. Certainly, in terms of *The Broken Cord,* I try to give a
thumbnail sketch of certain federal Indian policies and so forth, but if
you come to it from a writer's perspective and context then you will
read it differently. A writer, I think, always tries not to make the accessibility of something dependent upon the reader being expert before
hand, but clearly the more you know, the more you bring to the book.

Chavkin: We want to ask about an article published by Katha Pollitt
in *The Nation,* called "A New Assault on Feminism," where she attacks
The Broken Cord. She suggests that you hold the women's movement
responsible for fetal alcohol syndrome and that you unfairly blame
Adam's alcoholic birth mother for Adam's FAS problems. She suggests
that you are part of what she calls a "fetal rights" social trend, which
is really about "controlling women," and she argues that fetal rights
"posits a world in which women will be held accountable, on sketchy or
no evidence, for birth defects." How do you respond to her attack?

Dorris: That article made me furious. I thought it was culpably
ignorant and elitist. It was so easy, so facile, to make that kind of a
critique; it reminded me of the sort of Bush approach against choice, the
argument that all unwanted children will be adopted. I resent Pollitt and
people who take the purist view that it's no one's fault that prenatal
exposure to alcohol causes such sadness in so many people's lives. I
wish they would spend a week with an FAS child and then come back
and justify that position. Pollitt went through *The Broken Cord* and
picked out part of a line here and part of a line there to support her
argument without looking at the overall picture. Her dismissal of maternal responsiblity has the potential of actually doing harm. As you know,
I'm sure, I responded to her attack but magazines always give the
initiator of a piece the last word. She responded to my response and so
forth and so on; I didn't choose to keep on after that. It is the only time
that I ever actually objected in print to a review that was that critical of

something I wrote, and I did so because I thought her harangue gratuitously misrepresented the spirit and the facts of my book that shouldn't go unchallenged.

Chavkin: In other words, her argument that the current scientific wisdom about the influence of drug abuse and alcohol consumption on fetal development as being alarmist will do real damage.

Dorris: Yes! If you read her article, you almost feel that it is politically correct to drink, and nobody can guarantee that that's okay. Nobody knows the effect on a pregnant woman or her fetus of even a few drinks. The prudent course of action, the course advised by the Surgeon General and the A.M.A., is not to take an unnecessary risk. I don't know what prompted Pollitt's attack. She was practically the only person who took that position on the book because, quite frankly, I believe that others read the book more carefully. Nobody has been more supportive of that book's message than female physicians, female health care workers, teachers, psychologists, and so forth, because *women* in those professions traditionally have a much more direct involvement with victims of FAS than men do. FAS is *not* a feminist issue. I consider myself a feminist. I found Pollitt's misreading of that book reprehensible and irresponsible.

Chavkin: She even complained that the media was responsible for what she called "media bias." "Studies that show the bad effects of maternal behavior make the headlines," while "studies that show no bad effects don't get reported"; she also claimed that "studies that show bad effects of paternal behavior . . . get two paragraphs in the science section."

Dorris: I'm sorry, but FAS is not an equal opportunity disease. It is something that happens in fetal development. There are certainly some studies that suggest that male alcoholics can do chromosomal damage to their DNA that have negative repercussions on their offspring, but that isn't what I was writing about. I was writing about something that happened to one boy as a result of his birth mother's drinking over the course of her pregnancy, and men didn't have anything metabolic to do with that. Those are the facts.

Chavkin: Were you pleased with the film that was made of *The Broken Cord*?

Dorris: I didn't see it, to tell the truth. I worked on the screenplay, and I went on the set for a couple of days while it was being made to make sure for myself that it would present the critical themes and that the presentation was not sentimental. People I know who have seen it and who knew our family situation well have had good things to say about it, and actually in the last couple of weeks, it has won a whole slew of prizes. It won the Gabriel Award for National Broadcasting by the Catholic Media Critics, the ARC, Association of Retarded Citizens Award for national media, the media prize in the American Psychological Association, a Christopher award, and the Scott Newman award for best program on drug and alcohol problems. It was a finalist for the Humanitas Prize. So it must be good, and it certainly accomplished the goal that we set out for it—that is, to impact a very large audience with a story that could be digested in one sitting. Thirty million people watched it, I think. It will be rescreened on the network and then be released on video. Jimmy Smits is a wonderful actor. I give him and also Ken Olin a lot of credit for keeping it non-sentimental. The filming itself was very hard for me to deal with because just before it went into production our son was hit by a car and subsequently died of his injuries. Naturally my impulse was to walk away from the project at that point and not even think about it anymore, but I thought that if this was to be Abel's one shot at letting his life be an example to a very large audience, then my responsibility was to make sure that it was done as well as possible. But I didn't want to watch it. It would make my own memories a little too surreal.

Chavkin: Is there a film going to be made of *The Crown of Columbus*?

Dorris: It is optioned. The people who optioned it certainly think that there will be.

Chavkin: We'd like to ask you a few questions about *The Crown of Columbus*. How different is your Columbus from the traditional view of Columbus?

Dorris: We didn't know and we couldn't figure out who Columbus actually was, so one of the benefits of having two characters, each being a first person narrator, is that they each get to present a strong position that is different, one from the other. Whichever Columbus you believe in, in *The Crown of Columbus*, he is much more complex than most of the simplistic lore about Columbus gives him credit for. He was a complicated individual, and he told so many versions of his life he couldn't be everything that he said he was—that's precisely why he is an interesting character for fiction.

Chavkin: Do you think the judgement of Columbus for his arrogant attitude toward Native Americans should be made in terms of the historical context? Some people claim that we should not judge a fifteenth-century man by twentieth-century standards.

Dorris: I don't see Columbus as a particular villain. He was very much representative of his time. It would all be very simple if you could attribute everything bad that has happened to Indians over the past five hundred years to one person, but in fact it's attributable to an attitude which is still quite pervasive. You don't have to go back five hundred years to find a myopic Eurocentric world view. What everyone says about the encounter of 1492 unfortunately is very applicable to the situation today, not just between non-Indians and Indians, but between, for instance, Americans and southeast Asians.

Chavkin: Do you think that racist attitudes towards Native Americans will increase or decrease in the coming years?

Dorris: Well, they're certainly not going to disappear because they are always exasperated by competition. The land competition and especially the water competition in the West are going to accelerate as resources diminish and as tribes end up having legal rights to resources that non-Indians want. That always forecasts hostility.

Chavkin: So as Indians assert their rights, then tensions will probably be increasing?

Dorris: Or maintain their rights. Refuse to go away.

Chavkin: In her review in the *Chicago Sun Times* Gretel Ehrlich faults *The Crown of Columbus* as being "more entertainment than grand literature and will not sit on the shelf in future years beside *Anna Karenina* and *The Grapes of Wrath*." How would you respond to that?

Dorris: Well, I assume that would have to do with alphabetical order, in terms of what shelf you sit on. It's presumptuous for anybody to think that his work can sit on the shelf with *Anna Karenina*. I think that *The Crown of Columbus*, in terms of its reaction by reviewers, suffered by coming out in the year of the quincentennial. I would hope that some time from now, when the book is read as part of the body of Louise's and my work, it will be taken less topically and more as a novel of discovery. The many genres that are represented in the book are very intentional on our part because what we were attempting to do was reflect the chaos of discovery. It's sometimes melodramatic; it's sometimes surprising; it's sometimes poignant; it's sometimes poetic; it's all of those things wrapped into one. So what we were trying to do was make the form follow the content. *The Crown of Columbus* was a book we'd been thinking of for ten years before we wrote it, and we would have written it whether there was a five hundredth anniversary of the first voyage or not. For instance, in the beginning of Nash's section, he describes Roger and Vivian coming out of the bat cave in a manner that replicates the Navaho creation myth in which first man and first woman emerge into a new world from an underground place. Whether the idea works or not, time will tell, but there weren't, at least in this country, as many reviewers who seemed to understand the novel as there were, for instance, in England. The reviews there were much more perceptive, and I can only hope that in the future when it isn't all wrapped up in the Columbus hoopla—whether or not we are pro-Columbus or anti-Columbus blah-blah-blah-—that book will be looked at as a serious novel and not as something that was strictly tied to a historical moment.

   Chavkin: The novel went through many drafts, didn't it?

   Dorris: Many, many drafts.

   Chavkin: Are there major changes in plot and character in the various drafts?

   Dorris: Yes. In the beginning, the question was whether the whole book would be in the style of the poem in Columbus's voice, interspersed with a modern voice. That was one plan. Roger's role in the book became increasingly important with the drafts because we saw him as a character who was experiencing a great deal of movement, of growth. When we first started out with Roger, he was not somebody who we particularly liked; he was almost a foil to Vivian, yet eventually he became for us very important, an equally important character. Nash, too, emerged at the conclusion. I think the best idea in the whole book—and it was Louise's—is the framing device of Valerie Clock at the beginning and the end. Almost no critic in this country quite understood what that was all about, but to us, the whole story is told in the vignettes of Valerie Clock. Another thing that I think disturbed some people is that *The Crown of Columbus* was fun to write. We enjoyed it thoroughly—the process of working together and being able to try a big expansive book that was full of information and populated with characters who were well-educated, who had at their disposal the lexicons of several traditions.

   Chavkin: Should Vivian and Roger be seen as representatives of Native American and white European viewpoints, or is that too schematic?

   Dorris: I hope that's too schematic, and I don't think either Vivian or

Roger would agree to be so typecast. It isn't as though we stand back and think, "Let's make this character representative of Indians," or something. Roger got a bad rap in some of these reviews—some people pure didn't like him. They thought that he was too stuffy, whereas we thought that he was a man trapped by his class and his fears but who managed to overcome his problems analogously to the way Christine dealt with some of her obstacles at the end of her section in *A Yellow Raft in Blue Water*. We were quite proud of Roger for daring to have some genuine emotional feelings by the end of the book.

Chavkin: Please comment on the long poem about Columbus and its connection to the rest of the novel.

Dorris: The poem was one of the first elements that existed in the book. It started out being in Columbus's own voice. It wouldn't have sustained a whole book, though it could have probably been published on its own—and in fact it was. Before the book came out, we submitted the poem to *Caliban*, under Roger William's name, and it was accepted. We were a little jealous because he got a first-submission acceptance. Certainly, there were those who disagreed with where we placed the poem in the book—the French publisher didn't use the whole thing. She thought it should either be shortened or stuck on as an appendix because she said we were at a very climactic moment in the plot, and suddenly there were all these pages of epic poem. But that was our entire point. In the first place, everything in the poem is paralleled in the book, structurally or vice versa. Secondly, the poem showed that Roger was who he said he was—not a bad poet. And the other thing is that it was a poem about a journey that never reached where it was headed—it got stalled the same way that Roger did. It's part of that whole notion of discovery that suddenly there is this other kind of mystical, strange component in the book, so we took a risk. Some readers would get to the poem, skip ahead, just pass over it and continue reading the plot. That's okay. They can come back and read it later and see the parallels.

Chavkin: Was the poem part of your collaboration with Louise or did one of you primarily write it?

Dorris: No, we worked on everything in the book together, though not simultaneously; the pages all went back and forth and back and forth. Louise probably did a lot more primary research on Columbus than I did, on the historical period, on all the books that Columbus read.

I was finishing and then touring with *The Broken Cord*, and she was taking notes about Spain.

Chavkin: Had you already done a lot of research on Columbus when you taught Native American studies in college?

Dorris: I had read his journal and thought some about the notion of discovery and inter-cultural encounter, but one of the things we thought was important to do, because Columbus does tell what books he liked, was to read everything that he read and get a sense of the world from his point of view. That took a lot of time. Louise did more of that than I.

Chavkin: What does *The Crown of Columbus* say about power?

Dorris: That it is illusory, and that the ultimate power is curiosity. Much apparent power, such as Cobb's, actually interferes with curiosity and passes away very quickly without much influence. One of the results of curiosity is that you're often led where you don't expect to go. When Valerie Clock gets the idea that the sea is a place to cross, she can't get it out of her mind. Curiosity is at the core of discovery, whether it's of oneself or of a relationship or a baby or a new world.

Chavkin: What's you view of Columbus's ancestry?

Dorris: I think he was probably Jewish, or descended from Jews. That evidence is pretty convincing.

Chavkin: Isn't that a minority view of the historians, or are we wrong about that?

Dorris: The thing about Columbus is that he has so covered his tracks that it's hard to know what's true, but let us say that he fits the profile of a converso very well. What other influences he had in his family background is anybody's guess.

Chavkin: Are you suggesting in *The Crown of Columbus* that Columbus was an ethically confused man?

Dorris: Well, I don't know if he was so much confused. Vivian thinks he was. Roger doesn't. I think he was intentionally deceptive. He was always hiding something, but what he was hiding, no one knows. He very consciously obscured details about himself, or told various versions of them, and that makes him intriguing.

Chavkin: The novel has a lot to say about the idea of history.

Dorris: I hope so.

Chavkin: In an article on Tony Hillerman, you praised Thomas Berger's portrayal of Native American lives in *Little Big Man*, and we were wondering if you would elaborate on that.

Dorris: The thing that I loved about *Little Big Man* is that the Indian characters had personality and humor, and you have to look long and hard for other books in which they have either one. Berger's Indians, in both the book and the movie version, were interesting, intelligent people who happened to be from a different culture, but who had an edge, a perspective on the world, who didn't conform to stereotypes. I continue to think *Little Big Man* is one of the best fictional books that deal with Indians that I know.

Chavkin: Are you sympathetic with Berger's view of history and myth and American heroes in that book?

Dorris: I think so; it's a wonderful book. It's his best book. I hate to say that about a living writer because it is such a curse to feel that one's best is already done, but I think it's a terrific book.

Chavkin: Yes, it's a marvelous book. We have the impression that the anthropology in that book is accurate. Berger seems to have done a lot of research.

Dorris: I agree. I think that the anthropology is better than, say, *Bury My Heart at Wounded Knee.* It's much less good-guys versus bad-guys. It makes a picture of a complex world and confused world, which is, I think, accurate.

Chavkin: Do you think Native American writers of today share and identify a world view? Is there such a thing today as "Native American literature," or is that a useless label?

Dorris: I don't know what Native American literature is. I wrote an article a long time ago called "Native American Literature in an Ethnohistorical Context." Does "Native American literature" mean literature about Indians? Does it mean a literature by Indians about Indian themes? Does it mean literature by Indians about anything? Is *Gorky Park,* for instance, "Native American literature" because Martin Cruz Smith is part Indian? I don't know. You can certainly talk about stories within tribal traditions. Louise's books are very squarely within an Anishinabe perspective, especially *Tracks.* I think that I possibly have a good deal in common with James Welch, in terms of setting and sensibility of the northwestern plains, but whether that circle expands to include fine Indian writers like Linda Hogan and Scott Momaday and Leslie Silko, I don't know. We're all tied together in classes sometimes, but I'm not sure that's the best idea.

Chavkin: You mentioned that there are other novels on Native American experiences by white writers that you also admire.

Dorris: Well, I like *When the Legends Die*. That's a very good book. I like *I Heard the Owl Call My Name,* which is, I think, primarily intended for younger readers. Certainly the La Farge books and *Man Who Killed a Deer*. Books like that are very interesting to read if only because they reflect sympathetic attitudes of their day toward Indians. I certainly don't think that there's anything prescriptive or proscriptive about a non-Indian writing about Indians anymore than I would think that I should be prohibited from trying to imagine a life of a person who wasn't of mixed blood.

Chavkin: You've suggested in some articles that James Welch is an important writer. Which of his novels do you think is his best?

Dorris: Well, again I hate to use "best," but I think that his first is a very important book because it transcended anybody's notion of the genre. I like his work in general, but I especially admire *Winter in the Blood*.

Chavkin: For writers who can not support themselves on writing alone, do you think that working as a journalist or an English teacher would help or hurt or have no influence on their creative writing?

Dorris: Well, of course, I taught for years in anthropology and Native American studies, when I wasn't supporting myself by writing. Academic writing is so different from either creative nonfiction or fiction that, for me, it took a lot of unlearning to be able to break the habit.

Chavkin: What do you mean by "break the habit"?

Dorris: Having to footnote everything, or basically rehashing other people's ideas rather than trying to have an original concept that can be defended by its consistency and its validity rather than by external proofs.

Chavkin: John Gardner in a discussion with William Gass suggested that you write a book "to understand and get control of in yourself things that you haven't been able to control and understand in the world," and he suggests "that we revise our lives in our work and with each revision we find a mistake we don't have to make again." He suggests that with each new book, a writer becomes a slightly better person. What do you think of his theory?

Dorris: If only it were true. More thoughtful people than I have these opinions about what they do and what its impact is. I don't know; I have no idea. I get involved with a story, and it's like reading—that's all I can say—it's like reading a very compelling book, except that I'm writing it. I follow it through, and where it comes from or what influence it has on me personally, I have no idea. I go back and I read parts of *A Yellow Raft in Blue Water* or any of the other books that I've done and I sometimes think, "Hey, that's pretty good. Where in the world did it come from?" So perhaps I lost some of my goodness along the way. Maybe I'm going in the opposite direction.

Chavkin: Have you learned anything by reading what reviewers and critics have written about your work?

Dorris: I've learned that there are things in the books that I didn't know were there, and I'm awfully glad to find that out. I really do think that sometimes, if you're doing it right, a book is like a dream and somebody else's interpretation can be quite accurate. There was a review of *Morning Girl* recently that said that I have effectively paralleled the sibling relationship between brother and sister with the complications of communication between two separate cultural traditions. I thought, "What a good idea; I wish I had thought of it." When you write a book, and you send it out to the world, it belongs to everybody, and you can't limit what people take away from it. You shouldn't even try. It isn't like you're sending out a puzzle; it's there for people to enjoy, and if they choose to write about it or think about it, it doesn't surprise me at all if they find things in it that I didn't know were there or Louise didn't know were there. They make their own contributions.

Chavkin: In one of your reviews, you suggested that a novel may have too many complications, a plot may be too complex and that not all psychological conflicts need to be resolved, that in short, less is more. We see this aesthetic principle in *A Yellow Raft in Blue Water* and were wondering, how conscious is that?

Dorris: I think it gets back to the question before when you asked, "When do you know when something is finished?" It's an intuitive quest, rather than tying up each loop end. That isn't the way life is, and I think my work is fairly realistic. Part of that realism is not to have everything be neat. Better to leave things much more as they are, expecially when you're doing first person because first-person narrators never quite get it all. So, I guess I agree with my own review. What a relief!

Chavkin: So what would make a good editor?

Dorris: Honesty—believing in a person's work, loving his or her work in its essence, believing that it can be fine and not settling for anything less than that, and fighting like crazy to make you, the writer, sure that the choices you've made are the choices you want to make— and then stepping back.

Chavkin: What sort of approach would you take if you were teaching a course in fiction?

Dorris: Approach in what sense?

Chavkin: If you were an English professor, what sort of critical approach would you use to examine a short story?

Dorris: I think encouraging students to appreciate technique, how hard it is to make something seem simple. That's a nice metaphor for life and for almost any profession. I remember one of my best English courses at college was studying the poetry of Robert Browning, which I didn't particularly like, but so much attention was devoted to under-standing his technique of first person point of views that I probably was influenced by it. That kind of artistic respect and technical attention makes for a more appreciative reader.

Chavkin: Would you ever have any desire to teach creative writing courses?

Dorris: No.

Chavkin: Some people criticize the proliferation of writing programs. What's your opinion?

Dorris: I've got to say, I'm awfully glad they existed because Louise went to Johns Hopkins and taught me, so I got it one step removed.

Chavkin: You work in so many genres. We were wondering if you would ever consider working in Hollywood and writing screenplays, or is this something in which you have no interest?

Dorris: I tried it, and I found it a very frustrating experience because there are so many layers a work has to go through in which people with their own agendas make decisions about it and changes in it and so forth and so on. One of the great advantages to being a writer of either fiction or nonfiction or some newspaper stuff, such as Op-Ed essays, is that the material is ultimately under your control and whatever gets printed is basically your choice. When a screenplay goes through directors and actors and others, it's much more of a collaborative process, and the only person I really want to collaborate with is Louise.

Chavkin: What about the role of humor in your work? How important is it?

Dorris: It's part of everything, and to me it's a mark of intelligence. I would have a hard time writing a book without hoping that there was some humor in it. And especially, anytime Indians have humor, it undermines stereotypes, it surprises. Yet, I've never known an Indian person who didn't have a sense of humor.

Chavkin: Undermines the stereotype of the stoic Indian that you find in . . .

Dorris: I've never encountered one of those.

Chavkin: Do you find it easier or more difficult writing fiction as opposed to nonfiction?

Dorris: I couldn't say. It depends on what I'm working on.

Chavkin: So you wouldn't say that you preferred writing . . .

Dorris: Writing fiction is extremely liberating after writing academic material, but I also love writing nonfiction. I wrote seven editorial pieces last summer and I thoroughly enjoyed doing them.

Chavkin: Do you see any weaknesses you'd like to correct in your writing?

Dorris: A billion. If I didn't, why would I ever write another word? I don't know that I could point to them except this tendency to overwrite and to overexplain and to be too conservative sometimes, but I think that's a question one asks of every sentence.

Chavkin: What do you see as your particular strength as a writer?

Dorris: I think in some respects I find plotting easier than character. I watch what happens, and then I have to go back and make it richer, but I don't know. I guess that's probably for critics to say.

Chavkin: You think you'll continue to write primarily using first person narrators?

Dorris: Yes, I think so. A couple of the stories in *Working Men*, due out next year, are third person and I probably worked more on them than all the rest of them put together. It's very hard for me to do third person and make it as immediate and as interesting as first person.

Chavkin: Is there also a philosophical reason for using first person?

We recall that one novelist said that politically the first person was more honest than the omniscient.

Dorris: He's another one of those smart writers who knows what he's doing. It's easier for me. That's all I can say. It is like getting into a character's skin and trying to persuade an imaginary somebody of my position and not having to know everything except what I'm sure I know, which is my own perspective—"my" in the sense of my character.

Chavkin: There are a number of strong independent women in your fiction. We think of Rebecca in "The Dark Snake" and the women in *A Yellow Raft in Blue Water*. Is this a deliberate attempt to try to help overcome stereotypes of women that one often finds in fiction?

Dorris: No; it is my experience. I was raised by two grandmothers, three aunts, and a mother, all of whom were very strong women, and that is simply my context. The only non-strong women I know are women who pretend not to be strong as a ploy. It is sometimes said that the women characters are stronger in Louise's and my fiction than the men—well, I think that the women are simply *equally* as strong as the men; and also when women are telling a story from their point of view, they obviously are more sympathetic to themselves than to somebody else. I think they simply appear strong because we are so used to seeing women portrayed as not strong. But it isn't a self-conscious choice on my part; it's just the reality that I know.

Chavkin: "The Dark Snake" and "The Benchmark," though different in some ways, are very powerful stories that center upon accidental death. Do you recall what prompted you to write the two stories?

Dorris: Parts of "The Dark Snake" are based upon a family story of my great-grandmother who did, in fact, lose a cherished son in a train accident with a cow. Everything else is invented. "The Benchmark" actually came about in an attempt to use the vocabulary of a man who came to build a pond on our property. All these wonderful words that I had never heard before that seemed to reverberate with meaning. The story was the result of the words, and the accidental death simply occurred within that flow. There was no particular reason for it.

Chavkin: Do you find it useful to meet with other writers?

Dorris: You mean, useful to the writing?

Chavkin: Yes, in terms of talking about craft.

Dorris: No. I mean, I don't. It might be, but I don't. We tend to live in a pretty isolated setting, and so there are only a few writers we've become friends with by phone or whatever, and we very rarely talk about work with them.

Chavkin: What prompted you and Louise to write "Bangs and Whimpers: Novelists at Armageddon?

Dorris: Good question. I think we just happened to be reading a lot of post-nuclear fiction and looked for commonalities. Louise may answer that question much more intelligently than I.

Chavkin: Are there some twentieth-century writers who have influenced your work?

Dorris: Well, I mentioned Barbara Pym. I love Updike's short stories. I love Paul Theroux's short stories. I like Toni Morrison. I like the work of Robb Forman Dew, who describes weather better than anybody I know. Sinclair Lewis, I love. Laura Ingalls Wilder, I love. Tennessee Williams. Gloria Naylor. Camus. Those just off the top of my head.

Chavkin: Do you feel compelled to write about Native Americans? Will Native Americans populate your books the same way that Russians populate Dostoevski's books or Jewish characters populate Isaac Bashevis Singer's books?

Dorris: I think I will always write books that deal with Native American characters. Maybe not every book will have a Native American at center stage, but, you know the famous advice of the professor to Jo in Alcott's *Little Women* is write what you know. You have to write about characters with whom you can empathize and sympathize. I would hate to be thought of as a spokesperson for anybody. Some of the stories in *Working Men* aren't about Indians at all. One narrator is a Prozac rep. One is a man who spends his entire Vietnam tour of duty working at the PX at Danang and only hears about the war from the people that come in to shop.

Chavkin: Can you tell us about your current projects?

Dorris: There's this collection called *Paper Trail*, selected essays over the past fifteen years, ranging from the very personal to the political. There is a book of short stories called *Working Men* in which I make the daring and challenging attempt to write more in men's voices than in women's. There is a novel of which "The Dark Snake" is probably the first chapter; it's set over a multi-generational time in western

Kentucky. There's a brief book of journalism on Zimbabwe. There's a bunch more children's books, both fiction and nonfiction.

Chavkin: Tell us about your background and your career.

Dorris: My father was Indian and my mother was not. They met at a USO dance at the end of World War II. I'm the only child, and my father died when I was very small. I spent my childhood and high school days, partly in Kentucky with my mother and her family and partly in the West with my father's family. I should say I wasn't a very popular kid. I went to mostly Catholic schools, then to Georgetown on scholarship. I was the first person in my family to go to college, where I majored in Classics—so that I wouldn't have to take Calculus—and English. Then I went to Yale in History of the Theater, and from there transferred into Anthropology. I did field work in an Alaskan Athabaskan community for two years, where I fished commercially. It was a community that was undergoing rapid social change as a result of oil discoveries. I learned a language there. I taught at two experimental colleges, founded the Native American Studies program at Dartmouth, adopted three children, married, had three more children, and my midlife crisis entailed giving up tenure and a full professorship in order to try to be a writer. In a nutshell.

Chavkin: Quite impressive.

Dorris: As they say, I took the available path.

An Interview with Louise Erdrich

Nancy Feyl Chavkin and Allan Chavkin/1993

This interview was conducted by mail from September 1992 through
April 1993.

Chavkin: In *The Beet Queen*, Karl is described as both Christ-like and
Satanic, and it is difficult for the reader to arrive at a final judgement of
him. Is that what you were trying to do, or have we misunderstood this
aspect of the novel?

Erdrich: There is no reason to come to a final decision about whether
he is one or the other. He incorporates both. We all have a little of both.

Chavkin: At what point in the writing of *The Beet Queen* did you
decide to include the "Night" sections?

Erdrich: I'm not certain, but it was probably somewhere around
halfway.

Chavkin: Jim Harrison says that writing poetry was good preparation
for him to write his novels. Is that true in your case?

Erdrich: I hope it is true since I can't go back and do it otherwise,
and certainly I think it is true for Jim Harrison's novels and wonderfully
deft, funny, large-hearted essays.

Chavkin: Perhaps because of your interrelated stories and interweaving divergent points of view, you have been compared to Faulkner. Is
that comparison useful? Has your reading of Faulkner's work influenced
your own work?

Erdrich: Faulkner is probably an influence on any writer, but yes, I
do love his work and I read it over and over, especially *The Hamlet* and
Absalom, Absalom! Is the comparison useful? I guess it depends on
what sort of use you might make of it. I don't think it is a comparison
that deepens the experience of the writing; however, it probably points
toward an interesting academic question—that is, how white Southerners and Native American writers might partake of a similar (contained,
defeated, proud, undefeated) sense of history, and of place. Strange
bedfellows.

Chavkin: Do you think there is any truth in the theory that serious
writing is prompted by unhappiness or a sense of loss?

Erdrch: There probably is some truth to that. Unfortunately I've noticed as I've grown older that most of us increase our understanding through experiencing personal sorrows and setbacks. Slowly, perhaps, my children are teaching me what it is to experience deep joy. They do it so effortlessly, and there is such wisdom in their direct embrace of joy, that I at least understand from being with them that I know very little of what it means to concentrate and be at peace with the world. I don't know how exactly we lose this talent. I'm trying to get it back . . .

Chavkin: Can you give us some examples of how ideas for some of your stories came to you?

Erdrich: Getting a first line is immensely satisfying. The first line of "Scales" is written on the back of a Travelhost napkin. The first line of "Saint Marie" came to me in the bathtub where I was sulking after Michael told me that the Nth draft of the story wasn't quite right. My grandmother once got irritated with a yapping dog and excused herself to "go pound the dog." It became a line in a story. She didn't end up pounding the dog, by the way. She loved animals. My father told me about his first ride in a barnstormer's airplane. My sisters and brothers and aunts and uncles like to talk. Stories came from just about any-where, unpredictably, and I try to stay open. Try to leave the door open.

Chavkin: One of the things we like so much about your writing is the feeling of unpredictability, that anything is possible—it's a feeling one often has when reading "magical realism." Joyce Carol Oates calls you a "magical realist." Do you see yourself as one? Do you think that's a useful term to describe your work?

Erdrich: That must have been a while ago, and it was very good of her, a great compliment, but I think now that the rage to imitate Mar-quez has declined. Probably your word unpredictable is more accurate. It is certainly the reaction I'd like. The thing is, the events people pick out as magical don't seem unreal to me. Unusual, yes, but I was raised believing in miracles and hearing of true events that may seem unbe-lievable. I think the term is one applied to writers from cultures more closely aligned to religious oddities and the natural and strange world.

Chavkin: Can you name some contemporary writers whose work you admire?

Erdrich: Linda Hogan's book *Mean Spirits,* Amy Tan's novels, *The Joy Luck Club, The Kitchen God's Wife,* Gretel Ehrlich's essays. Annie

Dillard. James Welch. Joanna Scott's *Arrogance*. A. S. Byatt. Jeanette Winterson. Of course, everything by Toni Morrison, Philip Roth, and Joyce Carol Oates. Doris Betts. Margaret Atwood. Alice Munro. Thom Jones. Charles Palliser.

Chavkin: Which of Welch's novels do you especially like?

Erdrich: *Winter in the Blood* is one of the most economically beautiful spare novels ever written, and I very much like *The Indian Lawyer*.

Chavkin: For which of your works have you done research?

Erdrich: I do research for all of them, but spent the most time on *The Crown of Columbus*. I love the inside of Baker Library at Dartmouth, and I like small town libraries too. I'm a very poor researcher and too impatient to really ground myself for long, but I do have an affinity for odd facts, far flung notions, ethnohistories, folktales, trivia and especially those books about scientific research written for the science-dysfunctional like myself. *Chaos. The Mind of God.* Etc.

Chavkin: When you did your research for *The Crown of Columbus*, were there some books that you found particularly useful for the novel?

Erdrich: *The Long Desire,* Evan S. Connell. The letter from Presbyter Johannes to Pope Alexander III and Emperor Frederick Barbarosa, in 1165. *The Travels of Sir John Mandeville. The Conquest of America,* Tzvetan Todorov. *Lost Tribes and Promised Lands,* Ronald Sanders. The Bible. The Other Bible (apocrypha). *Admiral of the Ocean Sea,* Samuel Eliot Morrison. *Living Karate,* Hidy Ochiai. *Biathanatos,* John Donne. *The Bahama Islands,* George Shattock. Pliny. Columbus himself especially in Robert Fuson's transcription of his diary. And stacks of other books, including Dunn and Kelley's *Diario*.

Chavkin: What were the basic contradictions in Columbus's character?

Erdrich: He had an unusual capacity for observing and even understanding others unlike himself—that is clear from his diary. He had, as well, such cruelty in his nature. When his plans to mine gold failed, he lobbied Queen Isabella, convinced her to accept Indians as slaves.

Chavkin: You became stuck while writing *Tracks*. What was the problem and how did you solve it?

Erdrich: I was pregnant, homesick for the open spaces, for the Plains. I was stuck, physically, too grounded, cut off from my sources. Michael did all that he could do, and through conversations and his kind attempts to lift me from depression, the desperation fell gradually away. I finished the book, but am not satisfied.

Chavkin: Critics were enthusiastic about *Tracks*. Why aren't you satisfied with it?

Erdrich: This is not a negative dissatisfaction, on the contrary, I think that parts of *Tracks* are completely *there*. I want more time with it, that's all. More time, more time!

Chavkin: You were a researcher for a TV movie? Did you learn anything from that work?

Erdrich: I paged through images, found photos, researched, took great pleasure in the work. That summer I also learned a few words of Lakota (I was at the University of Nebraska) and spent some time with a friend at the Crow Dog's place in South Dakota. Leonard Crow Dog's mother, Mary, was an extraordinary, tough-minded, infinitely kind and generous woman who lived out her culture. I'm sure that many people miss her presence in the world, as I do still.

Chavkin: What were your responsibilities as a writer-in-residence at Dartmouth? Did you teach courses in creative writing and literature?

Erdrich: This was a wonderful chance for me. I gave readings, worked with students, but mainly concentrated on writing the first version of *Tracks*.

Chavkin: Although "I'm a Mad Dog Biting Myself for Sympathy" reveals serious themes, there is much humor in the story. Is one of the purposes of the humor to make this first-person narrator more sympathetic than he might otherwise have been?

Erdrich: I wasn't trying to elicit sympathy for this guy, but just telling what happened to him. There is so little purpose in the choices I make. It is mostly feel, instinct, and blind luck.

Chavkin: Despite some comic scenes, *The Beet Queen* is a bleaker book than *Love Medicine*. Would you agree?

Erdrich: On balance, I think they're similar, but *The Beet Queen* hasn't got Lipsha Morrissey, whose personality seems to transform personal pain into wonder. It's almost impossible for me to be objective, here, but the landscape and closed emotions of *some* of the characters in any of the books certainly are bleak.

Chavkin: Do Gerry and the mother in "A Wedge of Shade" represent two opposing or different Native American ways of life?

Erdrich: Just different ways, not opposing. Celestine is fairly assimilated and Gerry, of course, is a traditionalist and activist. That doesn't mean they are at odds in their common goals, and in fact I think there is a sense that they recognize and even like something similar in one another.

Chavkin: Is it correct to assume that in *Tracks* Pauline is not a reliable narrator, and even Nanapush is not completely reliable?

Erdrich: I think it is me, the writer, who in the end is unreliable and continually searching for the truth of an imagined story, a truth which changes with each consciousness and each point of view. It is, however, the "failed narrators" I feel closest to in the stories. Lipsha, for instance, the fallen character of Lyman Lamartine, heroically sensual Lulu, even Albertine is something of a failure as she narrates "Scales."

Chavkin: Both Sita and Russell Kashpaw lose the ability to talk. Is that a coincidence or a deliberate parallel?

Erdrich: It is both, as often is the case when some resonant incident occurs in thought and one keeps coming back to it again and again.

Chavkin: One reviewer praised *Love Medicine* but claimed that there were minor flaws in the novel. "Saint Marie" ended flatly and there should have been more about the younger generation of characters, Lipsha and especially Albertine. Are these flaws?

Erdrich: Probably, but nothing I write is perfect.

Chavkin: Why does Pauline hate Fleur?

Erdrich: She is afraid of Fleur, as many women who allow themselves to be controlled are threatened by women who do as they please.

Chavkin: What were you trying to suggest by interweaving "real" and imaginary events in *Tracks*?

Erdrich: There is no quantifiable reality. Points of view change the reality of a situation and there is a reality to madness, imagined events, and perhaps something beyond that.

Chavkin: Why did you have Pauline tell Fleur's story? Is "Fleur" as much about Pauline as it is about Fleur? Did you ever consider having Fleur tell her own story?

Erdrich: I don't have omnipotent control over the characters and voices, and the answer to these questions is that this is the only way I could write the story. Pauline's was the voice that presented itself, that I "heard."

Chavkin: Any predictions when the final volume in your tetralogy will be published?

Erdrich: I don't know how many books are related and how many not. *The Bingo Palace* will be published at almost the same time as the additions to *Love Medicine* appear, that is late fall and early winter 1993–94.

Chavkin: Fleur's destruction of the trees on her land reveals her noble defiance, but how should the reader perceive her departure without her child?

Erdrich: Fleur makes a mistake, a desperate mistake, and she pays for it the rest of her life, as does Lulu.

Chavkin: What will the next book in the series be about?

Erdrich: Father Damien, or perhaps Lipsha.

Chavkin: An important structural technique in *The Crown of Columbus* is the inclusion of the long poem at the end of Chapter 19. This poem, which is quite fine in its own right, also enriches the novel considerably. Why did you place the poem at this point of the novel?

Erdrich: The poem fit where it was in the narrative. It wouldn't be right to make Roger a poet and never have him read or think a poem, would it? He would thank you for the compliment; you're very kind.

Chavkin: An effective structural technique is your beginning and ending *The Crown of Columbus* with Valerie Clock. At what point in the writing of the novel did you decide to frame the novel this way?

Erdrich: Three-fourths of the way through, in desperation.

Chavkin: Why "in desperation"?

Erdrich: We always knew that she was crucial to the story, but couldn't figure out how.

Chavkin: Is it true that when you and Michael were writing *The Crown of Columbus* you did not have the plot planned completely in advance and that one of you might create a difficult situation for a character and then give it to your collaborator to figure out what should come next?

Erdrich: That's completely true and I felt great happiness when turning over to him the scene where Roger has just blown a hole in his raft with his baby aboard, the boat is sinking and there is a shark in the water. I had Roger jump in, and then I gave the manuscript to Michael. It was a pure moment of mingled generosity and sadism and I must say, he met the challenge.

Chavkin: Did he ever present you with such a difficult challenge?

Erdrich: He's a much kinder person. He did not.

Chavkin: Is it possible to collaborate closely with another writer and to still maintain an individual imagination?

Erdrich: The heart of our collaboration is a commitment to one another's separateness. I certainly respect the solitude and silence it takes for Michael's work, and he does the same for me. The idea of linking brains or even working in the same space—I find that impossible. As would anyone. An imagination is composed of all the signs and wonders of childhood, as well as the range of trivialities and possibilities that come with age. In a collaboration such as *The Crown of Columbus* we shared in one book the creations of our own selves, but the source itself, that is a well closed except to the free wondering of an individual mind. In each of the books we've written separately, it is that source, naturally, that dictates the substance of the work. However, there is no putting aside the sheer volume of sweaty maneuvering it takes to shape books, and we have done so much of that between ourselves that I find it impossible to ever thank Michael enough for his passionate commitment.

Chavkin: One of the qualities we especially like about your work is a sympathy, a real compassion, for your characters—a quality one finds so often in Chekhov's short stories but often lacking in many contemporary writers, where there's a cold–heartedness disguised as ironic detachment. Is that sympathy something you consciously attempt to inject into your work?

Erdrich: I'm glad that you find it there, and no, I'm not conscious of putting it in the work. I don't think that compassion is a quality that can be injected or added as an afterthought. Either it is there, or it is not, and certainly the reader brings hidden shades of that sympathy into existence during the act of reading.

Chavkin: Now that you have proven yourself, do you feel less pressure when you sit down to write—is the writing more enjoyable now?

Erdrich: It depends, for one sets up expectations, too. I just try to do my work and get along with these books. They have their own life— that exists comfortingly apart from mine.

Chavkin: You often seem to prefer first-person narratives. Why?

Erdrich: More natural, at least to me.

Chavkin: At what point in the writing do you know how the story will end?

Erdrich: Sometimes I don't and write past the end and then Michael notices I could drop off two paragraphs—it is common for writers to do this, he does the same. We always try to make the reader "get it" when so much more can be said enigmatically.

Chavkin: You have written in a number of different genres, which do you most enjoy?

Erdrich: I enjoy each for different reasons. Each gives different satisfactions, and I really have no favorite.

Chavkin: Can you think of specific examples where you or your spouse saved the other from a serious mistake or made suggestions that dramatically altered the work?

Erdrich: Michael woke me up the other morning to say that two of the characters in *The Bingo Palace* were really one character. This happens in every book—I write two sides of one character and give them different identities. Once I went down on my knees before Michael and begged him for revenge (on Clara, in *A Yellow Raft in Blue Water*).

Chavkin: You are not associated with a university, as so many American writers are these days. Do you think this influences your writing in any way?

Erdrich: While I love university atmosphere and get along fine there, I become very restless and soon need to get out. I think others can be the judge as to how it influences my writing—I think it does, but wouldn't know how to analyze the relationship or non-relationship, except to say that since the characters I relate to most are smart but undereducated, living and working in a university is not probably where I'd ultimately flourish. I like living in the country and knowing a broad variety of people. Having grown up in a small town, I often find that setting rich, but also choking, a mixture. I've lived in many different places but feel most attached to the outdoor West and Great Plains, the sky, the mountains, the broad reaches.

Chavkin: How do you select the names for your characters?

Erdrich: I keep notebook lists, and then sometimes they just come to me. Dreams. Others I discuss with Michael, and still others are suggested by old family trees or tribal rolls or local newspapers or the local cafe. I do love names.

Chavkin: Do you regard yourself as a religious writer?

Erdrich: It depends upon how that is defined. If I take it to mean a person whose characters ask questions about their origins in space and time, well, yes, and of course someone is often bumping up against crucial church dogma. Life is religious, I think, and that includes writing.

Chavkin: Does your work suggest there is no theological or epistemological certainty?

Erdrich: I have found none, and so the work most likely suggests the same.

Chavkin: Are you aware of common themes and preoccupations in your work?

Erdrich: Abandonment and return. Pleasure and denial. Failure. Absurdity. The inability to get a sound night's sleep.

Chavkin: How do you know when a story is finished and ready to be published?

Erdrich: I've often made mistakes and sent things out too soon. But when I think it is finished I feel right about it in a deep way, more certain than not certain, that is, in my case. Actually "right" for me is probably just a state of less intense doubt.

Chavkin: Can you tell us about the incident when you made a deal with Michael to remove what he considered to be some obvious symbolism in which a character imagines wings in the air during a love scene, on the condition that he would impose a severe fate on an unpleasant character in *A Yellow Raft in Blue Water*?

Erdrich: That was the revenge I mentioned, and now I don't remember what I traded off in order to acquire vengeance. Perhaps it *was* a lot of fluttering wings!

Chavkin: Your books in condensed form are available on audio cassette tapes. Who is responsible for condensing these books and what principles were followed in the production?

Erdrich: Another source of disatisfaction! I wish I'd never allowed them to be condensed.

Chavkin: Do you enjoy reading your work in public performances?

Erdrich: I love the performance itself but hate all that leads up to it—the cramped plane ride, lonesomeness for my daughters, the dislocation and combustion if they come along, the play-dough airline food, the packing, the unpacking, the uncertainty, the nervousness, the lack of

or too abundant audience, the strange rooms, the insomnia that follows
. . . Otherwise, yes, I enjoy reading from my work!

Chavkin: Grace Paley suggests that it's good for a writer to have
children, even though other writers argue otherwise. What do you
think?

Erdrich: I think, obviously, it's best to do what's best for children. It
was certainly best for Grace Paley's children that Grace Paley was and
is their mother. On the other hand, I can think of a number of writers
who probably shouldn't reproduce.

Chavkin: What's your opinion of publishing in small presses and the
"little magazines"?

Erdrich: Small presses and little magazines are run on sheer
idealism, and since I once worked for Joe Richardson of Plains Distribution, a small press bookstore distribution service, I'm quite familiar with
the joys and headaches involved in such operations. I greatly admire
those who persist. Without small magazines we would not have a
literary life in this country.

Chavkin: What's your view of the controversy in academia about
"opening up" the canon and studying minority and women writers?

Erdrich: I don't see why it is controversial. There is nothing unrea-
sonable about it provided the work is enlightening.

Chavkin: Do you have any advice for people who want to write a
novel?

Erdrich: Don't take the project too seriously.

Chavkin: Did you take the writing of your first novel too seriously?
Was that part of the reason for the trouble that you had with it?

Erdrich: That's the main trouble I have with everything!

Chavkin: Native Americans and others have responded enthusi-
astically to your work, but were you ever afraid that some overly-
sensitive people might misinterpret your work and accuse you of
depicting Native Americans in a negative way?

Erdrich: At first I didn't think that many people would read the
work. It was all a very private exercise. Later when I understood the
books were more widely read, I had something of a reaction that involved, I guess you might say, personal embarrassment. It was not that
the characters were so negative, since I think most people understand
that there are good and bad people of every ethnic group, it is that I
revealed myself to be more complicated, sexual and angry, especially

angry that I behave in my everyday encounters. I reverted to my small town persona, in shock, and wanted to hide.

Chavkin: Are you concerned that being labelled a "Native American writer" or a "woman writer" might result in your being marginalized? Do you object to those labels?

Erdrich: I think they originate in course descriptions and that there is some use in them. If the work survives, perhaps they'll fall away. If not, there isn't much I can do about it. After all, I don't think we read George Eliot, Jane Austen, Virginia Woolf, or Flannery O'Connor as "women writers" anymore, but as vital voices of their time. I know that, for instance, Toni Morrison will be read in this fashion. She is already. The point we're striving for is one at which the criteria for the work is its worth to readers, its excellence, the qualities that shine out and endure.

Chavkin: Obviously, you admire Toni Morrison's work a great deal. What attracts you to her work? What makes her a "vital voice"?

Erdrich: She writes such complicated, interwoven, shocking, comforting, rich internal lives for her characters. She is a master of physical sensation and description and demanding narratives. And she is a very brave writer, too, as well as a funny down-to-earth person. I once heard her read, and began to cry, her voice has such a quiet and moving power. Vitality.

Chavkin: In an article published in *American Literature* in September 1990, Catherine Rainwater argues that you include in your work structural features that "frustrate narrativity" in order to produce in the reader an "experience of marginality." What do you think of this argument?

Erdrich: I think it is true although of course I don't do it with such an object directly in mind. I am on the edge, have always been on the edge, flourish on the edge, and I don't think I belong anywhere else.

Chavkin: In your work is a Native American's knowledge of Roman Catholic beliefs and Native American religious beliefs an advantage, or is he/she torn between two systems of belief?

Erdrich: Torn, I believe, honestly torn. Religion is a deep force, and a people magnetize around the core of a belief system. It is very difficult for one individual to remain loyal to both although my own grandfather managed the trick quite well, by not fully participating in either traditional or Roman Catholic Church, and also by refusing to see distinctions between the embodiments of spirit. He prayed in the woods, he prayed in the mission, to him it was all connected, and all politics.

Chavkin: In his essay "Opening the Text: *Love Medicine* and the Return of the Native American Woman" published in *Narrative Chance,* edited by Gerald Vizenor (Albuquerque: University of New Mexico Press 1989), Robert Silberman suggests that in Native American literature the book is accepted as a necessary evil—the story and story-telling are the ideals. How important is the oral tradition in your work?

Erdrich: It is the reason so many stories are written in the first person—I hear the story told. At the same time I believe in and deeply cherish books and believe the library is a magical and sacred storehouse. A refuge. I'm a poorly-educated person in some ways. Not even Dartmouth could catch me up in having missed an intellectual life in high school. The town library was my teacher every bit as much as sitting in the kitchen or out under the trees swapping stories or listening to older relatives. So the two are not incompatible to me. I love the voice and I love the texture of writing, the feel of the words on the page, the construction.

Chavkin: Do you think that it's useful to view contemporary Native American writers such as James Welch, Simon Ortiz, N. Scott Momaday, Leslie Silko, and you and Michael as forming a literary movement, "Native American Literature"?

Erdrich: I think that literary movements often issue a manifesto. I'm stumped by the very idea.

Chavkin: Is one of your goals to undermine not only racist ideas but also romantic notions many people have about Native Americans?

Erdrich: This is not a specific conscious goal, but one which I hope would occur as a result of a reader following a story in which Native people were portrayed as complex and unpredictable.

Chavkin: Why are romantic notions (Native Americans as the first ecologists, as stoical) harmful?

Erdrich: Any notions that categorize a people limit a people, even such perfectly romantic notions.

Chavkin: Yeats, Henry James, Gore Vidal, and other writers have substantially revised previously published work. You have revised previously published work—how substantial are those revisions?

Erdrich: I have not revised previously published work, but I do add to it, as stories or additional scenes occur. There is no reason to think of publication as a final process. I think of it as temporary storage.

Chavkin: Yes, "temporary storage" is a good way of looking at it. The story "Destiny," published in *The Atlantic Monthly,* is told again but in a different form in Chapter 11 of *The Beet Queen.* Does the retelling of this story become more complex in the second published version?

Erdrich: Perhaps short pieces become more connected, more resonant, within the context of a novel, and then again, I miss how as short stories these pieces once stood alone. I'm not so thrifty about the work that I do this on purpose, it is just that the novels consume the short pieces while at the same time the pieces suggest additions to the novel.

Chavkin: When did you begin writing your first novel?

Erdrich: It is difficult to say exactly when, as bits and pieces of writing I did in the late nineteen seventies continue to find their way into later novels. I usually think of titles years before the books are written and in the interim I believe that there is a continual feeding of that title going on through dreams, experience, reading, other voices.

Chavkin: Was the acceptance of a poem of yours in *Ms.* magazine when you were a senior important in your apprenticeship?

Erdrich: It was very important. Very! I told everyone about it and showed the acceptance letter around . . . the poem didn't appear in print for two years! Still, I had real credibility.

Chavkin: Who were your favorite authors in your apprenticeship years?

Erdrich: Flannery O'Connor, Gunter Grass, Jean Rhys, Flann O'Brien, Alejo Carpentier, Mark Twain, John Barth, Willa Cather, William Faulkner, W.B. Yeats, John Tanner, Vladimir Nabokov, William Gass.

Chavkin: Who are the writers who influenced your work or served as models?

Erdrich: Michael Dorris, of course: believer, critic, beloved, and the person I most admire. Other than Michael, it is hard to pick out lasting influences. I'm a browser, prey to temporary enthusiasms. In my reading life, I usually have a number of books "going" at once. Last year I read nature essays. This year, women's politics and Henry James. My favorites over the years include Flannery O'Connor, William Faulkner, Angela Carter, Garcia Marquez, Marguerite Duras, Robert Stone, Jane Smiley, Robb Forman Dew, Jean Rhys, Adrienne Rich, Toni

Morrison, Rene Char, Larry Woiwode, Christina Stead, Katherine Anne
Porter, Willa Cather, Jim Harrison, the poets Louise Gluck, Mary
Oliver, Sharon Olds and Donald Hall. I read *Madame Bovary* and Jane
Austen and George Eliot over and over. Most of the reading these days
is nonfiction, the lives of saints, a history of Catholic devotions, and
captivity narratives.

Chavkin: Are you doing this nonfiction reading as a preparation for
a specific project?

Erdrich: I think so, but I'm not sure. Perhaps another novel. I'm
writing an introduction to John Tanner's narrative, an old family favorite, one I'm pleased to finally see re-issued. Also, I think that perhaps
Father Damien has more to say.

Chavkin: Before beginning work, Hemingway sharpened twenty
pencils and Willa Cather read a passage from the Bible. Do you have
any tricks to help you begin writing each day?

Erdrich: Actually, I just sit and stare disconsolately at the wall.

Chavkin: When did you decide you wanted to be writer?

Erdrich: By the time I was twenty it was clear to me that I was good
for, and good at, nothing else. I hated every job I had because I couldn't
tolerate authority and found any sort of repetition painfully tedious. I
hadn't the abstract mind of a philosopher or academic, or the physical
patience of an artist. I knew that if I were to have any chance at all for
happiness in work I had better throw myself at the writing life.

Chavkin: What were these jobs? Were you writing much while
working at them?

Erdrich: Picking cucumbers, hoeing beets, selling popcorn, life-
guarding, waitressing, selling Kentucky Fried Chicken, short order
cooking breakfast shift, (I can crack two, sometimes four, eggs at once,
one-handed), construction crew, and later, North Dakota Poet in the
Schools, ad-manager, psychiatric aide, candy-striper at an elderly care
center, newspaper deliveries, and others I can't remember.

Chavkin: What is your opinion of the reviewers of your work?

Erdrich: I have no general opinion, and I don't know them personally.

Chavkin: Your novels have received enthusiastic reviews, but it
seems some reviewers misunderstand your work at times—for example,
one review refers to June Kashpaw as a "prostitute" and calls the love-
making in "Wild Geese" a rape by the teenaged Nector. That's not accurate is it?

Erdrich: I guess it is a matter of interpretation, and I really try not to take reviews too much to heart. As a matter of fact, I wouldn't call June a prostitute, although she has sex with a man and notices that he's got some money. And the encounter between Marie and Nector was mistakenly ambiguous. I never meant it to be a rape and took a word or two out in the republished *Love Medicine* to make that clear. Reading it over, I too found it confusing and wanted to clarify his act (wrong, but not technically a rape).

Chavkin: Does it disturb you that your work prompts different reactions and interpretations, some of which you never intended?

Erdrich: I like the unexpected, and certainly can't predict the reactions, positive or negative, of other people. I don't really intend people to have reactions anyway, or interpretations. I'm wholly selfish about the work and write it for the characters on the page.

Chavkin: When you taught literature, what was your critical approach?

Erdrich: I had no critical approach.

Chavkin: Well, what kinds of topics did you focus on when you taught a novel or short story or a poem? Did you focus mainly on technique?

Erdrich: I taught students to read for pleasure, and I criticized their writing, worked on it with them. I can't seem to get a feel for critical theory. Either I soak up the writing . . . or not.

Chavkin: Which book of yours is your favorite?

Erdrich: Always the one I'm working on, at present, *The Bingo Palace.*

Chavkin: What's *The Bingo Palace* about?

Erdrich: Anxiety, money, chance, obsessed love, age, small griefs, failed friendship, self-denial, repressed sexual ardor—the usual.

Chavkin: When did you decide to write a series of interrelated novels?

Erdrich: It was never a decision, it just occurred once Michael pointed out the fact that they were related.

Chavkin: Once the final book in the series is published, one will be able to read the series in chronological order and that experience will be quite different from the experience of reading the books in the order they were published. Are we correct to assume that the ideal way to read the books is in chronological order?

Erdrich: That probably would be the ideal way, but for the fact that I don't really know when these books will begin and end, and the movement is so circular.

Chavkin: Have your experiences as a teacher and a journalist made you a more astute critic and editor of your own work?

Erdrich: I don't think there's a connection.

Chavkin: Well, can you tell us about your experience in journalism? You edited a Native American newspaper in Boston, didn't you?

Erdrich: The best aspects of that job were the people at the Boston Indian Council. I got out of myself a little, worked for idealistic reasons, felt assurance about telling what I needed to tell. Many of the stories I worked on evenings became part of *Love Medicine*.

Chavkin: Is part of your intention in some of your work to instruct and to reform?

Erdrich: God, no!

Chavkin: One of the remarkable aspects of your writing is that it "instructs" in subtle ways without seeming to instruct. That is, it enables the reader to see the world through the eyes of people from different cultures, different classes, and different historical periods. Sensitive readers come to understand that people from different cultures with different values and beliefs are human and similar to themselves in the most basic ways. Was this your conscious intention?

Erdrich: Thank you, that is very kind, but none of this is conscious intention. My one intention is to tell stories, or maybe just tell one long convoluted story. I don't think I can do much else.

Chavkin: Are you religious?

Erdrich: Yes, I am.

Chavkin: Can you elaborate?

Erdrich: My religious feelings are very private, and consist, in some general sense, of the need to work on tolerance and wonder, no dogma, much confusion.

Chavkin: Are there any disadvantages to being famous?

Erdrich: I'm not famous.

Chavkin: Well, if Thoreau, Melville, and other great American writers of the nineteenth century wrote as solitaries ignored by the public, the media industry has made major writers at least minor celebrities. Of course, no major writer has the name recognition of Madonna, but stories about you have appeared in *Life, The New York*

Times Magazine, and other national publications. Has this kind of attention put pressure on you that you didn't have before?

Erdrich: Probably a little, but I'd rather not think about it too much and just let it pass.

Chavkin: Are any of your friends writers? Do you discuss literary matters with them?

Erdrich: Michael has a great and generous talent for friendship and is acquainted with and close to lots of people in the writing world. You should ask him this question.

Chavkin: Did you feel you had to make compromises in your earliest work published under pseudonyms?

Erdrich: I had a good time writing those stories, but yes, they were pureed. I was desperate for money.

Chavkin: Some writers, Graham Greene for example, make a distinction between what they consider to be "entertainments" and what they consider to be serious works, works of art. Of course, in Greene's case the distinction does not seem to be as clear as the terms would indicate. But do you make such a distinction with your own stories? Would you prefer to see included in the literature anthologies such stories as "Fleur," "A Wedge of Shade," and "The Red Convertible" instead of one of your stories written under a pseudonym?

Erdrich: The pseudononymous stories were written to make money, and while I'm not ashamed of that, they're meaningless and sentimental. I doubt anyone would ever anthologize them.

Chavkin: Is *The Crown of Columbus* historically accurate?

Erdrich: It could be, but of course none of the things that happened to the characters really happened except for the part where they are practically devoured by no-see-ums on an idyllic Caribbean Island.

Chavkin: What about the Columbus parts—are they historically accurate?

Erdrich: As accurate as possible, given the academic disagreements about Columbus in the first place. I did barge around the library fully pregnant, that's true too, and in fact I became almost obsessed with Columbus for several months. I didn't expect him to come alive, or to become such an unwieldy, slyly teasing, deceptive, wholly frustrating subject. I used to throw my head down on the table sometimes and wish, just *wish*, I could talk to him. I know I could have made him understand what was going to happen, made him understand cultural history and ethnocentrism. He was brilliant, strange, and emotional, and very, very cruel.

Chavkin: Would it be accurate to say that *The Beet Queen* is a reworking and expansion of the sequence of poems entitled "The Butcher's Wife" in *Jacklight*?

Erdrich: Come to think of it, I do think that those poems had a great deal to do with *The Beet Queen*, or at least with one character's voice.

Chavkin: In writing *The Beet Queen*, did you have to overcome some technical challenges you had never confronted before?

Erdrich: The play between first and third person. Juggling all those voices. Nursing a baby while holding a pen.

Chavkin: In a review entitled "Here's an Odd Artifact for the Fairy-Tale Shelf" published in *Impact/Albuquerque Journal* (October 8, 1986), Leslie Silko attacks your work for its supposed postmodern literary aesthetic. For example, she sees *The Beet Queen* as an auto-referential text and therefore as outside the Native American oral tradition. She characterizes your writing as the product of "academic, post-modern, so-called experimental influences" which de-emphasizes the referential dimension of words. Usually, professors and critics of your work have said the exact opposite of what Silko says. Who is closer to the truth—Silko or the other critics?

Erdrich: The other critics.

Chavkin: In her review Silko also states: *"The Beet Queen* is a strange artifact, an eloquent example of the political climate in America in 1986. It belongs on the shelf next to the latest report from the United States Civil Rights Commission, which says black men have made tremendous gains in employment and salary. This is the same shelf that holds *The Collected Thoughts of Edwin Meese on First Amendment Rights* and *Grimm's Fairy Tales."* What do you think prompted Silko to say this?

Erdrich: Drugs.

Honestly, here is what I think happened. Leslie Silko didn't read the book carefully. It happens, I've done it myself. She thought the main characters were Chippewa when they were actually depression-era Poles and Germans. It is no wonder that she wrote a diatribe. They must have seemed shockingly assimilated.

Chavkin: Silko suggests you are ambivalent about your Native American origins. How would you respond to this charge?

Erdrich: Of course, I'm ambivalent, I'm human. There are times I wish that I were one thing or the other, but I am a mixed-blood. *Psychically doomed*, another mixed-blood friend once joked. The truth is that my background is such a rich mixed bag I'd be crazy to want to be anything else. Nor would Silko, probably, or any Native writer who understands that through the difficulty of embracing our own contradictions we gain sympathy for the range of ordinary failures and marvels.

Chavkin: Silko suggests your work lacks political commitment. Has she misunderstood your work or is this criticism accurate?

Erdrich: Any human story is a political story.

Chavkin: What do you think of Silko's creative work?

Erdrich: What's all this about Silko? I've always liked her work, and especially admire *Ceremony*.

Chavkin: What kind of influence did your education have on your writing?

Erdrich: Every kind of influence, I suppose, since my education gave me the tools and confidence to use in writing of and understanding my own past, the lives of others, which I do imperfectly, and language itself.

Chavkin: How did *Tracks* originate?

Erdrich: *Tracks* is very tangled, problematic for me, difficult. It was the first manuscript I finished, but I have since divided up and re-used pieces of that manuscript elsewhere. It has become the old junked car in the yard front, continually raided for parts. It is the form of all else, still a tangle.

Chavkin: One would never guess from reading *Tracks* that its origin was a tangled manuscript. Why did *Tracks* give you so much more trouble that *Love Medicine* or *The Beet Queen*?

Erdrich: Because I love it so much.

Chavkin: Do you recall the origins of your novels? For example, did you begin with a particular structure or certain characters that served as the genesis of the work?

Erdrich: *The Bingo Palace,* the novel I'm working on right now, originated from my consistent failure to break even at the blackjack tables. *Love Medicine* wouldn't have become a novel if Michael hadn't pointed out that it was a novel and I should finish it. *The Beet Queen* began with the image of an airplane vanishing, and then the opening sequences, the children jumping off the train, the scent of those pure white blossoms.

Chavkin: So you had in your mind those images of the airplane vanishing, the children jumping off the train, and so forth—did you then discover what those images meant by writing the novel, or did you know the basic plot of the novel as soon as you had those images in your mind?

Erdrich: I never know the basic plot, it becomes more evident during the writing as the images evoke questions and explanations must be concocted.

Chavkin: Do you recall what you read when you were a child?

Erdrich: What most children read, I think—Nancy Drew, the Bobbsey Twins and Hardy Boys, Jack London, *Marjorie Morningstar, Animal Farm* and Shakespeare's history plays, because with my father, I watched all of Educational TV's *The Age of Kings,* and then listened to *Macbeth* and *King Lear* records over and over. I read every single *Readers Digest* Condensed book, all kinds of household magazines, nature guides, Victoria Holt, Robert Ruark, Leon Uris, all the big fat books in the front shelf at the local library. I remember having books splayed open, under pillows and jackets all over the house because, as the oldest of several children, I had lots of responsibility and not much time to read.

Chavkin: What's your view of the value of writing workshops?

Erdrich: The criticism of your peers is very helpful, as is the presence and direction of other more established writers. Every story has to have a basis in experience and be driven by imagined risks, so of course what I'm saying is that writing breaks from the mess and elegance of life and the intellect and cannot be taught. And yet, it is good to find situations when you feel compelled to write and improve.

Chavkin: Were there any established writers whom you knew and were important to your writing career during or after your apprenticeship period?

Erdrich: Mark Vinz, Cynthia MacDonald, Richard Howard, Charles Newman, Edmund White, M. L. Rosenthal, and then, although *Love Medicine* went out with absolutely no expectations or any prepublication notes or hype, none at all, Toni Morrison, Kay Boyle, Philip Roth, Peter Matthiessen, Anne Tyler, and Rosellen Brown read an unknown manuscript and responded with those quotes and marks of approval that appear on book jackets. These were completely unsolicited and I still find it remarkable that these writers, overwhelmed with pleas and manuscripts, picked up *Love Medicine* and responded.

There were a great number of people kind along the way. One hears much more about the egomania and posturing of writers than one does about the devotion that writers have for one another's work.

Chavkin: Have any reviews influenced your writing in any way?

Erdrich: I wait about a year, at least that, before reading reviews. By then I've started a new book and the old book isn't so vulnerable, which is a way of saying I'm not so easily hurt by or helplessly grateful to reviewers. I do have a superstition about the book in its first year. It seems in need of protection, silent protection, from me, and that is partly why I find publishers' book tours excruciating.

Chavkin: Why else do you find these book tours excruciating?

Erdrich: An old friend of mine recently observed that book tours must be difficult since I am shy. It was such a relief to know the reason. I hadn't known how to say it. *Shy.* That's the reason I end up after three weeks of interviews and readings drinking Maalox from wineglasses, and why I carry sleeping pills along. I don't know how public people endure the constant pressure of being with and trying to please others. Trying to amuse people, being constantly judged, sizing up interviewers, repeating stories about oneself—all of these things make me acutely nervous. Michael once called me from a book tour and said woefully, "I'm *so* tired of myself." I knew how he felt, though *he's* wonderfully original and entertaining in person.

Chavkin: Is it accurate to say your writing forms an organic whole?

Erdrich: It's more like a compost pile.

Chavkin: Can you think of any non-Native American writers who portray in their fiction Native Americans as individuals and not as stereotypes?

Erdrich: Howard Norman.

Chavkin: Any others? Thomas Berger?

Erdrich: Yes, and Tony Hillerman.

Chavkin: Sartre and others argue that writers must be committed, they must be concerned about social issues, and this concern must be reflected in their writing. What's your view?

Erdrich: Everyone should be politically and socially committed in personal life, but not in art. Political art is polemic and boring. The greater danger to artists in this country is commercialism. I have been approached to sell Gap clothes and soap, etc., but haven't done so because it seemed wrong, not to mention embarrassing.

Chavkin: Do you think film and TV will alter the form of the novel?

Erdrich: I suppose they already have.

Chavkin: Do you think film has influenced the form of your fiction? Can you think of specific examples?

Erdrich: I'm sorry, I can't think of any examples, although I'm sure there must be some influence. I don't watch many films, I wasn't raised watching much television, so perhaps the influence upon me specifically is fairly minimal.

Chavkin: You write a lot of stories—do you write them between novels? while you are working on a novel?

Erdrich: I write them whenever I can. I am disorganized and never certain about exactly what I am working on, when, what time frame.

Chavkin: You have written two highly-regarded volumes of poetry and are one of the youngest poets to be included in *The Norton Anthology of Modern Poetry*. But we assume you have abandoned poetry for writing novels and short stories—if this statement is accurate, can we assume that this shift from poetry to fiction is at least partially because of the lack of interest in poetry these days?

Erdrich: No, no! When I am able to write poetry, I do so. It is like being touched and held by a force that I don't understand, can't will.

Chavkin: For you, then, the process of writing prose is quite different from that of poetry?

Erdrich: Yes. I know if I regularly sit down and try to write every day something will happen, some connections will form. Poetry is much more the result of strong emotion and beyond my control.

Chavkin: Why did you decide to use water as the controlling imagery in *Love Medicine*? How does this imagery help unify the novel?

Erdrich: It wasn't a decision. I didn't notice it for a long while.

Chavkin: You usual work intuitively and don't deliberately unify a work with patterns of imagery?

Erdrich: I'm much more responsible and deliberate in life I hope than I am in writing. When I notice a pattern of imagery emerging I certainly work with it in a very slow formal way and try to develop and transform characters through metaphor. But I never count on noticing it before it happens.

Chavkin: Do you think that any of your novels might be made into good films? Would you want to write the screenplays?

Erdrich: It's all the same to me, and I wouldn't want to even get near the writing of a screenplay.

Chavkin: Are any of your stories *somewhat* autobiographical?

Erdrich: If my stories were even somewhat autobiographical, I'd be pretty well played-out, wouldn't I? My life's quiet as I can make it, and for that reason I've got time to daydream.

Chavkin: You don't believe, as Hemingway did, that a writer needs to seek out experiences in order to acquire material for writing. But at least some of your work experiences become the work experiences of some of your characters, right?

Erdrich: I do think that attending deeply to one's own experience, whatever it is or becomes, is part of a writer's job. When younger, I wrote in order to understand my experience, and now I find that I seek out experience in order to understand why I write.

Chavkin: Have any of your friends or family seen themselves or people you know in your fiction?

Erdrich: I hope not. I'm always glad when strangers do.

Chavkin: Did any of your stories evolve out of their settings?

Erdrich: I think that setting is integral, but I can't pinpoint exactly how it influences plot.

Chavkin: Would you agree that in such stories as "Fleur" and "A Wedge of Shade" setting becomes a crucial part of the action?

Erdrich: Absolutely, and in fact place and setting have always been a difficult personal issue with me, for I have never stopped missing and loving the Great Plains although for the last eighteen years I've been east or west of their definition. Right outside the margin. Longing is as much a part of "Fleur" and "Wedge of Shade" as is the setting itself.

Chavkin: What sets you apart from other contemporary writers?

Erdrich: The particularities of who I am, I suppose.

Chavkin: Do you ever worry your work might be too difficult for the average reader and then change it as a result of that concern?

Erdrich: The average reader of my work is very literate.

Chavkin: Your novels have sold very well, but they are not the kind of books one usually finds on bestseller lists. *Love Medicine* is experi-

mental in form, and in general, your books probably would be regarded
as complex and difficult by the public. How do you account for their
popularity?

Erdrich: Luckily, it's not my job to accout for it, but I don't feel
they are all that popular. By now, I've got a small exchange going with
a few passionate, intelligent readers. Mostly through Michael's hard
work of getting the books published well, I might add. Most Americans,
and most people in general, prefer sitcom TV to reading, so only a
small percentage of Americans actually read. TV has made world leaders more accountable and strengthened chances for peace, still, prime
time is boring, maddening, and violent. An irresistible combination.

Chavkin: So you don't see your books as having sold very well? In
an interview Saul Bellow divided modern writers into two groups—
large public writers and small public writers. Both are good, he suggests. A large public writer would be someone such as Dickens who
was trying to please a large public, and in fact Dickens had many thousands, perhaps millions of readers. On the other hand, a small public
writer, such as Flaubert or Bellow, perceives himself as a writer who is
an artist and therefore does not expect a large readership. What do you
think of this division and does large public writer or small public writer
best describe you?

Erdrich: I'm not kidding when I say that this is *not* something that I
think about a great deal. There is really no way for me to be a public
writer of any type unless I think first about the story I'm telling, so I try
to do that and let the other aspect, like water, find the appropriate level.

Chavkin: When you write, do you have an ideal reader in mind?

Erdrich: Michael.

Chavkin: Is the process of writing a novel one of merely following a
detailed outline, or do you discover the novel as you compose it?

Erdrich: The novel comes to light as it is written. It gathers its own
material and acquires life, substance. I've got everything and nothing to
do with it.

Chavkin: Have you noticed your attitudes changing as a result of
creating your fictional characters and having them experience certain
things?

Erdrich: It's usually the other way around.

Chavkin: Which of your novels gave you the most trouble? Which
was the easiest to write?

Erdrich: *Tracks. The Bingo Palace.*

Chavkin: Why do you think that is? Do you think that in the future you'll be able to avoid the trouble that *Tracks* gave you and duplicate the writing experience of *The Bingo Palace*?

Erdrich: No, probably not. Every so often you get a break as a writer. Most of *The Bingo Palace* was written in six weeks. Of course, now I'm toiling at rewrite after rewrite. Still, because of Lipsha, it is a work that involves the lighter and perpetually bewildered aspects of my own personality. I'd been thinking that *Tales of Burning Love* would come next but that book will be published in two years. *The Bingo Palace* just intervened, proposed itself, took over.

Chavkin: Can you tell us what *Tales of Burning Love* will be about? We seem to recall reading that the novel is about a group of people who pass the time by telling stories they've never told any person before—is that an accurate description of the novel?

Erdrich: The novel is about women and the complexity of their love for one man, for their children, for God, for other women. I'm hoping that along with the novel I'll finish a book of essays I've been working on for quite a while. Every time I think of an essay I think it is the new title. *The Bluejay's Dance, The Names of Women, Rising Wolf, Foxglove,* or maybe *The Veils.*

Chavkin: Do you find it difficult to write from the point of view of the opposite sex?

Erdrich: No, because I'm one of those rare daughters (I guess, so the self-help books say) who has and always had an interesting, interactive, social, challenging and loving friendship with her father. That is, Ralph Erdrich!

Chavkin: Did you ever find yourself frustrated by having to restrict yourself to the limited point of view of a first-person narrator?

Erdrich: Yes, that's why third person narratives are usually included in the books.

Chavkin: Did you find it difficult to shift from writing poetry to fiction?

Erdrich: As I've said, I usually just can't do it.

Chavkin: Do you complete a project before moving on to another one, or do you work on several things more or less at the same time?

Erdrich: I like working on a number of things all at once, and hate the process of finishing anything.

Chavkin: Why do you hate the process of finishing anything?

Erdrich: Because I don't want to die, I hate death, and living things keep growing. I hope I live long enough to cultivate a civilized attitude about the end of things, because I'm very immature, now, about letting go of what I love.

Chavkin: How do you relax after a day of writing?

Erdrich: I have children, smart, beautiful, striking, eccentric daughters. We play. When they have to go to bed, I talk to Michael, who has never said a boring word to me in our eleven-year relationship. If he's on the phone, I pet the dog or my cat. I play the piano (badly), draw (poorly), practice Ojibway, French, or German (atrociously). Or read, there is always that. If all else fails, I drink red wine and stumble out into the woods.

Chavkin: What have you done with the early drafts of your work? Will they be available for scholars to study your composing process?

Erdrich: There's nothing to learn from my composing process, but the manuscripts are slowly filling cardboard boxes.

Chavkin: Do you ever show your early drafts to people other than your spouse?

Erdrich: Once in a while, an editor, the editor of a magazine, a writer friend. Rarely.

Chavkin: Can you think of any instances in which they made comments that resulted in significant changes in your work?

Erdrich: Susan Moldow, an editor with a long and impressive publishing title, did such thoughtful work on *The Bingo Palace* that I know it has changed, significantly. I'm still working on it so I can't say exactly how. Judy Karasik, who edited *Love Medicine*, is an extremely talented writer and editor. Richard Seaver worked on *The Beet Queen*. Marian Wood on the additions to *Love Medicine*. With no one do I have the sort of relationship I share with Michael Dorris.

Chavkin: How many drafts of a story do you usually write? How many for a novel?

Erdrich: I have never counted and don't think I'll ever start. It would make me worry, and, perhaps imagine there was a magic number.

Chavkin: Your style no matter how lyrical is always precise. Do you do a lot of "polishing" of your language?

Erdrich: Yes, I polish, and Michael does extensive and demanding work on the draft as we go along. He's very particular about word repetitions and awkwardness. In addition to all else, he is a fine editor.

Chavkin: Do you serve as his editor? Are you as particular as he is about such matters as word repetitions and awkwardness?

Erdrich: I love being ruthless, yes. I'm very hard on Michael's work, but often my ideas are less line editing than character insights. Of course, he does the same for me. We have a merged writing relationship in many ways, it's very close, and yet we are able to break away for months and months and become solitary and in charge of our own imaginative lives. I completely respect his judgements, even when we disagree and we have learned to leave each other alone when that is necessary. Sometimes the struggle is interior, sometimes it can be mutual. I do admire Michael's work with all of my heart. He is a true, staunch friend and in so many ways a great-hearted soul.

Chavkin: Did your poems typically require extensive revision?

Erdrich: Yes, and as I've said I don't write many anymore although I wish that the poetry would return.

Chavkin: Where is your greatest effort made—in the first draft or in subsequent revisions?

Erdrich: My greatest effort is made in living in such a way that the writing is possible in the first place. Writing is an escape from my own sins and failures, so although there is a great deal of work involved, I don't think of it as effort.

Chavkin: At what point do you begin revising? Do you write a whole draft and then rewrite it, revise as you go along, or follow some other procedure?

Erdrich: I revise all of the time, as the work demands. The procedure changes all of the time. Some pieces are so old that they've gone through a hundred drafts. One piece included in the expanded *Love Medicine* was written well before *Love Medicine*. Once in a great grand while I get "a piece" as though it is dictated to me from the character. This usually follows an intense solitary experience, or a long frank talk with Michael, or after a long drive through open country, alone, no radio, just wind, or a walk in the woods, or a run. Often, words drop into my head while I slog pathetically along the side of the road with our dog.

Chavkin: When John Fowles published *The Magus: A Revised Version* he meant for it to replace the first published version because he felt this revised version corrected mistakes made in the first published version and thus was better. On the other hand, that's not the case with

Marguerite Duras' *The North China Lover* and *The Lover*. They tell the same story but are different novels with different points of view. *The North China Lover* presents a new perspective and new material not in *The Lover*. Is the expanded version of *Love Medicine* meant to replace the original version, as Fowles meant with *The Magus: A Revised Version,* or will we have two different versions of the same story, as Duras intended with *The North China Lover* and *The Lover*?

Erdrich: The original will go out of print, but of course there are always libraries. I have no great plan for the reader here—some may prefer the first version without the additions, others the next. I don't think of the books as definitive, finished, or correct, and leave them for the reader to experience.

Chavkin: How elaborate are your outlines before you begin writing? Do you depart much from your original plans?

Erdrich: I have no rules about writing. Sometimes a book has an outline and other times I feel my way along, piecing it together bit by bit until the book answers itself.

Chavkin: Jerzy Kosinski has stated that he begins a novel by writing the opening and the end of the novel. When you are writing a novel, do you write chronologically from beginning to end or do you skip around, or do you have some other procedure?

Erdrich: I skip around everywhere, writing the pieces that I can't wait to write. It's like always eating your favorite part of the meal first. It's a greedy habit. But, why not?

Chavkin: Your ability to capture the voices of your first-person narrators is quite impressive. Do you ever use a tape recorder to capture these voices or act out parts of a story?

Erdrich: Absolutely not!

Chavkin: You have been quite prolific, publishing much in a relatively short period of time. Do you write quickly? Are you disciplined in your work habits?

Erdrich: Thank you, but I don't see it that way and am not satisfied with the work and the time it has taken. I am driven and become depressed without the writing. I'm not disciplined, I just like being happy. Writing is a pleasure for me even when I fail.

Chavkin: Do you write for the sheer joy of writing?

Erdrich: Yes, I do, I find solace in work.

Chavkin: Do you try to write seven days a week?

Erdrich: I'm always trying to write, to get to the writing, to play around with it, and so I do try to write seven days a week, yes. I never thought of it that way before. I sound like maniac here, but I am not so impossible as all of this, I hope. Even more than writing, I love doing nothing. Nothing.

Chavkin: How many pages can you write on an average day?

Erdrich: I really don't know because I've never had an average day. Either they are good days or dismal ones, impossible days or delicious ones when I don't worry about the writing at all. I never count up pages in any case.

Chavkin: Why do you prefer to write early drafts in longhand?

Erdrich: I can write anywhere and need no equipment. Longhand feels more personal, as though I'm physically touching the subject. If I get a good idea in a bar I can walk back to Women, Females, Damsels, Does, etc., shut and lock the stall, then jot.

Lately I've been writing nonfiction directly onto the computer. It all seems magical and goes so quickly, but most of the pieces started as journal entries.

Chavkin: How important is your writing in your journal? How does it "feed into" your fiction and nonfiction?

Erdrich: I keep several notebooks going all at once besides daily diaries and letters and I go back to notebooks I kept many years ago for emotional context or to get a sense of character, or to turn up ideas. I keep scraps, keep drafts, it all collects. That's what I mean by compost.

Chavkin: Do you ever write up biographical sketches of your characters when you are writing a novel?

Erdrich: Sometimes I try to do a page or two of character sketching, but I usually don't end up using a thing I've written. The characters seem to appear via their reaction to story events, in the first instance, and then once they are written down they seem somehow called into being and I can't get rid of them.

Chavkin: Too much planning and outlining for a work of fiction are not useful, then? They hamper your creativity?

Erdrich: I don't know, maybe I could really get something perfect if I plotted, but I don't think I'd have such a good time uncovering the plot day to day. Of course, around ¾ through I do get a plot and write down what I know—and then there are frequent conversations with Michael. I'm not a completely instinctive writer, but I do have a high level of tolerance for chaos and disorder.

Chavkin: Some writers have stated that writing is a painful, exhausting, and frustrating process for them. What's your experience?

Erdrich: It's easier than hoeing sugar beets.

Chavkin: What were you writing before you started getting published?

Erdrich: Poetry and small experimental pieces of prose.

Chavkin: Were some of these small experimental pieces later included in your novels?

Erdrich: No, they're still sitting around, somewhere in an appropriately dark corner.

Chavkin: Can you tell us about your work as a "poet-in-the-schools"?

Erdrich: I went to a new place (prisons, schools, hospitals, etc.) in North Dakota every week and taught and through the kindness of the North Dakota State Arts Council, managed a year's survival and a writing space. I learned a great deal—not to drink from taps in cheap motels, give out my address indiscriminately to inmates, how to entertain large fourth grade classes. I still recall some of the poetry written by young children, the surprise of the inner lives. I worked very hard with them, and put together a raft of poetry booklets before the shocking finale—a tough case of hepatitis, for which I was quarantined and hospitalized.

Chavkin: Your literary relationship with Michael began in 1979 when he was living in New Zealand. Can you tell us about that?

Erdrich: While at the MacDowell colony, Peterborough, New Hampshire, Michael and I began to correspond. He sent poetry, and we wrote obscure hints about a possible relationship into our letters.

Chavkin: Were your parents apprehensive when you decided to be a writer? Did they encourage or discourage you?

Erdrich: They were always encouraging, never concerned about my possible failure or the fact that for a while I had an Ivy League education and a below minimum wage job. They never worried about prestige but happiness was important. They told me that they wanted me to do whatever made me happy. My parents still read the manuscripts and make changes. I've written with one of my sisters, Heid Erdrich and I exchange manuscripts with Lise Erdrich. Both of my sisters are extremely interesting and very, very talented writers, and they are now finishing collections of poetry and fiction.

Chavkin: When you were growing up in North Dakota, did you ever feel as if you were an outsider because of your background? Did you feel as if you were an outsider at Dartmouth?

Erdrich: Sure, always an outsider, but that's a gift for a writer because one is schooled early on in observation, in reading others for survival. People who belong don't become writers, they're immersed and have no edge, or so I tell myself, anyway, when I need reassurance.

Chavkin: Is "Captivity" about the psychological state of the outsider unable to find a place in society?

Erdrich: I can't say exactly what it is about, although the beauty and anguish of one voice may be enough. I read so many captivity narratives around that time that they merged in my head and I'm afraid that the quote in the beginning isn't even accurate. A student at the University of North Dakota noticed this, and told me so. Still, the woman's voice to me has a psychological truth. She doesn't trust her emotions, she is tortured with longing, and yet her captors aren't who she thought they were. That problem, she can't resolve, for it means admitting her common humanity as did Mary Jemison and John Tanner and Cynthia Parker.

Chavkin: What prompted you to write "Bangs and Whimpers: Novelists at Armageddon"?

Erdrich: Fascination with post apocalyptic writers, terror for the future.

Chavkin: "Indian Boarding School: The Runaways" challenges conventional assumptions about reservation life? Is that what prompted you to write the poem?

Erdrich: No, memory of friends who ran away from school.

Chavkin: What is your opinion of your early work, such as "The True Story of Mustache Maude"?

Erdrich: The story was, as early work often is, an experiment in voice and form. It was also about a lot of raw and unresolved emotion, I'm sure, and it may turn up in later work. (In fact, echoes occur in "Saint Marie," the veil with a cutting edge and the erotic undertones.) Mustache Maude was a real person, a North Dakota maverick, and perhaps it's wrong to play so fast and loose with a real person's life. I wouldn't do it now in exactly the same way, although I'm working on a book of the same title now. When I started writing I had no idea my work would be read. You must have gone to great lengths to find this one. Is the magazine still around? I think there was some controversy about the possible lesbian sado-masochism, a letter or two, and it certainly never became anthologized, or gained much notice. Still, it is part of what comes next.

Chavkin: Yes, you're right, it wasn't exactly "a piece of cake" finding the issue of *Frontiers* in which "The True Story of Mustache Maude" was published, but eventually we did find it in one of the libraries at the University of Texas at Austin and photocopied it. Tell us about the real Mustache Maude and how she differs from your fictional character.

Erdrich: I'd have to find my copy of "Extraordinary North Dakotans" and I fear it is still in the boxes of unopened books upstairs. However, she did rustle hogs and I don't think she was a lesbian. Still more difficult—I can't find a copy of the story in question.

Chavkin: Will your book on Mustache Maude be rooted in or inspired by or totally different from "The True Story of Mustache Maude"?

Erdrich: Inspired by, most likely. She is an inspirational historical figure.

Chavkin: In your story, Mustache Maude is the child of "an Italian Lothario" and "a Chippewa beauty." How important is her background, her being of mixed blood, her growing up "wild and alone," in understanding her behavior as an adult?

Erdrich: I wish I had the story so I knew how she did behave as an adult. Remember, this tale was a Gothic experiment.

Chavkin: One of the early versions of "Saint Marie" was told by a different narrator—what kind of story was it in this early version?

Erdrich: There were several versions, one third person, others told by lesser characters, all, perhaps predictably less intense.

Chavkin: There are few references to political and historical events outside the small community where the action of *Love Medicine* occurs. Is this a way of suggesting the marginality of the Native Americans— that is, events in the outside world do not much concern them because they cannot influence those events and do not consider themselves part of that world?

Erdrich: In later books, there is more involvement with the political life of the country, and of course reservation people are gravely impacted. There wasn't room for a large political spectrum but I think the suggestion that great events influence the way people live day to day is implicit. In *Love Medicine*, the effects of Roman Catholicism, missionary zealots, termination, boarding schools, The Great Depression, World War II, Vietnam and the siege of Wounded Knee are all touched upon. That seems, come to think about it, enough.

Chavkin: Albertine's mother says: "I raised her an Indian and that's what she is." Is being Native American to some degree a state of mind?

Erdrich: I don't think that follows from Zelda's statement. No, of course you can't help being an Indian, a mixed-blood, or whatever you are, but certain choices bring you closer to your background and others lead away. Identity is a complex mixture of circumstance, chance, faithfulness and need.

Chavkin: What allows some characters in *Love Medicine* to survive while a character such as June dies?

Erdrich: They were not abused as children.

Chavkin: In "Love Medicine," Lipsha suggests that "love medicine" is a Chippewa specialty. Is that really true or does Lipsha's claiming that reveal his ethnocentricity?

Erdrich: Are you asking me to comment on whether Chippewas are better lovers, to be objective about this? Why would it be ethnocentric to claim that your people are charming and loveable? Especially when it's true?

Chavkin: It's not an accident, is it, that Gerry Nanapush's name echoes the traditional Chippewa trickster hero Nanabozho?

Erdrich: No, you are right, it's not an accident!

Chavkin: In *Love Medicine* there are places where you switch from the past tense to the present tense. For example, in "The Plunge of the Brave" Nector Kashpaw suddenly changes from past tense to the present tense as he tells his story. The change is quite effective, but how do you know when to switch from the past to the present? In John Haffenden's *Novelists in Interview* (London: Methuen 1985), Malcolm Bradbury explains his use of the present tense this way: "It diminishes the moral reference as it diminishes the casual reference, precisely because it suggests the dominance of action—it's the tense of film scripts, after all—over interpretation of action." Do you have some ideas on the use of present tense?

Erdrich: This is such a carefully structured question, such an admirable question really that I'm abashed to say I don't have an answer that measures up. I write present tense when I think the character would be talking that way. In the book I'm working on now, *The Bingo*

Palace, the tense changes from past to present because the character becomes increasingly desperate to explain and clarify his actions.

Chavkin: Do you ever fear that your work might be regarded as too bleak and that readers will miss the humor in it?

Erdrich: I don't write to please readers, but out of a sense of necessity, which is not to say I don't *want* to please readers. I like to, and especially love that people find the work comic in certain episodes. If you're really living, life encompasses extremes.

Index

Winterson, Jeanette, 222
Woiwode, Larry, 233
Woman, 37, 115
Wood, Marian, 245
Woolf, Leonard, 84
Woolf, Virginia, 84, 230
Wouk, Herman, *Marjorie Morningstar*, 106, 239
Wounded Knee, 148
Wright, James, 161

Y

Yale University, 19, 30, 65, 90, 105, 163, 219
Yeats, William Butler, 231, 232
Yoknapatawpha County, 163

Z

Zimbabwe, 184, 191, 219